TIME-HONORED WISDOMS ON WEALTH CREATION

A High Performer's Handbook On Tapping The Perennial Wisdoms For Inner and Outer Success

By

Emerson Lee

ISBN: 1-4033-6027-8 (e-book)
ISBN: 1-4033-6028-6 (Paperback)

Library of Congress Control Number: 2002093625

This book is printed on acid free paper.

Printed in the United States of America
Bloomington, IN

1stBooks - rev. 12/03/02

To Dr Deepak Chopra,
for his profound insights into the spiritual laws of success.

To Dr Huston Smith, Dr Stanislav Grof, Ken Wilber,
Dr Roger Walsh, Dr Wayne Dyer, Dr Fritjof Capra,
Dan Millman and Gary Zukav
for guiding us back to the perennial philosophy.

To Dr Denis Waitley, Zig Ziglar and Dr Stephen Covey
for implanting the seeds of greatness in the new
generation.

To Anthony Robbins,
whose self-empowering techniques and metaphors
continue to revitalize me.

To Ms Oprah Winfrey,
whose uplifting words galvanize me to
rise to the plane of fruitful living.

To Dr Gerald Jampolsky and Charles Swindoll,
for brightening the spiritual skyline
with touching messages of love, hope and healing.

To Dr Jack Kornfield,
whose transmission of the Buddha's wisdom
underpins the awakening of many modern minds.

To Thich Nhat Hanh,
who exemplifies the ideal of living Buddha, living Christ.

To Lama Surya Das, Sharon Salzberg and
Pema Chodron
for leading us back to the sacred dimension of our being.

To Wes Nisker and Dr Jon Kabat-Zinn
for imparting to us the essence of the art of meditation.

To my teacher, Brother Noel,
whose Christ-like lovingkindness and patience
continue to reverberate in my heart.

To my wife and daughter,
whose affection is a source of daily inspiration.

I always feel if you do right, right will follow.
Oprah Winfrey

CONTENTS

7

v

PART I

A Road Map To The Perennial Wisdoms & Inner Wealth

Emerson Lee

Wealth-Creation Wisdom 1
Nurturing A Healthy Abundance Consciousness

Blessed is the man who finds wisdom,
the man who gains understanding,
for she is more profitable than silver
and yields better returns than gold.

Proverbs 3:13-14

We have what we seek. It is there all the time, and if we give it time, it will make itself known to us.

Thomas Merton

We human beings can be nourished by the best values of many traditions.

Thich Nhat Hanh

Let us take a quantum leap and be attuned to a pivotal truth. It can elude us for many years before genuine success beacons at us:

Wealth creation is not a zero-sum competition.

This truth resonates in a memorable question posed by Dr Gerald Jampolsky in his inspiring book *Forgiveness*: Do we *"see that our search for the pot of gold at the end of the rainbow is only hiding the fact that we are both the rainbow and the gold?"*

What is the essence of the higher truth that creating wealth is not a zero-sum competition, that *"we are both the rainbow and the pot of gold?"*

3

Does it mean that wealth creation need not be narrow-minded or self-centered? Does it mean that it need not undermine the well-being of others, and that it involves unlocking our inner wealth?

During younger days, I thought that fighting for survival and scoring victories were vital, that I need to internally armor myself. Life was perceived as a brutish battle, an ongoing crisis and emergency. Wealth creation was perceived as zero-sum competitions. *Either* we win and earn our riches *or* our rivals would triumph and seize the riches.

Since scoring victories and creating wealth were perceived as zero-sum competitions, I fervently pursued tertiary education to master technical knowledge. At mid-twenties, armed with post-graduate business and accountancy degrees, I thought that my professionalism as a leader-manager was guaranteed. I thought that climbing the corporate ladder hinged on technical expertise, on applying positive thinking, persuasion and human relations techniques.

Years of soul searching, leadership studies, managerial experiences and professional accomplishments convince me that this line of thinking is inadequate. It dawns on me that effective leadership, management and wealth creation require *something more foundational* than technical expertise. They require *something more foundational* than positive thinking and interpersonal skills.

It dawns on me that creating affluence is not a zero-sum competition. Guided by wisdom, it emerges as a constructive win-win process that develops our deep potential. Having a "win-lose perception" is the huge obstacle. It is the essence of a scarcity mindset.

The liberating insight is that we have the choice to shed this scarcity mindset. We need not be trapped by its pattern of self-struggling thoughts, discontent and frustrations. We need not be ensnared by its misperception that our goals in life are self-aggrandizement and sense enjoyment. We need not be entangled in the misperception that others' achievements would threaten us.

Rather, we can attune ourselves to the higher truth that wealth creation entails transforming a competition-riven scarcity mindset that is blocking the flow of wealth into a healthy abundance mindset that is naturally receptive to the inflow of affluence.

The Secret of secrets unveils. It dawns on us that inner wealth precedes outward affluence; inner contentment precedes outward joy; inner peace precedes outward serenity; inner vivacity precedes outward enthusiasm; inner resilience precedes outward fortitude; inner kindness precedes outward affection; inner wisdom and character precede emotional maturity and leadership ability.

.........success, including the creation of wealth, has always been considered to be a process that requires hard work, and it is often considered to be at the expense of others. We need a more spiritual approach to success and to affluence, which is the abundant flow of all good things to you.

Deepak Chopra
The Seven Spiritual Laws of Success

> *Wealth-Creation Secret #1*
> *The discovery, mining and sharing of our inner wealth*
> *lay a firm foundation for inner and outer success.*

Discovering Genuine Inner Worth

The greatest good you can do for another is not just to share your riches, but to reveal to him his own.

Benjamin Disraeli

Let us share a memorable story from Zig Ziglar.

Years ago, on the streets of New York City, was a balloon seller. When business was poor, he would patiently release one of his helium-filled balloons. Floating into the air, it would capture the children's attention and his business would improve.

One day, when the seller released one of his colorful balloons, a little African American boy approached him, tugged on his coat sleeve and asked, "Mister, if you released a black balloon, will it fly high?"

With kind understanding, he looked into the boy's eyes and replied, "Son, the color of the balloon does not matter. It is what is inside it that enables it to fly high."

Eckhart Tolle's refreshing book *The Power of Now* contains an equally illuminating parable.

A pauper had been begging by the roadside for over thirty years. One day, a stranger walked by. Instead of offering some coins, he enquired what was the object on which the beggar was sitting.

"Nothing," the beggar replied. "It is an old box. I have been sitting on it for as long as I can remember."

When the stranger enquired whether he ever looked inside the box, the beggar replied in the negative, "There is nothing in there."

The stranger urged the beggar to look inside the old box on which he was sitting "for as long as he can remember" and which he had all along assumed to contain nothing. When the beggar finally pried open the box, he discovered to his utter astonishment that it was filled with gold.

When our inner worth eludes us, are we acting, in a metaphorical sense, like the beggar in the parable? Can we realize our potential and become contributing members of our families, organizations and societies if our heart wisdom and inner wealth elude us?

All of us in this world want to feel useful, be it through service to the community, through work in our profession, or by involvement in a variety of actions. Yet first we must experience the inner reality that is a nontransferable, deep part within us.........

Carlos Warter
Acres Of Diamonds Tale

Without touching the higher truth that inner wealth precedes outward affluence, we are hemmed in by a scarcity mindset. We become fixated on material acquisitions and external goals, enmeshed in "lives of quiet desperation".

Let us share the poignant "Acres of Diamonds" tale of Dr Russell Conwell. As our life circumstances evolve, its layers of meaning will dawn on us.

It began in 1870 when Dr Conwell was traveling on the Tigris River, visiting the ancient cities of Assyria. Their guide, an elderly Arab, told the following tale.

There once lived a Persian farmer near the River Indus. He owned a large farm with gardens and grain fields. One day, a priest visited him and told him that if he possessed a diamond the size of his thumb, he would be immensely rich. If he possessed a mine of diamonds, he and his children could enjoy luxuries, power and status beyond their dreams.

The Persian farmer thereupon became discontented and gnawed by restlessness. He was told by the priest that diamonds were hidden in rivers running over white sands between high mountains. Soon he sold off his farm and went searching for diamond mines in neighboring countries and eventually in Europe. His efforts were in vain and he became penniless. Totally disheartened, he ended up throwing himself into the Bay of Barcelona.

At the hometown of the Persian farmer, the person who bought his farm caught sight of sparkling stones in a stream that ran through the farm. Upon verification, these sparkling stones turned out to be precious gems and diamonds.

When seeking external wealth, did we ignore the importance of discovering our deep essence? Did we neglect to nurture the spiritual foundation which sustains our resilience? Did we neglect to nurture the spiritual foundation which underpins a fulfilling life that is not plagued by self-centered pursuits?

Without discovering our deep essence and nurturing wisdom, our life purpose will elude us. Inner abundance will elude us. We are unconscious of our ability to enjoy inner peace, contentment and fulfillment that cannot be bought by material riches. Our worldview, self-perception and perception of others are contorted by ego-protecting self-seeking energies. Our efforts to develop our potential and unique talents are hampered.

Without discovering our deep essence and nurturing wisdom, like the Persian farmer, many of us are lured by external diamonds. We are gnawed by unease, restlessness, feelings of discontent and insecurity. When we earn our first million, instead of becoming contented, we begin to crave for our second and third million. When we earn our first million, we purchase luxurious cars and properties, and become heavily indebted. The more fervently we pursue external possessions, the deeper is the entanglement, the wider is the breach with our pristine serenity, the more severe is the disconnection from our inner peace.

Did you notice that more and more of us are working at a frantic pace and many hours overtime, enduring intense work-related stress, and sacrificing time with our families? Is our physical, emotional, mental and spiritual health being gnawed away by this frenzied pace?

Are we acting like a medieval warrior driving a eight-horse chariot, lashing the whip against the sweaty beasts to gain turbulent speed, our minds fixated on winning the

9

laurels.........*but not realizing that we are racing toward a precipice?*

When genuine self-understanding eludes us, we are psychologically at war with ourselves. Assaulted by discontent, we also become enmeshed in psychological strife with other people, with our spouse, siblings, neighbors or colleagues. We resist changes in life circumstances and combat them in unconstructive ways. Without healing these aggressive energies, they constrict and warp our daily consciousness, *propelling us toward the precipice.*

For a long time I thought the most tragic thing that could happen to a man during his lifetime would be to discover an oil well or a gold mine on his property as he lay on his death bed. Now I know that it is infinitely worse to never discover the vastly greater wealth that lies within the individual.

Zig Ziglar

Let us share another story.

Once upon a time in Greece, a young man with unrivaled physical prowess was triumphant in sporting competitions one after another. Brimming with arrogance, he decided to challenge the mightiness of Apollo, the sun-god.

Apollo accepted his challenge and proclaimed, "If you are able to touch me, I will offer my throne to you."

The young man was exuberant and began his arduous chase after Apollo who sometimes appeared faraway and sometimes nearby, but always beyond his grasp. Eventually, after chasing many months, the young man, totally exhausted, died in disappointment.

To me, this story contains a paradox with two levels.

The first level is: If the young man were *aware* that he was bathed in resplendent sunlight, he could have reasoned with Apollo that he was already "touching" the sun-god. From this angle of witty logic, the young man could have won.

The second level is: If the young man were *genuinely aware* that he was blessed with resplendent sunlight, he would not yearn to usurp Apollo's throne. Instead, he would be contented, at peace with himself.

In the language of psychology, this young man may be trapped by subtle superiority or inferiority complex. But his yearning for recognition by others arises from basic inner dislocation prevalent in modern societies. He has yet to touch his deep essence, the wellspring of healthy self-acceptance. He has yet to be at ease with himself, to be mindful of inner wealth.

To be oblivious of our inner wealth is crippling. To mire in spiritual unconsciousness is to cloak the inner Light. To be disconnected from the deep significance of our lives is to forfeit our freewill, forgo the unique capacity to reinvent ourselves and strangle the invigorating source of life. To passively wait for strong wake-up calls or traumatic events to jolt us from spiritual unconsciousness is defeatist. It is like searching desperately for a compass when we lost our way in a grim forest, only to realize that we did not carry a compass in the first place. In due course, our passiveness proves to be a baneful self-imposed handicap.

Even though you live for just one day, if you can be awakened, that one day is vastly superior to one endless life of sleep……

Zen Master Dogen

Cardinal Newman once wrote: "Fear not that thy life shall come to an end, but rather that it shall never have a beginning." If we remained stuck in the quagmire of spiritual torpor, sooner or later, we would become trapped in the labyrinth of egoistic cravings, unable to unravel and heal the inner morass of afflictive emotions. Our higher intelligence becomes stunted, our higher creative potential stultified. We unconsciously undermine our lives.

Cultivating wisdom and deeper self-understanding can remedy this handicap and heal inner dislocation and disharmony. We learn to let go of the facade of security based on amassing outward prizes, to see through the artificial aspects of our existence and nurture healthy simplicity in personal needs. We awaken to the pernicious effects of being trapped by spiritual unconsciousness. Many aspects of our lives are being trampled by this black mammoth unless we acknowledge and name it. Our inner luminosity can thereby transmute its chaotic anarchic energies into purposeful commitment to positive growth.

In narrating the Acres of Diamonds tale and the story of the young man challenging Apollo, we are applying what Dr M. Scott Peck identified with a dose of humor as the Sutton's law. This law is named after Willie Sutton, a notorious bank robber. When asked why did he rob banks, he replied, "Because that's where the money is." We have been pondering on the negative consequences of pursuing external goals at the expense of discovering our deep essence. It serves to awaken us to the real *pay-off:* healing inner discontent, restlessness and unease.

However, when we practice acceptance, non-resistance and accessing inner peace to heal discontent, restlessness and unease, we are not lapsing into negative surrender. We should not equate broadminded acceptance and non-resistance, which evolve from gaining insight into the higher reality, with passiveness, apathy or a fatalistic-defeatist attitude.

Rather, as we tread along the path of wisdom, it will dawn on us that we are nurturing a healthy proactive type of higher acceptance and non-resistance. Being the offspring of wisdom, such insightful acceptance and non-resistance subsist along the same spectrum of spiritual maturity that bears the fruits of resilience, courage and perseverance.

Thus, nurturing this higher type of acceptance and non-resistance means that we dwell into our sanctified source to rejuvenate our body and soul, obtain inner nutrition, derive intrinsic fulfillment from performing worthwhile deeds and dislodge fixation on external goals and meretricious rewards. Nurturing this higher type of acceptance and non-resistance means that we sustain a healthy perspective of life priorities, that we learn to perceive adversities as catalysts for growth, as opportunities for forging a sound character.

This higher type of acceptance and non-resistance are proactive as they are attuned to our inner resources and resilience. Revealing the futility of evading life, they induce us to be receptive to and learn from each blooming or trying moment. They enable us to face changing and adverse circumstances with equanimity and open-mindedness. They endow us with inner vivacity, optimism and trust, aligning our words and deeds with the realization of our deep potential. They imbue us with the determination and courage "to do what ought to be done".

The most valuable result of all education is to make you do the thing that you have to do, when it ought to be done, whether you like it or not. It is the first lesson that ought to be learned. And however early a man's training begins, it is probably the last lesson that he learns thoroughly.

Thomas Huxley

Wealth-Creation Secret #2
To passively wait for strong wake-up calls or traumatic events to jolt us from spiritual unconsciousness is crippling. Without awakening to our higher dimension, outward success is relatively meaningless, superficial and cannot be sustained.

The Hapless Vinedresser

Once upon a time in France, there was a hardworking vinedresser who faithfully assisted his rich master to take care of a huge vineyard. For ten years, he conscientiously and skillfully tended the vineyard. During this period, the plantation of grapevines under his care produced large juicy grapes that were used for making the best wine in his country. However, his affluent master was miserly and the vinedresser's monthly income amounted to a mere pittance. Thus, he remained poor and lived in a simple cottage.

One wintry night, the affluent vineyard owner suffered a stroke and passed away. His son who inherited all the vineyards was a generous person. He appreciated the efforts of the vinedresser and gave him a bag of silver coins to start a small business.

The vinedresser was overjoyed. He promptly returned to his cottage and untied the bag. A hundred sparkling silver coins met his eyes. He gazed at the coins in disbelief for he had never seen so many silver coins before. Recovering from the pleasant shock, he meticulously counted the silver coins over and over again. After counting the silver coins for one full day, he began to fret over where to hide his bag of coins. After pondering for several hours, he decided to hide it under his bed.

That night, the vinedresser kept tossing in his bed and could not fall asleep. He was afraid that the silver coins would be stolen.

For the next three months, the vinedresser could not eat or rest well. He was filled with anxieties about losing his silver coins. He was filled with uncertainty on what business to engage in or how to use the coins. Finally, he fell ill. When he visited the town's physician and recounted the background of his ailment, the physician advised that he need to let go of his anxieties to be restored to good health.

The vinedresser returned to his cottage and pondered over the matter for another three nights. Finally, he could no longer contain his worries and anxieties. The next morning, he returned the bag of silver coins to his master's son, explaining his predicament and expressing his wish to continue to be a vinedresser.

What is our mindset and attitude toward material wealth? How do we gain insight into the true significance of material wealth?

The bag of silver coins can be regarded as the fruits of the vinedresser's ten years of honest labor. It is commendable for him to choose to continue cultivating and pruning grapevines that utilize his unique skills. Nonetheless, shouldn't he be awakened to the true significance of material wealth? Shouldn't he cultivate a wiser mindset and a more healthy attitude toward material wealth? Shouldn't he learn to tap upon his inner wisdom and creatively harness the fruits of his labor toward realizing worthwhile goals that contribute to the well-being of others?

Wealth-Creation Secret #3
Gaining insight into the true significance of material wealth
enables us to enjoy and share the fruits of our endeavor.

The Four Noble Truths Of Wealth Creation

[The righteous man] is like a tree planted by streams of water, which yields its fruit in season, and whose leaf does not wither. Whatever he does prospers.

Psalm 1:3

But the wisdom that comes from heaven is first of all pure; then peace-loving, considerate, submissive, full of mercy and good fruit.........James 3:17

God has literally laid all the bountiful gifts of the universe at your feet..........

Pastor Kirbyjon Caldwell
The Gospel of Good Success

The process of life taking form is a mystery. That mystery is governed by a creative energy that is knowable when we genuinely feel worthy of receiving its blessings in form. Abundance is the way of the creative force in the universe. You are entitled to have abundance in your life, and to radiate prosperity to all that you encounter in your world.

Dr Wayne D. Dyer

Transforming a constricted scarcity mindset into an abundance mindset entails that we attune ourselves to the Four Noble Truths of Wealth Creation. Distilled from the life-affirming perennial wisdoms, they reveal that nurturing a healthy mindset and attitude toward material wealth is conducive to the realization of our deep potential.

First Noble Truth of Wealth Creation:

Material wealth is a means to an end.
Being neutral and instrumental in nature, material wealth is not intrinsically bad. It is the quality of heart wisdom that we bring to the creation and usage of material wealth which enables us to step into the arena of fruitful living, to be attuned to the sanctified source of inner and outer affluence.

On the other hand, *mental attachment* to material wealth or *mental attachment* to sense pleasures that can be bought by material wealth will lead to inner dislocation and anguish.

Second Noble Truth of Wealth Creation:

Based on wisdom, kind intentions and activities that are aligned with our authentic life purpose, wealth creation becomes a positive process that creates value for others.

Wisdom can be defined as "the attunement of our intentions, thoughts, words and deeds to the deep harmony and constructive potential of our true essence". Cultivating wisdom leads to a clearer vision of the sacredness and unity of life, of the meaning of our existence. We can thereby more effectively define our life priorities and harness material wealth to contribute to the well-being of others. Our authentic life purpose is to nurture and manifest this higher wisdom.

It is therefore useful to distinguish *positive* wealth creation based on wisdom, kind intentions and constructive activities from *negative* wealth creation which is driven by self-seeking motivations. Mindful of this distinction, we do not trap ourselves into thinking that wealth creation is necessarily bad and motivated by egoism and selfishness.

Third Noble Truth of Wealth Creation:

Positive wealth creation hinges on discovering our true essence and authentic life purpose.

Discovering our true essence precedes positive wealth creation. It enables us to catch glimpses of the cosmic intelligence vibrant within us. In due course, we arrive at the stage where we realize that everyday reality is suffused with divinity, that each of us has the divine spark. Deeper insights into our authentic life purpose and the true significance of wealth creation will dawn on us.

Fourth Noble Truth of Wealth Creation:

The cultivation of wisdom and spiritual qualities are essential to positive wealth creation. Nurturing a healthy abundance consciousness, they align our life goals and daily activities with our authentic life purpose. It reveals that engaging in constructive activities that create value for others is inherently fulfilling. Material wealth emerges as a by-product of a healthy commitment to contribute to the well-being of others.

Guided by wisdom and kind intentions, wealth creation is no longer perceived as zero-sum competitions. Deep in our hearts, we understand that we create external wealth to provide for our family, to help the needy, to realize worthwhile goals. Wealth creation is fallaciously perceived as zero-sum competitions when our goals are self-centered. Upon shedding the egocentric mindset, inner affluence unveils. By cultivating spiritual qualities like patience, compassion, forgiveness, broadmindedness, contentment, empathy, generosity and reverence for life, we can more effectively tap our inner resources to create value for others.

…….. money is not the end; it's only a means. You and I must make sure that we find a way to share its positive impact with the people we care about, or the money will have no value. When you discover ways to contribute that are proportionate to your income, you will tap into one of the greatest joys in life.

Anthony Robbins
Awaken The Giant Within

There are many aspects to success; material wealth is only one component. Moreover, success is a journey, not a destination. Material abundance, in all its expressions, happens to be one of those things that makes the journey more enjoyable. But success also includes good health, energy and enthusiasm for life, fulfilling relationships, creative freedom, emotional and psychological stability, a sense of well-being and peace of mind.

Deepak Chopra
The Seven Spiritual Laws of Success

Wealth-Creation Secret #4
By seeking and manifesting the inner kingdom of wisdom
and resources, fruitful living unfolds on our lap.
Upon shedding the egocentric mindset, wealth creation
is no longer perceived as zero-sum competitions,
but emerges as ongoing collective efforts
to create value for others.

Spiritual Exercises: Nurturing A Healthy Abundance Consciousness

Let us bring our minds to rest in
The Glory of the Divine Truth.

Rig Veda

Meditation is a worldwide practice that has an honored place in the history and heart of all the great traditions.

Dr Roger Walsh

Regular meditation assists you in reconnecting to the aspect of your inner self that is connected to God. That connection is already there, but you have to become aware of it to experience it.

John Gray

We are slaves to what we do not know; of what we know we are masters. Whatever vice or weakness in ourselves we discover and understand its causes and its workings, we overcome it by the very knowing.

The primary purpose of meditation is to become conscious and familiar with our inner life.

The ultimate purpose is to reach the source of life.

Sri Nisargadatta Maharaj

Visualization can help us retool and rethink our self-concepts. We all have certain images and concepts of self that we cling to erroneously. Some people think of themselves as overweight even when they are not; others think of themselves as incompetent or lacking in some basic way. We can all visualize ourselves in more satisfying and edifying ways............We can use these techniques to help us grow our spiritual selves by seeing ourselves as compassionate, warm and loving.

Lama Surya Das
Awakening To The Sacred

Indian folklore has an illuminating story about a little musk deer, an amiable creature which lived on the lower slopes of the Himalayas. One bright morning, the little musk deer detected a deep lingering fragrance. He briskly went to his mother and enquired, "What is this wonderful fragrance? Where is it coming from?"

The mother deer smiled and said, "Perhaps you can visit some of your friends to ascertain its source?"

Immediately, the little musk deer visited the rabbit, the squirrels, the birds, the monkey, the chimpanzee, the horse, the tortoise, the giraffe, the bear and the elephant. However, to his dismay, none of his friends was able to identify the source of his fragrance. Dejected, the little musk deer returned home. On seeing him, the mother deer smiled and suggested, "Why don't you smell your own paws? Remember, you have washed them in the lotus pond last evening?"

21

The little musk deer lifted one of his paws, sniffed at it and cried out in joy, "The fragrance comes from me!..........."

How do we rediscover our inner fragrance? How do we retouch our inner wealth? How do we transform a competition-riven scarcity mindset into a healthy abundance mindset?

An effective way of nurturing a healthy abundance consciousness is to undertake meditation, silent contemplation and creative visualization exercises. These are time-honored methods and stepping-stones for spiritual cultivation. Their benefits are profound and manifold, which cross-fertilize each other. Apart from inducing relaxation and alleviating stress, they enable us to connect with our higher unitary consciousness and nurture a healthy insightful awareness. They enable us to calm the untrained wandering mind and its feverish energies. We can thereby better understand the subtle dynamics, pitfalls, snares and ambushes of the untrained roaming mind. Effective self-mastery and positive reinvention of our phenomenal self begin with recognizing and avoiding these pitfalls and traps.

For beginners, we can undertake the following meditation, silent contemplation and creative visualization exercises at a quiet spot at home twice a day, eg. 20 minutes in the early morning and 20 minutes before we go to bed. Their beneficial effects will dawn on us within two weeks.

Ideally, we can visit a tranquil and beautiful seaside during the weekend to undertake meditation. As we walk along the seaside, positively focus our attention on the bright blue sky, the floating white clouds, the resplendent sunshine, the refreshing sea breezes, the sparkling surface of the ocean, the seagulls at the horizon, the carefree voices of children who are building sandcastles and playing games, the soothing soul-touching rhythm of the waves, the liveliness, vibrancy and deep harmony of Mother Nature.

Focus our attention on the reality that we can enjoy such beauty and serenity at the seaside without competing with anybody. No amount of material wealth and treasure could offer us such splendor. This is the higher reality. We are continuously being blessed with and embraced by natural abundance.

Find a quiet spot at the seaside. Sit comfortably on a mat, cross-legged, with straightened back, neck and head. Our clothing should be comfortable. Place our hands gently on the knees. Keep a watch nearby.

Broadly speaking, meditation follows a four-stage cycle. The first stage involves gentle relaxation and calming down. The second stage involves stabilizing our growing sense of inner composure and serenity. The third stage arrives when we touch the immensity of inner spaciousness, boundlessness and freedom. The fourth stage is the state of pure awareness, a kind of composed alertness and vividness, where we can comfortably watch the interplay of our conditioned thoughts, feelings and emotions, and we can choose to repose ourselves in the sacred gaps and spaciousness between our thoughts and sensations.

We shall begin our meditation by relaxing and calming down. Inhale deeply through the nostrils. Hold our breath for five seconds and exhale gently through the lips. Repeat this deep breathing several times. As we compose ourselves, allow our awareness to gently scan through our body to identify muscle tension. If there is muscle tension in the neck, shoulders, hands, legs or other parts of the body, adjust our posture to reduce the tension to a comfortable level.

Close our eyes. Breathe gently, relax and smile. Let the sea breezes blow away all our worries. Gently remind ourselves that we have made a salutary decision to allot half an hour to connect with the higher dimension of our being, to dwell into our authentic life purpose. Gently remind ourselves that during this time, we shall let go of our frenzied thoughts about unfinished work assignments and projects, about future plans and endeavors. Gently let go of our sense of time urgency by sprinkling the awareness that meditation offers the precious opportunity to connect with the true essence of our being and immerse us in authentic living. Gently let go and release our sense of compulsiveness and desperation.

Inhale gently through our nostrils and count silently at the bottom of our heart as "one". Exhale gently through our nostrils and count as "two". Repeat this silent breath-counting process up to "ten". Thereafter, repeat the entire cycle for ten minutes. Alternatively, if we are uncomfortable with counting, we can silently label our inhalation as "in" and exhalation as "out". The crux of this "mind concentration" exercise is to nurture and sustain a composed attentiveness.

While counting our breath silently, we also let our attentiveness to gently follow the tingling rhythmic inflow of the breath through the nostrils and into the lungs, and the subsequent outflow through the same nostrils. Let the wandering and meandering mind to settle down and compose itself. We are remolding our frenzied mind, gently prodding it to become "more aware and attentive" in a healthy therapeutic way. The benefits of transforming a frenzied mind into a clear, tranquil, discerning and insightful mind are profound. Attuning us to the unseen order and processes of natural abundance, we are raised to a new trajectory of fruitful living.

For beginners in meditation, during this ten minutes, all kinds of thoughts, feelings, memories, worries and neurotic projections would assail us. Do not be fretful. Gently label them as "thinking" at the back of our mind. Do not cling to them or invest emotional energy in them. Instead, divert our attentiveness back to our silent breathing.

This continuous process of patiently "catching" the roaming of the ordinary thinking mind during meditative moments has manifold benefits. It is a route to developing a valuable skilful mindset that underpins authentic living and cultivates effective responses to external events. It nurtures a healthy insightful awareness of the many reactive egoistic injunctions and exhortations of the thinking mind during normal waking hours. It sharpens our awareness that these unhealthy injunctions and exhortations originate from years of negative environmental conditioning as well as egocentric self-conditioning where, shrouded by spiritual torpor, we recycle mental stories on the overriding importance of self-protection. Gradually, we become aware of the evanescent nature of these egoistic injunctions and exhortations. Our capacity to watch them "arise and pass away" during meditative moments and during normal waking hours is enhanced. A healthy mastery over them is being fostered. By undertaking daily meditation, as time passes, our mental-

25

emotional attitude and behavioral pattern toward external events become positively transformed. It will dawn on us that the wellspring of authentic living lies in nurturing a healthy insightful awareness with genuine freedom to sprinkle kind intentions into our thoughts, words and deeds.

Gently remind ourselves that by practicing meditation, by relaxing and releasing our grasping, sense of desperation and myriad neurotic anxieties, we are accessing the innermost state of non-aggression, peace, tranquility, ennobling grace and pure sacred awareness. This innermost state integrates our phenomenal being with the Divine Source of life. It allows us to rejuvenate, retouch and rekindle our altruistic heart and to dedicate its natural compassion and radiance to the wellness of all beings.

When the ten minutes are up, our breath counting can stop as our mental state would have been more stabilized and composed. Continue to close our eyes. Relax into the great abundance of Mother Nature. Enjoy the sea breezes and the rhythm of the waves. Gently focus our awareness on the inner spaciousness, expansiveness and calmness of the meditative mind. Gently focus our awareness on how the untrained wandering mind has composed itself and becomes permeated with a healthy insightful awareness.

Gently watch and witness the arising of any thoughts and emotions, and develop the attentiveness, patience and wisdom to comprehend their transitory nature, their "thusness" evanescence, non-solidity and hollowness, their "thusness" arising and passing away. This attentive "watching and witnessing" of the non-substantial nature of our thoughts, feelings and emotions will mature. As time passes, it will evolve into an insightful understanding that our thoughts, feelings and emotions do not comprise our deep essence, that they are not the building blocks of the sanctified source of our being.

It will dawn on us that meditation and creative visualization enable us to lift the veil of everyday consciousness which is filled with dualistic subject-object notions and dichotomous concepts, filled with fractious "I-against-you", "I-against-other-people", "I-against-other-objects" and "I-against-the-world" ideations and thoughts. They enable us to discover and connect with our higher unitary consciousness, to heal inner fragmentation and strife.

Next, visualize that we have become a glittering white pebble sinking slowly to the bottom of a clear lotus pond. Visualize the blessed stillness and silence as we rest at the bottom of the lotus pond. Visualize that we have reached this sacred resting place where all our frenzied thoughts and emotions have dissipated. They are replaced by a deep sense of calm and serenity. Our normal consciousness has taken a quantum leap. It has discovered its deep essence and sanctified source. It is positively transformed and illuminated. It is knighted by its pristine sentient quality of "divine thusness". We become both the glittering white pebble and the fragrant lotus pond. We have witnessed the arising and passing away of the dancing ripples of thoughts and emotions on the shimmering surface of the lotus pond, realizing that these ripples, whether haphazard, feeble, pattern-like or vigorous, cannot disturb the beyond-the-surface inner peace and profundity of the lotus pond.

Wealth-Creation Secret #5
A healthy insightful awareness is the golden key
that unlocks our inner wealth.
Guided by the perennial wisdoms, it unlocks the Mystery of
mysteries.

In the beginning, meditative awareness is like a small flame, which can easily be extinguished and needs to be protected and nurtured. Later, it is more like a huge bonfire, which consumes whatever falls into it............. Emaho! Everything is food for naked enlightened awareness!

Dzogchen Master Jigme Lingpa

Every act done in the sunlight of awareness becomes sacred.

Thich Nhat Hanh

Next, visualize Golden Light streaming and emanating from our heart, from the depths of our being. Visualize that we are comfortably enveloped and embraced by Golden Light. Visualize inner abundance emanating from the depths of our being, abundance of wisdom, compassion, understanding, patience and forgiveness. Visualize our inner negativities being dissolved and healed by the outpourings of Golden Light from the depths of our being.

Gently sprinkle some of the following contemplations into our creative visualization exercise:

- Our thoughts, sensations, feelings, memories, thinking and emotional patterns do not constitute our true essence. They are not substantial or solid entities, but transient. They arise and pass away.

- Our "ego", "personality", "sense of personal identity", "self-concept" and "self-image" are not independent, substantial or solid entities. Rather, they are habitual thoughts and thinking patterns. Thus, they are intrinsically transient and porous in nature and we should not be fixated on them. We can undertake inner cultivation to foster a healthy character and personality that exude kind intentions, broadmindedness, compassion and empathy.

- Our physical body and physical appearance do not constitute our true essence. The millions of cells that make up our body undergo countless miniscule changes and transformations every moment of our life. They are not permanent, substantial or solid entities. They are subject to the natural laws of birth, growth, aging, death and disintegration.

- Our cognitive intelligence, technical knowledge and expertise, interpersonal skills, family and social roles, occupation and job title, academic achievements, external wealth, material possessions and social status do not constitute our true essence. They do not comprise the sanctified source of our being.

- Like all phenomenal things, our physical body emanates from the divine Nonmanifest Realm. Our true essence partakes of Divinity. It is innately wholesome, sanctified, eternal, beyond time, space and causation. Past, present and future events cannot undermine our divine essence. External circumstances cannot impair our innate wholesomeness. Our deep essence is part and parcel of divine Cosmic Consciousness and Intelligence. From the very beginning, our true essence is resting in the arms of Divinity. From the perspective of the higher truth, we are localized or individuated Cosmic Consciousness and Intelligence, permeable pockets of sacred awareness. As we mature along the spiritual path, we realize that such individuation is, in a higher sense, conceptual. By tuning, heightening and refocusing our insightful awareness, we can transcend this conceptual individuation and touch the radiant Source of our being, the holiness of ultimate reality. Epiphanic moments emerge as sacred blessings, as beacons of inspiration, as the natural kaleidoscopic flowering of an altruistic heart.

- Our innate wholesomeness and sanctity resemble the pristine purity of the clear blue sky. Our pleasant or unpleasant sensations, feelings, emotions, thoughts, memories, intentions, motivations, urges and inner energies are like the white, grey or pinkish clouds floating across the clear blue sky. They arise and pass away. They cannot diminish the pristine beauty, vastness and purity of the clear blue sky.

- Our authentic life purpose is to attune our intentions, thoughts, words and deeds with the deep harmony and wholesomeness of our divine essence. Inner peace, contentment and fulfillment are the natural fruits of such authentic living.

- Let us be gently aware that we have availed ourselves to this deep insight and understanding for the purpose of healing inner negativities, inner dislocation and existential confusion. We thereby rediscover our spiritual essence and innate wholesomeness. We touch the sacred and vibrant oasis of inner peace.

- Let us be gently aware that we are not generating unhealthy attachment to a new specious spiritual identity. Rather, we are learning to heal and dissolve unhealthy attachment to erroneous concepts in a substantial and separate self and unhealthy attachment to external forms and appearances. We are learning to disentangle from egoistic thinking and emotional patterns by fostering a healthy insightful awareness. We are learning to avail ourselves to the higher truth of the deep kinship of humanity, of the interwoven fabric of life. Guided by this insight and higher understanding, we touch our heart wisdom and innate goodness. We learn to extend kind understanding, compassion, patience, forgiveness and acceptance to ourselves and others. We learn to substitute healthy commitment to worthwhile goals for unhealthy attachment to narrow-minded pursuits.

- For beginners treading the path of wisdom, it is valuable to affirm to ourselves that external forces, events and circumstances cannot impair our innate sanctity. Such affirmations connect us with our innate wholesomeness. Our inherent healing capacity is restored. Subtle fears that arise from distorted concepts of a substantial, isolated and separate self slowly dissolve. By awakening to erroneous self-concepts, by healing subtle fears and destructive self-seeking urges, we rejuvenate our emotional and spiritual health.

Just as a jewel that has been buried in the earth for a million years is not discolored or harmed, in the same way this noble heart is not affected by all of our kicking and screaming. The jewel can be brought out into the light at any time, and it will glow as brilliantly as if nothing had ever happened.

Pema Chodron
When Things Fall Apart

The ultimate dimension is a state of coolness, peace, and joy. It is not a state to be attained after you "die". You can touch the ultimate dimension right now by breathing, walking, and drinking your tea in meditation. Everything and everyone is dwelling in nirvana, in the Kingdom of God.

Thich Nhat Hanh
Living Buddha, Living Christ

Wealth-Creation Secret #6
By affirming the higher truth that external forces and events cannot impair our innate wholesomeness, our inherent healing capacity is restored. We retouch the higher dimension of our being. This is a stepping stone to emotional and spiritual maturity.

Visualize that our physical body is slowly merging with the Golden Light emanating from the depths of our being. Visualize that we are dissolving into the Golden Light, partaking of its divinity and sanctity. Visualize that we have awakened from spiritual unconsciousness, resting in that sacred place within us, the wellspring of innate wholesomeness.........We have returned home. Like the numerous sparkling streams flowing naturally back to the immense ocean, like the early morning rays of beatific sunlight dissipating the last vestige of mist in our heart, revealing the fountain of hope and joy in the depths of our being, we have truly come home.........

This innocent heart, our Buddha Nature, the Child of the Spirit, the Holy One is never degraded nor lost. It is never born and never dies. To see in this way is to see, as the Tao says, "with eyes unclouded by longing". When we awaken this innocent heart, we find our true home.

Jack Kornfield
After The Ecstasy, The Laundry

When we touch the simplicity and goodness of things and realize that fundamentally we are not stuck in the mud, then we can share that relief with other people. We can make this journey together.

Pema Chodron
When Things Fall Apart

Gently open our eyes. Relax into the embrace of Mother Nature, into our inner peace, tranquility and spaciousness. Gently sprinkle the awareness that we can enjoy inner peace without competing with anybody. Deep inner peace is the ground of genuine fulfillment.

The Buddha said that the potential for enlightenment lies within our fathomlong body. May we awaken to the source of authentic living and ever-flowing wealth within us. May we awaken to the rich cadence and harmony of inner music within us. May we wisely receive the true inheritance of inner freedom and non-grasping gracious living.

Stop being like the man in the Lotus Sutra, who looked all over the world for the gem that was already in his pocket. Come back and receive your true inheritance. Don't look outside yourself for happiness. Let go of the idea that you don't have it. It is available within you.

> *Thich Nhat Hanh*
> *The Heart of the Buddha's Teaching*

.... each of us is here to discover our true Self, to find out on our own that our true Self is spiritual, that essentially we are spiritual beings that have taken manifestation in physical form. We're not human beings that have occasional spiritual experiences — —it's the other way around: we're spiritual beings that have occasional human experiences.

> *Deepak Chopra*
> *The Seven Spiritual Laws of Success*

Wealth-Creation Secret #7
Discovering that we are surrounded by natural abundance, and discovering our capacity to enjoy and be revitalized by the wonders of Mother Nature, unlock our inner wealth.

Becoming Bridge Builders

Let us share a traditional Chinese fable.

A young horse wanted to cross a stream. However, he was unaware of its depth. He decided to consult three good friends.

His first friend was a huge water buffalo. "Don't worry, little horse," he bellowed. "I just took a bath in the stream. It is shallow and safe."

His second friend was a puny lamb. "Don't try to cross the stream," the little lamb bleated out. "I heard from a few friends that the middle of the stream is deep."

His third friend was a sagacious deer. "I have waded into the stream several times in my life," he counseled. "During spring time, the water appears to be deeper. During summer time, the water appears to be shallower. Nevertheless, whether the stream is deep or shallow, it crucially depends on your height. You need to experience it yourself. Ask your older brothers to accompany you while you attempt to cross it. If necessary, they can assist you."

The little horse requested his older brothers to keep watch while he attempted to cross the stream. As he waded into the cool water, it rushed up to his knees. As he approached the middle of the stream, the water rose to his chest. Thereafter, he waded safely across it and galloped light-heartedly to the lush green meadows on the other side.

The little horse finally understood the importance of personal experience. No words of advice could substitute for experiential and intuitive understanding.

Similarly, to gain insights into our true essence, we need to commit ourselves to nurturing inner wisdom and spiritual qualities. We need to avail ourselves to experiential understanding which no words can adequately describe.

Upon opening ourselves to experiential and intuitive understanding, we catch glimpses of the inner Light within each of us. The deeper recesses of our consciousness are illuminated. A profound sense of higher purpose is ignited, unmasking our unique gifts and talents, authentic potential and capabilities, revealing that we are intimate partners of Divinity engaging in constructive co-creation. Like the Northern Star illuminating and sanctifying the path of all truth-seekers, the inner Light reveals that we are ingenious designers, architects, craftsmen, artists and molders of our lives.

We all want to believe deep down in our souls that we have a special gift, that we can make a difference, that we can touch others in a special way, and that we can make the world a better place.
Anthony Robbins
Awaken The Giant Within

………let us pursue the things which make for peace and the things by which one may edify another.
Romans 14: 19

Wealth-Creation Secret #8
To awaken to the fact that we are intimate partners of Divinity engaging in acts of constructive creation is to discover Life.

The inner Light has always been there, awaiting our discovery. With its guidance, we can tap our inner wealth. With its guidance, a clearer vision of our life purpose and direction will dawn on us. With its guidance, we can awaken together to a fulfilling and fruitful path.

May we embrace authentic living and manifest the full measure of our humanity. May glimpses into our inner Light, innate sanctity and wholesomeness continue. May we realize that we are destined to awaken to them and to be guided by them. May we become tireless bridge builders for each other, for our children and posterity.

Whenever we awaken, we begin to feel ourselves being carried............by the holy spirit, by the Tao, the Dharma, the sacred river of life. We realize we belong to this earth. Whoever we are is the right person, wherever we are is the right place to awaken, the place we have been given to serve.

Jack Kornfield
After The Ecstasy, The Laundry

The Bridge Builder
An old man, going a lone highway,
Came, at the evening, cold and gray,
To a chasm, vast and deep, and wide,
Through which was flowing a sullen tide.
The old man crossed in the twilight dim;
The sullen stream had no fears for him;
But he turned, when safe on the other side,
And built a bridge to span the tide.

"Old Man," said a fellow pilgrim, near,
"You are wasting strength with building here;
Your journey will end with the ending day;
You never again must pass this way;
You have crossed the chasm, deep and wide—
Why build you the bridge at the eventide?"

The builder lifted his old gray head:
"Good friend, in the path I have come," he said,
"There followeth after me today,
A youth, whose feet must pass this way.

This chasm, that has been naught to me,
To that fair-haired youth may a pitfall be.
He, too, must cross in the twilight dim;
Good friend, I am building the bridge for him."

Will Allen Dromgoole

* * * * *

Wealth-Creation Wisdom 2
Gaining Insight Into The Higher Dimension

Therefore everyone who hears these words of mine and puts them into practice is like a wise man who built his house on the rock. The rain came down, the streams rose, and the winds blew and beat against that house; yet it did not fall, because it had its foundation on the rock.

Matthew: 7: 24-25

To know that what is impenetrable to us really exists, manifesting itself to us as the highest wisdom and the most radiant beauty...............this knowledge, this feeling, is at the center of all true religiousness. In this sense, and in this sense only, I belong to the ranks of devoutly religious men.

Albert Einstein

Deeper roots make for stronger lives.

Charles Swindoll

A learned university professor visited an old Zen master for teachings. The Zen master offered him tea and began pouring it into his cup until it overflowed. Instead of stopping, the Zen master continued to pour tea into the overflowing cup.

The university professor was astonished and quickly enquired why he didn't stop. The Zen master explained patiently, "A mind that is already full cannot take in anything new."

In a similar vein, the Buddha once told a story about a man who loved his son deeply. One day, while he was away on business, bandits ravaged his village, burned his house and kidnapped his son. When the man returned and saw the debris, he was overwhelmed with grief. He mistook a burned corpse to be that of his son and sadly organized a cremation ceremony. Thereafter, he kept the ashes in a velvet bag, carrying it with him all day long.

Days passed, and his real son, who managed to escape from the bandits, returned. He knocked on his father's new cottage to announce his return. The father, who was still clinging to his velvet bag of ashes, refused to open the door. He thought that it must be a mischievous youth seeking to mock him. The real son, after many knockings, finally decided to leave. The father missed the opportunity to be reunited with his real son.

The Buddha said, "If we assume something to be the truth and cling to it tenaciously, when the genuine truth comes in person and knocks at the door, we are not receptive to it."

In our quest for wisdom, are we able to guard against a cloistered mind? Are we able to shift our perspective and avail ourselves to the higher truth? Are our minds similar to the cup overflowing with tea, filled with self-opinionated views and rigid mental references?

The Conventional Paradigm Of Personal Development

During younger days, I thought that for leader-managers and high performers seeking to thrive in profit-driven workplaces, the crucial question would be:

"How can we effectively contribute to the creation of economic value and wealth for our organization?"

Nevertheless, years of soul searching, leadership studies and managerial experiences reveal that my mental references and assumptions underlying this question are unclear. It gradually dawned on me that they are derived from an inadequate *conventional paradigm* of personal development.

This conventional paradigm is imparted by mainstream business education, MBA courses and leadership development programs. It can also be distilled from best-selling books on self-improvement and peak performance. In essence, its equation for external success emphasizes the need to:

- *build up functional-technical knowledge, analytical, problem-solving and creative thinking skills;*
- *apply self-motivational, positive thinking and Neuro-Linguistic Programming (NLP) techniques;*
- *build up organizational, communication, listening, inter-personal and persuasion skills;*
- *build up management and leadership skills;*
- *cultivate emotional intelligence.*

In striving for personal excellence, these components are important. However, if we aim to sustain optimum performance and rise to the higher plane of creative living, we need to recognize the inadequacy of this paradigm.

If we do not clarify this inadequacy, it will impede the realization of our deep potential and unique talents. We are unable to cultivate healthy emotional dynamics at our workplaces. Genuine managerial and leadership effective-

41

ness will elude us. Our efforts to contribute to organizational wealth creation will be impeded.

What is the inadequacy of this conventional paradigm? What is the missing dimension in its equation for personal success?

Wealth-Creation Secret #9
The time is ripe to bring conventional management thinking and our ordinary five-sensory worldview to a higher plane.
The time is ripe to take a quantum leap.

The Four Majestic Sights

There is one spectacle grander than the sea, that is the sky; there is one spectacle grander than the sky, that is the interior of the soul.

Victor Hugo

May I translate my quest for wisdom in the past fifteen years into a story.

There was once a youth filled with ardor to attain outward success. He was told by his well-intentioned elders that to fulfill his dreams, he ought to seek the guidance of a wise old man living peaceably in a hut near a beautiful seaside.

After several days of travel, the youth reached the hut. Upon seeing the wise old man whose countenance shone with compassion and serenity, the youth bowed at him and explained the purpose of his visit.

With lovingkindness, the venerable old man patted the youth on his back. He decided to show him four things to broaden his mental and spiritual horizon.

He first brought the youth to a giant redwood, hundreds of years old, a symbol of steadfastness, resilience and determination.

As the youth admired the giant branches of the towering tree and its immense trunk, the old man said, "Wouldn't we like to be as steadfast and resilient as this tree? Examine closely its huge trunk and deep roots. Without developing a sturdy foundation, when the winds blow and the storms strike, it will collapse. With a firm foundation, it has withstood many turbulent storms during its hundreds of years of existence."

Next, the old man brought the youth to see the great pyramids of Egypt, one of the Seven Wonders of the World. The youth was astounded by the magnificence and mystery of these great architectures.

The old man said, "These great pyramids, undaunted by the numerous storms that swept across them during their thousands of years of existence, continue to inspire us. Examine closely their firm foundation, without which they would have collapsed many centuries ago. The awe-inspiring majesty of these great pyramids arose from their firm foundation. They symbolized the impregnable human spirit aspiring to attain union with the highest dimension of life."

Next, the old man brought the youth to a plateau where they could admire a range of mountains. The famous Mount

Rushmore came within their sight. When the youth saw the faces of the great Presidents of the United States carved on the mountain, he was captivated and enthralled.

The old man narrated the history of these great men, their courage, noble character, fortitude and dedication to the progress of humanity. The youth was deeply touched.

The old man said, "Great men and women of all ages understood the importance of cultivating a sound character which in turn hinges on nurturing a strong spiritual foundation. It is their firm spiritual foundation that provides them with indomitable strength, tenacity, broadmindedness and inner resources to realize their vision for the betterment of society."

Lastly, the old man brought the youth to a hill overseeing his hut at the beautiful seaside. The old man asked the youth to further extend his vision, where the immense boundless ocean came into sight. The ocean was a beatific blaze of sparkling blue diamonds, bathed in resplendent springtime sunlight in the early morning.

"Notice the numerous little streams that flow down from all these lush green hills, meandering toward the deep blue ocean. Each of us is similar to these sparkling little streams. When we discover the true essence of our life and build up a firm spiritual foundation, the boundlessness of the ocean would fill our hearts. The outward storms in our lives would arise and pass away. The boundlessness, deep understanding and profundity of the ocean will stay in our hearts."

The Wisdom Paradigm Of Personal Development

The fruit of the Spirit is love, joy, peace, patience, kindness, goodness, faithfulness, gentleness and self-control.

Galatians 5: 22

Let us reconsider: *What is the inadequacy of the conventional paradigm of personal development? What is the missing dimension in its equation for personal success?*

Wealth-Creation Secret #10
Our conventional five-sensory worldview and mindset
have been building castles in the air.
The time is ripe to lay a firm spiritual foundation.

The conventional paradigm of personal development is inadequate. It did not differentiate between the *foundational attributes* (ie. wisdom and inner qualities) for attaining personal success and the *instrumental knowledge and skills*. It emphasizes the acquisition of instrumental knowledge and skills. But it omits the foundational attributes that should guide the development and application of these knowledge and skills.

Without emphasizing the importance of cultivating the foundational attributes, a clearer vision of our life purpose and direction will elude us. The *true meaning and significance* of cultivating a sound character, emotional intelligence and a positive mindset will elude us.

We will forgo the rewarding experiences of how wisdom and inner qualities are foundational to the cultivation of a sound character and emotional maturity. We will forego the rewarding experiences of how wisdom and spiritual qualities are conducive to and augment positive thinking and effective communication, listening, interpersonal and creative thinking skills.

Without the guidance of wisdom, functional-technical knowledge and skills may be insincerely used to achieve self-centered goals. Browse through the newspapers and everyday there were reports of highly educated professionals who committed fraudulent or illegal acts to advance personal interests.

Let us consider the following Wisdom Paradigm of personal development. This conceptual framework is distilled from the time-honored truths espoused by the wisdom traditions. Incorporating the Four Noble Truths of Wealth Creation, it is useful in guiding us toward cultivating wisdom and developing our deep potential. It enables us to commit to values and life-goals that are attuned to our deep essence. By differentiating the *foundational attributes* from the *instrumental knowledge and skills*, we have a clearer understanding of our life priorities in the context of positive growth and maturation.

The Wisdom Paradigm Of Personal Development

(A)   *The Foundational Attributes For Inner And Outer Success*

- *Wisdom: The cultivation of wisdom (ie. the attunement of our intentions, thoughts, words and deeds with the harmony and deep potential of our divine essence and with our authentic life purpose) is pivotal to inner and outer success. Nurturing inner peace and an abundance mindset, it leads to deeper self-understanding and the discovery of inner wealth.*

- *Inner qualities: The cultivation of positive spiritual qualities, like compassion, kindness, patience, empathy, broadmindedness, forgiveness, generosity, reverence for life and commitment to serve and create value for others are essential to developing our deep potential.*

The cultivation of wisdom and spiritual qualities lay a healthy foundation for cultivating a sound character, emotional maturity, a healthy personality and a positive mindset.

(B) Instrumental-Functional Knowledge and Skills:

- *Self-motivational, auto-suggestion and Neuro-Linguistic Programming (NLP) skills*
- *Functional and technical knowledge, skills and expertise*
- *Analytical, problem-solving, positive and creative thinking skills*
- *Organizational, communication, listening and inter-personal skills*
- *Management and leadership skills*

Guided by wisdom and spiritual qualities, we can sincerely and more effectively harness functional-technical knowledge and skills for working toward worthwhile life goals.

Thus, based on this Wisdom Paradigm, the key question is not: "How can we effectively contribute to the creation of economic value and wealth for our organization?"

Rather, it would be: "*Without attaining genuine self-understanding, without cultivating foundational wisdom and positive spiritual qualities,* can we effectively contribute to the creation of economic value and wealth for our organization?"

Wealth-Creation Secret #11
The cultivation of wisdom and spiritual qualities
lay a healthy foundation that enables us
to quantum-leap to the higher plane of fruitful living.

The Courage To Gain Insight Into The Higher Dimension

A human being is part of a whole, called by us the "Universe", a part limited in time and space. He experiences himself, his thoughts and feelings, as something separated from the rest — — a kind of optical illusion of his consciousness. This delusion is a kind of prison for us, restricting us to our personal desires and to affection for a few persons nearest us. Our task must be to free ourselves from this prison by widening our circles of compassion to embrace all living creatures and the whole of nature in its beauty.

Albert Einstein

As a self-designated Christian....... I personally not only believe that there is a "Higher Power" behind the visible order of things, but also that It is not neutral — — — that It actively wants us to be in harmony with It.

Dr M. Scott Peck

On a dark night somewhere in Arabia, a man was crawling on his knees under a street lamp. His friend walked by and enquired what he was searching for. The man explained that he was looking for a lost key. Out of kindness, his friend volunteered to assist in the search.

After a lengthy search, the friend was tired and enquired, "Are you certain that you lost your key under this lamp? Is it possible that you could have lost it in some other places?"

At that instance, the man stood up and sheepishly stretched out his arm, pointing toward the bushes. "Actually, I lost my key over there. However, since there is no lamp in that area, I decided to try my luck under this bright lamp. If I were to commence my search among those bushes, I believe I won't stand a chance of finding it."

Let us recount the famous story of how Siddhartha Guatama, the young prince, commenced his path to enlightenment.

Before his birth, soothsayers predicted that the prince would become either a powerful monarch or a world-redeeming sage. Siddhartha's father, the king, was alarmed. Desiring his son to succeed him, he took pains to surround his son with luxuries. The prince grew up in a highly comfortable and sanitized environment. Even when the prince went riding outside the palace, his guards would clear in advance all sights relating to human illness, disease, the infirmities of old age and death.

However, while riding outside the palace on several occasions, despite the care taken by his guards to clear all unpleasant sights, the young prince came into contact with the stark realities. He saw a man suffering from ugly diseases; an elderly person suffering from the common afflictions of senility; and a dead human body that was soon to be cremated. He also saw an ascetic monk in ochre robe, carrying a begging bowl.

This is the legendary "Four Passing Sights" which filled Siddhartha, the Buddha-to-be, with perplexing questions on human sufferings and finitude, the impermanence of joy and life. At the age of twenty-nine, the young prince made the firm decision to leave the luxuries of his palace and embark on a journey of self-discovery.

Let us ponder: *Why did the conventional paradigm of personal development omit the important dimension of cultivating wisdom and spiritual qualities?*

When searching for the possible answers, we cannot act like the Arabic man searching for his key under the street lamp, when we are intuitively aware that the answer lies somewhere else. Instead, we need to emulate the courage of Buddha Guatama and be receptive to the time-honored truths. We need to retrace the rise of Western scientific thinking to which modern management subscribes and ascertain its impact on the modern consciousness.

Wealth-Creation Secret #12
We have shunned and buried the higher truths in the subterranean regions of our mind. The time is ripe to unearth them andlet their divine glow to re-ignite our inner wisdom.

The Great Chain Of Being

Nonexistence is eagerly bubbling in the expectation of being given existence.........For the mine and treasure-house of God's making is naught but nonexistence coming into manifestation.
                                                        Persian poet, Rumi

God's nothingness fills the entire world.

Christian mystic Meister Eckhart

As we progress and awaken to the soul in us and things, we shall realize that there is consciousness also in the plant, in the metal, in the atom, in electricity, in every thing that belongs to physical nature.

Sri Aurobindo

In *Forgotten Truth*, Huston Smith explained that the wisdom traditions uphold an organic-unitary worldview which was described by many Eastern and Western scholars and philosophers as the Great Chain of Being. In *The Marriage Of Sense And Soul*, Ken Wilber summarized the essence of this worldview as *"reality is a rich tapestry of interwoven levels, reaching from matter to body to mind to soul to spirit. Each senior level "envelops" or "enfolds" its junior dimensions – – – a series of nests within nests of Being – – so that every thing and event in the world is interwoven with every other, and all are ultimately enveloped and enfolded by Spirit, by God, by Goddess, by Tao, by Brahman, by the Absolute itself."*

It is also eloquently presented by Dr Roger Walsh in his classic *Essential Spirituality*:-

There are two realms of reality. The first is the everyday realm with which we are all familiar, the world of physical objects and living creatures............But beneath these familiar phenomena lies another realm far more subtle and profound: a realm of consciousness, spirit, Mind or Tao............this realm creates and embraces the physical realm and is its source. This domain is not limited by space or time or physical laws, since it creates space, time and physical laws, and hence it is unbounded and infinite, timeless and eternal.

Human beings partake of both realms. We are not only physical but also spiritual beings. We have bodies, but we also have, at the core of our being, in the depths of our minds, a center of transcendental awareness. This center is described as pure consciousness, mind, spirit, or Self and is known by such names as the neshamah of Judaism, the soul or divine spark of Christianity, the atman of Hinduism, or the buddha nature of Buddhism.

In his treatise on the Great Chain, Arthur Lovejoy emphasized that this view of reality as comprising the Manifest and Nonmanifest Realms was *"the dominant official philosophy of the larger part of civilized humankind throughout most of its history."*, ie. for more than four thousand years prior to the emergence of Western science in the sixteenth century.

Thus, the perennial wisdoms hold that all phenomenal objects and sentient beings are interconnected, interrelated and non-separate. For example, let us consider the current book in your hand. It came into existence because of the combined efforts of many people, like the logger who sawed down the tree, the driver who transported the timber to the factory, the factory workers and technicians who processed the timber into paper-making materials, the scientists who specialized in paper-making technology, the managers of the publishing firm who supervised the manufacture, design, publication and marketing of this book, etc.

It came into existence because its author had the precious opportunities of learning the perennial philosophy and encountering many teachers over two decades. These teachings are time-honored, transmitted and passed down by many sages. From this unitary worldview, the contents of this book reflect the deep insights and wisdom of many sages of the past centuries.

In addition, this book came into existence because the tree from which it originated was nourished by energy from the sun, nutrients from the soil and rainwater from the sky. Hence, the preconditions of its existence include solar energy, soil, rainwater, the natural processes of photosynthesis, planet Earth and the sun. The existence of planet Earth and the sun depend on the existence of the Milky Way, and the Milky Way is connected with other galaxies. Thus, from the macro-cosmic perspective, the existence of this book in your hand subtly and miraculously reflects the existence of the cosmos. This macro-vision is axiomatically captured by William Blake's oft-quoted poem:

To see a World in a Grain of Sand
And a Heaven in a Wild Flower,
Hold Infinity in the palm of your hand
And Eternity in an hour.

This paradoxical and profound aspect of the interwoven and intermeshed fabric of reality is also exquisitely expressed by Thich Nhat Hanh in *The Heart of The Buddha's Teaching*:

"Dear Buddha, are you a living being?" We want the Buddha to confirm the notion we have of him. But he looks at us, smiles, and says, "A human being is not a human being. That is why we can say that he is a human being." These are the dialectics of the Diamond Sutra. "A is not A. That is why it is truly A." A flower is not a flower. It is made only of non-flower elements — — sunshine, clouds, time, space, earth, minerals, gardeners, and so on. A true flower contains the whole universe.

Persian poet Rumi also expressed this insight beautifully in the following poem. The entire natural world, its inhabitants and phenomena, is depicted as inseparably "held in the divine", subsisting within the bosom of the divine Nonmanifest Realm:

The whole world lives within a safeguarding,
fish inside waves, birds in the sky, the elephant,
the wolf, the lion as he hunts, the dragon, the ant,
the waiting snake, even the ground, the air,
the water, every spark floating from the fire,
all subsist, exist, are held in the divine. Nothing
is ever alone for a single moment.

Thus, the perennial wisdoms hold that all phenomenal things and events, inclusive of human beings, are interconnected, interdependent, interwoven, non-separate and are manifestations of the Nonmanifest Realm. Divine cosmic consciousness, intelligence and affection pervade all earthly beings and things. Lucinda Vardey, the editor of *God In All Worlds* wrote: "*In the Vedas, the five-thousand-year-old yogic scriptures, it is recorded that we are constituted of two bodies — the corporeal and the spiritual — and that it is the spiritual that defines us, sustains us, and provides meaning and purpose to our existence.*"

That which does the seeing, cannot be seen; that which does the hearing, cannot be heard; and that which does the thinking, cannot be thought.

The Vedas

Taoism also emphasizes the transcendental unity of all things and that all phenomena and material objects arise from the ineffable transcendental One. Confucianism emphasizes the unity of Nature, man and all myriad things. Mahayanic Buddhism propounds the importance of attaining a non-dual non-dichotomous perspective whereby all conceptual categorizations of things and events are transcended and everyday reality is perceived as suffused with divinity.

> There was something formless and perfect
> before the universe was born.
> It is serene. Empty.
> Solitary. Unchanging.
> Infinite. Eternally present.
> It is the mother of the universe.
> For lack of a better name,
> I call it the Tao.
>
> Lao-Tzu

In *The Archetypes And The Collective Unconscious*, Swiss psychologist Carl Jung wrote, "Being that has soul is living being. Soul is the living thing in man, that which lives of itself and causes life. Therefore God breathed into Adam a living breath, that he might live." In *Lines Composed A Few Miles Above Tintern Abbey*, William Wordsworth also memorably described the affinity and alliance of subjective human consciousness with the sacred presence of Divinity:

> *A presence that disturbs me with the joy*
> *Of elevated thoughts; a sense sublime*
> *Of something far more deeply interfused*
> *Whose dwelling is the light of setting suns,*
> *And the round ocean and the living air,*
> *And the blue sky, and in the mind of man:*
> *A motion and a spirit, that impels*
> *All thinking things, all objects of all thought*
> *And rolls through all things.*

To summarize, the perennial wisdoms emphasize that genuine self-understanding is nurtured by tapping our higher unitary consciousness and by being attuned to an organic worldview. This worldview espouses the ontological Higher Truth relating to (i) the basic unity and interconnected nature of the cosmos; (ii) the intrinsically dynamic, ever-changing and impermanent nature of phenomenal things; (iii) the emanation of the Phenomenal Realm of forms and appearances from the divine Nonmanifest Realm, and the ultimately non-dual unitary nature of Higher Reality, ie. the Phenomenal Realm and the Nonmanifest Realm are two aspects of the Ultimate Reality; (iv) the primacy of cosmic consciousness, intelligence and affection as the basic creative principle of this universe; and (v) the immanence of the "divine spark" in human beings.

All of creation, everything that exists in the physical world, is the result of the unmanifest transforming itself into the manifest. Everything that we behold comes from the unknown.

Deepak Chopra
The Seven Spiritual Laws of Success

That deeply emotional conviction of the presence of a superior reasoning power, which is revealed in the incomprehensible universe, forms my idea of God.

Albert Einstein

............we use the word 'believe' when we think that something is true but we don't yet have a substantial body of evidence to support it. No. I don't believe in God. I know there's a God.

Carl Jung

However, with the emergence of Western science in the sixteenth century, the seeds of materialistic secularism were being sown. By the end of the nineteenth century, the progress and achievements of Western science finally collapsed it into the currently dominant worldview of scientific materialism.

This modern worldview upholds the primacy of the Manifest Realm. It upholds that there is no spiritual and sacred dimension beyond the boundary of the Manifest Realm. Non-material stuff such as human consciousness, feelings and thoughts are by-products of the neuro-chemical processes of the physical brain. If the brain is destroyed, human consciousness would cease. Similarly, divine cosmic consciousness is considered to be mental projection and unreal. The spiritual dimension of existence and related spiritual-ethical values are gradually displaced from the modern consciousness. The modern spiritual wasteland emerged. Many of us consigned ourselves to it. We misinterpret our higher intuitive-unitary consciousness as spurious and illusory, as a remnant of infantile yearning for the blissful state of existence when we were in our mother's womb. Striving in a misguided way to be pragmatic and empiricism-minded, we lost touch with our authentic potential to creatively transform ourselves into a positive force in the world. We lost touch with the higher form of realism and wisdom which underpin fruitful living. We lost our sense of the sacred, of the intrinsic sanctity of our being, of the higher dimension of life.

Wealth-Creation Secret #13
To embrace the organic-unitary worldview and the interwoven
fabric of life is to see through the porous nature of our ego
boundaries. Our egocentric mindset arises from habitual self-
centered thoughts and thinking patterns.
By gaining insight into their transient porous nature
and dissipating our fixations on them,
our scarcity egocentric mindset can be healed.

Scientific Materialism And The Conventional Paradigm Of Personal Development

The Cartesian Revolution has removed the vertical dimension from our "map of knowledge"; only the horizontal dimensions are left. To proceed in this flatland, science provides excellent guidance: it can do everything but lead us out of the dark wood of a meaningless, purposeless, "accidental" existence.

E. F. Schumacher

The difference between most people and myself is that for me the 'dividing walls' are transparent.

Carl Jung

Not everything that counts can be counted.
Not everything that can be counted counts.

Albert Einstein

The birth of Western positivistic science in the sixteenth century was marked by the use of instruments for measurement, quantification and gathering empirical evidence, by its emphasis on objective observation and study of natural phenomena, and by its growing confidence in human reason to unravel the secrets of nature. It was characterized by its satisfaction at the gradual accumulation of piecemeal empirical knowledge about natural processes, rather than the ambition to build vast systems of thoughts encompassing all spheres of human life. It was also characterized by the adoption of a detached, critical and skeptical attitude toward all things and phenomena, withholding acceptance of any idea or proposition until it could be verified based on the scientific method of careful observation, quantification, hypothesis-testing and analysis. Further, even when a scientific proposition was accepted, such acceptance could be regarded as "tentative", in the sense that a scientific proposition could be disproved or modified if sufficient contrary evidence emerged in the future. In *The Spectrum of Consciousness*, Ken Wilber wrote: "Within the span of a century, European man had become totally intoxicated with this new idea of measure-ment...............All knowledge was to be reduced to objective dimensions, to the "primary" objective qualities of number, position, and motion, while the subjective aspects, the "secondary" qualities of the emotions, senses, and intuitions were to be completely exterminated............"

Measurement has become a kind of scientific idol. The result is an attitude on the part of many scientists of not mere skepticism but outright rejection of anything that cannot be measured. It is as if they were to say, "What we cannot measure, we cannot know; there is no point in worrying about what we cannot know; therefore, what cannot be measured is unimportant and unworthy of our observation."

Dr M Scott Peck
The Road Less Traveled and Beyond

The birth of Western Science was also accompanied by the development of a dualistic "spirit/matter" model of thinking. It was popularized by French philosopher Rene Descartes in the seventeenth century who divided nature into two realms, namely that of mind and matter.

In accordance with this Cartesian philosophical dualism, scientists could assume the role of detached impersonal observers. Scientists could study matter and natural phenomena as completely separate from their subjective selves. They began to conceive and view the universe as a cosmic machine, a vast and complex assembly of different objects. They could objectively perform experiments, quantifying and measuring data. Their findings yielded generalized scientific propositions and laws concerning the processes and operations of the natural world. These scientific propositions and laws enabled humankind to control many events in the natural world.

This mechanistic-deterministic worldview was adopted by Sir Isaac Newton when formulating his great theories, namely the three laws of motion and the law of gravitation. Newtonian physics held that the world was governed by immutable physical laws. By studying such laws, humans could control and manipulate many events in the universe.

I do not know what I may appear to the world, but to myself I seem to have been only like a boy playing on the seashore, and diverting myself now and then in finding a smoother pebble or a prettier shell than ordinary, whilst the great ocean of truth lay all undiscovered before me.

Sir Isaac Newton

It should be clarified that for Newton himself, the existence of the material universe was inconceivable without the intervention of divine intelligence. However, his followers dispensed with his belief in divine creative intelligence and retained only his mechanistic-deterministic paradigm of the universe. Newton's followers also held that the basic constituents of matter were "atoms" which were perceived to be isolated, indivisible and indestructible. The success of Newtonian physics and atomistic worldview also influenced eighteenth century social philosophers. For example, John Locke held that individuals were the basic constituents of a society. The collective whole was an illusion. Only the rights and needs of individuals were primary.

Against the backdrop of the rise of individualism and rationalism in Europe, this Cartesian-Newtonian conceptual model of the universe dominated scientific thinking from the second half of the seventeenth century till the end of the nineteenth century. Prior to the advent of Western science, human civilizations were mainly the achievement of cities whose rulers, administrators, mercenaries, merchants, craftsmen, artists, philosophers and teachers were dependent on the agricultural surplus produced by the peasants. However, with the rise of modern science and technicalization, agricultural productivity gradually improved. The eighteenth and nineteenth centuries were also marked by the emergence of modern governmental institutions and the accumulation of capital which were conducive to industrializations and economic modernization. Technical mastery accorded unprecedented power to scientists, administrators and businessmen who could pursue their separate fields of activities without excessive dependence on the peasantry and the vagaries of the weather. In *A History Of God*, Karen Armstrong wrote: "......the process of modernization involved the West in a series of profound changes: it lead to industrialization and a consequent transformation of agriculture, an intellectual "enlightenment" and political and social revolutions......these immense changes affected the way men and women perceived themselves and made them revise their relationship with the ultimate reality that they traditionally called "God".........By the beginning of the nineteenth century, atheism was definitely on the agenda. The advances in science and technology were creating a new spirit of autonomy and independence which led some to declare their independence of God. This was the century in which Ludwig Feuerbach, Karl Marx, Charles Darwin, Friedrich Nietzsche and Sigmund Freud forged philosophies and scientific interpretations of reality which had no place for God."

Western positivistic science had "no place for God" as it enshrined only the *conceptual* mode of knowing, ie. through conceptual-logical observation, study and analysis. This *conceptual* mode of knowing yields "conceptual-symbolic knowledge" which can be described by mathematical or dualistic language, with immense practical value. The successes of positivistic science in endowing us with a growing body of knowledge that enables humankind to control many events in the external world gradually lead to the deification of "conceptual-symbolic" knowledge. "Primary" objective qualities of number, position, and motion emerge as the legitimate concerns of scientific studies, while the "secondary" qualities of the emotions and intuitions are rejected as unreliable and unreal. Positivistic science could not accept the *intuitive* mode of knowing and the intuitive-unitary insights and knowledge yielded by it.

There are two ways of knowing things, knowing them immediately or intuitively, and knowing them conceptually or representatively.

Dr William James

We have two kinds of knowledge which I call symbolic knowledge and intimate knowledge.......... [The] more customary forms of reasoning have been developed for symbolic language only. The intimate knowledge will not submit to codification and analysis; or rather, when we attempt to analyze it, the intimacy is lost and it is replaced by symbolism.

Arthur Eddington
Man And The Universe

The recognition of the symbolic mode and the non-dual mode of knowing....... figures prominently in the work of Henri Bergson (intellect vs. intuition), Abraham Maslow (intellectual vs. fusion knowledge),............Krishnamurti (thought vs. awareness)....... Spinoza (intellect vs. intuition)............

Ken Wilber
The Spectrum of Consciousness

There was a reaction in the West against the radical empiricism of positivistic science. It was led by poets, novelists and philosophers of the Romantic Movement who were appalled by the reductionist nature of modern science that sought to cast aside our innate intuitive capacity and transcendental awareness as well as the sacred and mysterious dimension of Life. In *The Marriage Of Sense And Soul*, Ken Wilber wrote that Romantics like Rousseau, Herder, the Schlegels, Schiller, Novalis, Coleridge, John Keats, William Wordsworth and Walt Whitman "took it upon themselves to heal this violent fragmentation" with the intuitive and subjective dimension of our being. In addition, philosophers like Friedrich Schelling, Georg Hegel and

Emerson Lee

Herbert Spencer propounded the idea of history as evolution toward a higher stage or toward the Absolute. This line of thinking also appears in the writings of Sri Aurobindo and Pierre Teilhard de Chardin who emphasized that we can undertake inner cultivation to discover the the higher dimension within us.

To a large extent, Einstein's conceptual breakthrough in the early twentieth century relating to his four-dimensional space-time continuum and the findings of modern quantum physics have displaced the mechanistic-deterministic worldview. They have effectively refuted the scientism prejudice that phenomena which cannot be detected by human senses or cannot be observed and measured by scientific instruments are of no significance. Modern physicists have discovered that atoms and sub-atomic particles are essentially energies or energy fields. They are not solid or isolated entities as conceived by the Newtonian mechanistic model. Instead, to quote Dr Deepak Chopra, "every atom is more than 99.9999 percent empty space" and the "subatomic particles moving at lightning speed through this space are actually bundles of vibrating energy". In addition, the "void between two electrons is proportionately as empty as the space between two galaxies".

The recognition that mass is a form of energy eliminated the concept of a material substance from science.......... Subatomic particles are not made of any material stuff; they are patterns of energy. Energy......is associated with activity, with processes, and this implies that the nature of subatomic particles is intrinsically dynamic. When we observe them, we never see any substance, nor any fundamental structure. What we observe are dynamic patterns continuously changing into one another – – – a continuous dance of energy.

> Dr Fritjof Capra
> The Tao of Physics

...........the whole universe is a quantum mirage, winking in and out of existence millions of times per second. At the quantum level the whole cosmos is like a blinking light. There are no stars or galaxies, only vibrating energy fields that our senses are too dull and slow to pick up given the incredible speed at which light and electricity move.

> Dr Deepak Chopra
> How To Know God

Modern empirical findings on the vastness of space within atoms correspond to the insights on the intrinsic non-substantial nature of matter and the overarching "nothingness" which underpins the phenomenal world as presented by the wisdom philosophy. Paul Dirac, one of the founders of quantum physics and the "father" of antimatter, wrote:

All matter is created out of some imperceptible substratum and...the creation of matter leaves behind a 'hole' in this substratum which appears as antimatter. Now, this substratum itself is not accurately described as material, since it uniformly fills all space and is undetectable by any observation. But it is a peculiarly material form of nothingness, out of which matter is created.

In his groundbreaking books *Quantum Healing* and *Ageless Body, Timeless Mind*, Dr Deepak Chopra explained that our physical body and its myriad physiological-chemical processes are permeated by a network of higher intelligence. When our consciousness is attuned to this inner complex network of higher intelligence, we experience the pulsating immediacy, vivacity and affection of Divinity coursing through the cells of our body:

The essential stuff of the universe, including your body, is non-stuff, but it isn't ordinary non-stuff. It is thinking non-stuff. The void inside every atom is pulsating with unseen intelligence. Geneticists locate this intelligence primarily inside DNA, but that is only for the sake of convenience. Life unfolds as DNA imparts its coded intelligence to its active twin, RNA, which in turn goes out into the cell and imparts bits of intelligence to thousands of enzymes, which then use their specific bit of intelligence to make proteins. At every point in this sequence, energy and information have to be exchanged or there could be no building life from lifeless matter............

Dr Deepak Chopra
Ageless Body, Timeless Mind

Dr Deepak Chopra's views on a form of higher intelligence coursing through our bodies are shared by an increasing number of physicians and scientists. For example, in her article *The Brain And Consciousness*, Dr Karen Shanor wrote: "*Today, some scientists assert that the human brain is not limited to the gray matter in our heads; every cell in our bodies, every functional combination contains properties of the whole. Even our big toes do some thinking and may have emotions too............*

Furthermore, Werner Heisenberg emphasized the crucial role of the observer in quantum physics. This means that scientific descriptions of external events cannot be wholly independent of human perception. Instead, human consciousness plays an active role in transforming reality. In his classic *The Tao of Physics*, Dr Fritjof Capra explained:

According to Heisenberg, we can never speak about nature without, at the same time, speak about ourselves.........I believe that it is valid for all of modern science, and I want to call it the shift from objective science to epistemic science. In the old paradigm, scientific descriptions were believed to be objective, that is, independent of the human observer and the process of knowledge. In the new paradigm, we believe that epistemology — — — the understanding of the process of knowledge — — — has to be included explicitly in the description of natural phenomena.

However, the post-Einstein scientific worldview which is being unfolded by modern quantum-relativistic physics has yet to become prevalent in modern consciousness. In addition, although prominent physicians like Dr Stanislav Grof and Dr Deepak Chopra uphold the spiritual dimension of existence, the scientific methods and findings of mainstream physical sciences, like quantum physics, astrophysics, astronomy, chemistry, psychiatry and medicine do not aim to present insights into the spiritual and sacred dimension of existence. They also do not adequately consider the natural boundary and limitations of conceptual-symbolic thinking and knowledge.

On the other hand, the wisdom traditions clearly recognize the natural limitations and inadequacy of conceptual-logical thinking and conceptual-symbolic knowledge. To reach the higher echelons of wisdom, we need to tap upon our higher unitary consciousness to rise to the level of intuitive understanding and embrace our heart wisdom. We can thereby experience the "thusness" impermanence and incessant flux of all phenomenal events, the "thusness" absence of an independent permanent "selfhood", the "thusness" absence of intrinsic solidity and substantiality of all forms and appearances, the "thusness" non-dual unitary nature of Higher Reality where our multi-layered multi-potential subjective consciousness is a microcosmic individuation and manifestation of cosmic consciousness. We also experience the "thusness" immanence of the deathless dimension within us, the immanence of divine wholesomeness and affection within us. It will dawn on us that we are individuated manifestation of the dynamic universal life force, that we are sacred vessels of the eternal verities. This is the ontological Higher Reality.

Within us, we carry the world of no-birth and no-death. But we never touch it, because we live only with our notions. The practice is to remove these notions and touch the ultimate dimension – – – nirvana, God, the world of no-birth and no-death.

Thich Nhat Hanh
The Heart of the Buddha's Teachings

However, it is useful to remind ourselves that when we critique the worldview of scientific materialism, we are not denying or denigrating the progress of modernity. Social scholars have pointed out that the most prominent feature which distinguishes the modern era from the pre-modern world is the "differentiation" of the cultural value spheres, namely the domains of the art, morals and science. People of the modern era could pursue legitimate activities within these different human domains without intervention and persecution by the religious authorities.

Nevertheless, in pre-modern days, this would not be the prevailing norm. As correctly highlighted by Ken Wilber in *The Marriage of Sense And Soul*, although pre-modern cultures also possessed art, morals and science, these spheres could be regarded as relatively "undifferentiated". He offered this memorable example:

……. in the Middle Ages, Galileo could not freely look through his telescope and report the results because art and morals and science were all fused under the Church, and thus the morals of the Church defined what science could – – or could not – – do. The Bible said (or implied) that the sun went around the earth, and that was the end of the discussion.

Thus, broadly speaking, in pre-modern societies with "undifferentiated" cultural value spheres, if teachers, poets, mystics or philosophers were to advocate beliefs which were antithetical to the official doctrines of the religious authorities, it is likely that they would be persecuted and punished. Moreover, in pre-modern societies, many of the modern social, economic and political institutions that underpin democratic government, law and justice, protection of individual human rights, freedom of speech, freedom of the press and religious tolerance were non-existent.

From this perspective, in modern societies, the "differentiation" of the cultural value spheres into the separate domains of art, morals and science whereby people could engage in legal and legitimate activities in a particular domain without intervention from the religious authorities is a significant progress. In addition, what social scientists identified as the "modern dignities" which include the whole range of political, social, economic and educational institutions and systems which safeguard democracy, individual human rights, the rule of law, social justice and equality, religious tolerance, etc are laudable and precious achievements of modern societies.

Further, it is useful to remind ourselves that when we critique the worldview of scientific materialism, we are neither rejecting nor launching a sweeping assault on Western science. We recognize the critical importance of the scientific method in the study of natural phenomena and in the acquisition of human knowledge.

Since the dawn of Western science when Kepler and Galileo began using measurement instruments for celestial studies, the application of the scientific method has brought enormous benefits to humankind. Its emphasis on objective observation and study of natural phenomena, the use of scientific instruments for accurate measurement, its hypothesis-testing approach and its requirement for empirical verification so as to arrive at generalized scientific truths contributed immensely to the progress of humankind.

For example, Western science resulted in great advances in mechanization and technology that raised the productivity of agricultural production. It also led to the mass-production of a whole range of consumer items. Modern sciences and technology made possible industrialization, urbanization and economic modernization in many countries around the world, raising the standards of living for millions of people in both developed and developing nations. There were also breakthroughs in the medical sciences, resulting in cures for many types of diseases that previously ravaged humankind. In the past 50 years, technological progress and innovations accelerated, further speeding up the economic development and modernization of many countries. The contributions of Western science to human civilization and progress are immense.

Nevertheless, the huge successes of Western positivistic science, with its deification of the conceptual mode of knowing and the resultant conceptual-symbolic knowledge, have spawned a reductionist and parochial worldview, namely "scientific materialism". To adopt E. F. Schumacher's and Ken Wilber's picturesque label, it is essentially a "flatland" conception of the universe. It is eloquently summarized by Dr Stanislav Grof in *The Cosmic Game*:

According to Western Science, the universe is an immensely complex assembly of material particles that has essentially created itself. Life, consciousness, and intelligence are insignificant and more or less accidental latecomers on the cosmic scene...............We are told that consciousness emerged in late stages of this evolution out of the complexity of the physiological processes in the central nervous system. It is a product of the brain and as such, it is confined to the inside of our skull.

This worldview upholds the primacy of the Phenomenal Realm. It ignores the spiritual dimension of existence. It claims that spiritual experiences are unreal or imaginary. Similarly, religious beliefs are considered as psychological or emotional crutches, as mental projections of the human imagination or egoistic glorification. It holds that our consciousness, feelings, emotions and rational thinking arise from matter, ie. from the neuro-chemical processes in the brain. There is no inner network of higher intelligence guiding and coordinating the numerous physiological-chemical processes occurring within our body every moment of our life. There is no divine cosmic consciousness or intelligence which is independent of these physiological-chemical processes. For many of us, this worldview subtly displaces the spiritual dimension from our everyday consciousness.

Your brain is hardwired to find God. Until you do, you will not know who you are.

Dr Deepak Chopra
How To Know God

Prominent physicians like Dr Stanislav Grof and Dr Deepak Chopra have urged us to avail ourselves to the multi-dimensional potential of our physical brain. They have postulated that it would not be entirely correct to adhere to the conventional notion that our subjective consciousness is solely a product of the physical brain. Rather, our brain should be viewed as having the potential to be receptive to cosmic consciousness and intelligence. To use an analogy, the brain functions like a TV set or a radio tuning in and receiving signals from an independent cosmic source. With forty years of researches in non-ordinary states of consciousness, Dr Stanislav Grof wrote in The Cosmic Game:

This can be illustrated by looking at the relationship between the TV set and the TV program. The situation here is much clearer, since it involves a system that is human-made.......... The final reception of the TV program, the quality of the picture and the sound, depends in a very critical way on proper functioning of the TV set and on the integrity of its components...............

............The fact that there is such a close relationship between the functioning of the TV set and the quality of the program does not necessarily mean that the entire secret of the program is in the TV set. Yet this is exactly the kind of conclusion that traditional materialistic science drew from comparable data about the brain and its relation to consciousness.

Many meditators and those who underwent spiritual experiences would find this analogy useful and refreshing. It offers a creative way to gain deeper understanding of the existence of cosmic consciousness and how we can align our subjective consciousness to it.

The latest research in physics, mathematics, biology, chemistry, and psychology tells us that the brain itself is in reality only one small part of the mind, the physical transmitter and receiver, if you will, of something much more comprehensive and profound.

Dr Karen Nesbitt Shanor
The Emerging Mind

A growing body of philosophers and scientists, like Dr Stanislav Grof, Dr Roger Walsh, Dr Deepak Chopra and Ken Wilber, upholds that there is no basic conflict between genuine science and spirituality. By adopting an open-minded attitude toward the study and analysis of spiritual and meditative experiences, psychologists and neuroscientists can apply scientific methods of objective observation, verification and reasoning to study and better understand these phenomena and how they affect physiological processes, human behavior and human thinking.

While Change is a defining character of the universe, I firmly believe in the unchanging idea that consciousness creates reality.

Deepak Chopra

Further, during the early 1990s, Canadian neuro-psychologist Michael Persinger performed experiments to identify a God spot in our physical brain. He fitted his head with a transcranial magnetic stimulator and discovered that by stimulating certain tissue of his temporal lobes, he could experience "God". Many modern scientists agree that there is a God spot in our brain which refers to an isolated module of neural networks in the temporal lobes. By appropriately stimulating this God spot, we can undergo spiritual experiences. Thus, by routinely undertaking meditation and visualization exercises, I believe that we can strengthen appropriate neural pathways in our brain to render them more receptive to cosmic consciousness, enabling us to experience our divine essence. As we mature along the spiritual path, we will realize that Divinity dwells within the gaps, the spaciousness, the "emptiness" between our intentions, thoughts, feelings and sensations. These gaps and spaciousness are pregnant with the holiness, harmony, affection, creativity and vibrancy of Divinity, of the Higher Reality. These gaps and spaciousness are replete with the natural abundance, bountifulness and ever-flowing resources of the Nonmanifest Realm. These gaps and spaciousness are the transformative vortex where we can obtain inner nutrition, rejuvenation, deep peace and healing.

The most beautiful and profound emotion we can experience is the sensation of the mystical. It is the sower of all true science.
Albert Einstein

The wisdom of thousands of years of mystical experience is walking hand in hand with the emerging knowledge of our science.
Fred Alan Wolf

Without nurturing a more broadminded conception of the multi-dimensional potential of our brain, we would tend to adhere to the conventional materialistic view that there is no cosmic consciousness and no divine spark within us, that human beings are essentially a conglomerate of animal instincts, without a higher dimension. Dispelling our sense of the sacred, this materialistic worldview would de-anchor us from our sense of innate wholesomeness. It would insidiously commodify our everyday consciousness.

A commodified consciousness confines itself to the five-sensory world of forms and appearances. It misperceives that our physical body, physical appearance, sensations, thoughts, emotions, urges and desires are the *essential* constituents of "selfhood" and personal identity. It is thereby oriented toward material possessions, outward achievements and self-advancement. It subtly assesses the worth of a thing or person based on their instrumental value. It subtly views human beings as chiefly "means to an end", and not "ends in themselves". It produces a scarcity mindset which views life as a relentless competition where the proverbial Darwinian principle of "survival of the fittest and fastest" reigns supreme. Life is seen as a continuous brutish win-lose struggle for self-preservation and self-aggrandizement. Negative self-seeking urges are reinforced by this commodified consciousness and scarcity mindset.

The conventional paradigm of personal development subscribes to the worldview of scientific materialism. By omitting the spiritual dimension of our existence, it is therefore inadequate. It cannot enable us to attain genuine self-understanding and cultivate foundational wisdom. Rather, it cloaks our deep potential and impedes us from taking a quantum leap to the higher plane of creative and fruitful living.

The time is ripe to avail ourselves to the perennial wisdoms. We are not proposing a simple-minded retrogressive return to the pre-modern worldview with its lack of knowledge of the natural physical laws and parochial views arising from lack of knowledge of the basic human rights upheld by modern political, social and economic institutions. Rather, we seek to tap our higher unitary consciousness, to touch the intrinsically dynamic, organic

75

and interconnected nature of Higher Reality, to discover the sacred dimension of our being and to rise to the higher plane of authentic living.

Modern consciousness research has generated important data that support the basic tenets of the perennial philosophy. It has revealed a grand purposeful design underlying all of creation and has shown that all of existence is permeated by superior intelligence. In the light of these new discoveries, spirituality is affirmed as an important and legitimate endeavor in human life since it reflects a critical dimension of the human psyche and of the universal scheme of things.

Dr Stanislav Grof
The Cosmic Game

Study the art of science.
Study the science of art.
Use and develop all your senses, especially your sense of vision.
In the light of all knowledge, remember that everything connects, in some way or another, to everything else.

The Four Laws of Lenardo da Vinci

I want to know God's thoughts............the rest are details.

Albert Einstein

Wealth-Creation Secret #14
To touch the sanctified source of our being, we need to heal
the commodified consciousness that is oblivious of
the intrinsic sanctity of all beings. We need to embrace the
higher truth that we are not "means to an end", but ends in
ourselves. We are divine beings in chrysalis with
the potential to co-create a bright future.

Obstacles To Spiritual Awakening

Modern society seems to me a celebration of all the things that lead away from the truth, make truth hard to live for, and discourage people from even believing that it exists.

Sogyal Rinpoche
The Tibetan Book of Living And Dying

Against the backdrop of the modern commodified consciousness that subscribes to the flatland worldview of scientific materialism, the following factors impeded spiritual awakening and the discovery of our true essence.

(1) Social, Political And Economic Environment

No matter how much territory the society acquires, how much glory, how much wealth, how much productivity and prosperity, each individual within it still will sicken, age, and die. The collective cannot help that individual beyond death. Only individuals' enlightenment – – – their clear knowledge of their own minds, conscious, instinctual, and subtle – – – and their confident mastery of their deepest reactions can assist them in their onward journey.

Robert Thurman
Inner Revolution

For the past 6,000 years, humans have been more interested in knocking holes in the decks of neighbor's boats than in patching up those holes. At last, as the water level is up to our eyes, we are beginning to see that we are all on the same sinking ship.

Dr Carlos Warter
Who Do You Think You Are?

Our social, political and economic institutions and systems correctly uphold the rule of law, the protection of human rights, democratic principles of government, fair and equal opportunities, meritocracy and religious tolerance. However, some aspects of these systems are not conducive to individual and collective spiritual awakening. They are driven by powerful materialistic and consumerist forces. Their negative orientations include competition for external power, outward achievements, cultural imperialism, ideological victory and narrow-minded nationalism.

The human race is a family. Men are brothers. All wars are civil wars.

Adlai Stevenson

A prominent example would be the "arms race" between the major powers of the world. Vast sums of money and resources continued to be spent on military research and expenditure, on upgrading nuclear arsenal and conventional weapons. It continued despite the fact that there are millions of children and people in less developed countries suffering from destitution, undernourishment, preventable diseases and abject living conditions. The negative energies which spawned the suspicions, misgivings, distrust, fear, antagonism and rivalry between nations, races, tribes, clans and people is eloquently described by Gary Zukav in *The Seat Of The Soul*:-

The need for physical dominance produces a type of competition that affects every aspect of our lives. It affects relationships between lovers and between superpowers, between siblings and between races, between classes and between sexes. It disrupts the natural tendency toward harmony between nations and between friends............The energy that separated the family of Romeo from the family of Juliet is the same energy that separates the racial

78

family of the black husband from the racial family of the white wife. The energy that set Lee Harvey Oswald against John Kennedy is the same energy that set Cain against Abel. Brothers and sisters quarrel for the same reason that corporations quarrel — — they seek power over one another.

Another salient example is the negative conditioning induced by the mass media. Significant portions of corporate advertising focused on fuelling our materialistic urges. Without the guidance of inner wisdom, we were lulled into believing that sense pleasures and amassing material possessions could eliminate the spiritual vacuum in our being. We were lulled into believing that it is sinful to be unhappy, to be deprived of sense enjoyment. Subconsciously, our roaming minds kept comparing our material achievements with those of our siblings, neighbors and colleagues. We became trapped in the dudgeon of discontent, frustrations and inner warfare. Aggressive energies insidiously engulfed us and imploded our inner harmony.

Similarly, our minds were bombarded by the mass media that sensationalized and glamorized sex, violence and the popular brand of heroism and bravery that returned aggression with aggression, that returned maliciousness with vindictiveness, that returned brutality with more brutality. These unhealthy messages seeped into our supple minds when we were young. Unless we learn to heal inner aggressive energies and dissipate distorted notions of "revengeful" heroism and bravery, we are barred from fulfilling our deep potential. As cogently expressed by Dr Jack Kornfield in *A Path With Heart*, *"Our war against life is expressed in every dimension of our experience, inner and outer. Our children see, on average, eighteen thousand murders and violent acts on TV before they finish high school. The leading cause of injury for American women is beatings by the men they live with. We carry on wars within ourselves, with our families and communities, among races and nations worldwide. The wars between peoples are a reflection of our inner conflict and fear."*

Hence, many of us grew up in an environment that was not conducive to spiritual awakening and authentic personal growth. It was an environment that emphasized self-advancement, outward achievements and showy heroism. It was an environment inciting us to pursue material wealth and social recognition. It was an environment oblivious to the intrinsic sacredness of life. It confined our mental horizon to the five-sensory world of forms and appearances. It negatively conditioned our thinking and emotional patterns. Our daily experiences became "inauthentic" as they are not aligned with our true essence. However, we became accustomed to this mode of "inauthentic" existence and misperceived it as "normal". In the absence of strong "wake-up calls", many of us would continue to be shackled by spiritual unconsciousness.

(2) Family Environment

Nothing is precious except that part of you which is in other people and that part of others which is in you.
Pierre Teihard De Chardin

My stand is clear; produce to distribute, feed before you eat, give before you take, think of others before you think of yourself. Only a selfless society based on sharing can be stable and happy. This is the only practical solution. If you do not want it, then — — — —fight.
Nisargadatta Maharaj

In materialistic consumerist societies, few of us were handed the pearls of the perennial wisdoms. Instead, since young, our parents, elders and teachers emphasized the importance of outward achievements and social success.

The higher truth is that most of our parents, elders and teachers were under the fetters of spiritual unconsciousness. Yet to awaken to their deep essence, their consciousness was confined to the five-sensory world of forms and appearances. Although we are grateful for their kind intentions, we should be aware of the inadequacy of their advice.

There is a crucial difference between sacred family upbringing and materialistic competition-based parenting. In his classic *Who Do You Think You Are*, Dr Warter Carlos contrasts the scenario of "spiritual family upbringing":

"Imagine if your beloved mother and father had recognized their own essential identity and thus were able to tell you, "Kathleen, we're calling you by name because in three-dimensional reality we need to be able to call each other by name. But you are not simply your name. Who you are is much more than your name, or your neighbourhood, or your country, or the color of your skin, or your occupation......Who you are is a majestic, perfect, delightful, spiritual being whose purpose in entering this world is to learn the transformation of matter into the brilliant light........."

with competition-based parenting:-

"Kathleen, you're American, you're white. Anything that's not white and not American is not part of us. You belong to our family and our neighbournood, and anything else is bad."

Our competition-driven parents, elders and teachers may not explicitly say these negative words. However, on many occasions, their behavior conveyed such a message, which are stronger than words. Subconsciously, we imbibed and internalized this message. As time passes, if we did not awaken to our deep essence, these messages will become part of our belief systems and influence our conduct. In turn, when we become parents, we subtly transmit these messages to our children and this vicious cycle continues.

Furthermore, when we were young, many of our parents, elders and teachers tend to emphasize "conditional" love. They were well-intentioned, eager that we should learn from their experiences in pursuing outward success. This is understandable. We appreciate their kind intentions.

However, in many instances, the message that seeped into our young supple minds was that affection would be showered on us only if we met their expectations. Gradually, the negative conditioning of this message barred us from experiencing the intrinsic worth and sanctity of our being.

Psychologists have identified that many young people led their lives based on the scripts handed to them by their parents or elders. From this perspective, if we were seeking largely to fulfill the dreams and ambitions of other people, without appraising whether such pursuits would lead to positive personal growth, genuine fulfillment and realization of our deep potential would elude us. As emphasized by Dr Stephen Covey in *The Seven Habits of Highly Effective People*, *"If our definition or concept of ourselves comes from what others think of us — — from the social mirror — — we will gear our lives to their wants and their expectations; and the more we live to meet the expectations of others, the more weak, shallow, and insecure we become."*

(3) Secular Education Environment

Knowledge is important, but much more important is the use towards which it is put. This depends on the heart and mind of the one who uses it.

The Dalai Lama

Modern secular education, which includes undergraduate business education and MBA courses, has much merits. They equipped us with functional-technical knowledge and skills that enable us to earn our livelihood in industrialized technology-driven societies. Nevertheless, it can be a major obstacle to spiritual awakening since it subscribes to the reductionist flatland worldview of scientific materialism.

We should be aware that modern professionals and knowledge workers with high levels of technical expertise are not necessarily "wise". Based on the wisdom philosophy, a wise person has deep self-understanding and a high degree of emotional and spiritual maturity. His words and deeds are guided by heart wisdom and positive values. Thus, to fulfill our deep potential and unique talents, to ensure that our functional skills and knowledge are used to realize worthwhile goals that contribute to the well-being of others, we need to tap upon the perennial wisdoms to nurture a healthy character.

As dangerous as a little knowledge is, even more dangerous is much knowledge without a strong, principled character. Purely intellectual development without commensurate internal character development makes as much sense as putting a high-powered sports car in the hands of a teenage who is high on drugs.

Dr Stephen Covey,
The Seven Habits of Highly Effective People

(4) Self-Induced Environment Of Negative Self-Conditioning

Popular literature on self-improvement emphasizes the importance of acquiring *"accurate"* self-understanding. For example, they encourage us to pen down our short-term and longer-term objectives, to draft our personal mission statement, to write down our core value systems. They offer useful self-assessment tests that enable us to better understand our psychological traits, our managerial and leadership style, our need for achievement, the strength of our ego, etc.

Nevertheless, the kind of "self-understanding" yielded by these self-assessment tests and the penning down of personal objectives and mission statement, belief and value systems, are inadequate. Without developing foundational wisdom and spiritual qualities, authentic personal growth will elude us. Our value system is unclear. Without awakening to our deep essence, can we ensure that our short-term and longer-term goals are aligned with the realization of our deep potential? Without the guidance of inner wisdom, can we ensure that our value and belief systems are conducive to positive personal growth? Without the guidance of inner wisdom, can we rise above the negative aspects of our personality or psychological traits? Can we rise above our "small egoistic self"? Can we ensure that our long-term goals, personal mission statement, value and belief systems are not distorted by negative self-seeking energies and thinking patterns? Can we effectively manage, lead, coach and mentor other people if we cannot rise above narrow-mindedness and an egocentric mindset?

The higher truth is that without tapping our higher unitary consciousness, without awakening to our deep essence and heart wisdom, we will engage in negative self-conditioning. Firstly, under the fetters of spiritual torpor, we engage in egocentric self-conditioning whereby we compulsively repeat mental stories on the supreme need for self-aggrandizement. Secondly, we utilize positive thinking, auto-suggestion, Neuro-Linguistic Programming (NLP) and human relations techniques to mechanically "condition" our neuro-physiological and psychological systems to advance self-centered goals. These techniques can enable us to achieve outward success. However, without the guidance of inner wisdom, outward success cannot yield genuine fulfillment. Instead, these techniques can become harmful tools that reinforce negative self-seeking energies.

If I try to use human influence strategies and tactics of how to get other people to do what I want, to work better, to be more motivated, to like me and each other − − −while my character is fundamentally flawed, marked by duplicity or insincerity− − − then, in the long run, I cannot be successful. My duplicity will breed distrust, and everything I do− −even using so-called good human relations techniques − −will be perceived as manipulative.
Dr Stephen Covey
The Seven Habits of Highly Effective People

Wealth-Creation Secret #15
To rise above negative environmental conditioning and
unhealthy self-seeking urges is to touch the wellspring of inner
wealth.

Our Modern Palliative

To summarize, why is modern consciousness receptive to the flatland materialistic worldview?

The root of this grand misconception of ultimate reality arises from losing touch with our true essence. Born into a secular, industrialized and consumerist society and non-receptive to the interwoven nature of all things, we experience self-isolation, loneliness, disconnectedness and meaninglessness. We experience feelings of insecurity and vulnerability.

We begin to rationalize, unaware that our thinking mind and its egocentric roaming thoughts do not comprise our deep essence. We begin to misconceive and misperceive that our thoughts, feelings, emotions, urges, physical body and related physiological-chemical processes are the only *realities,* are the essential constituents of our "self-identity". We begin to misconceive that it is *rational and normal* to fight for survival and advance our personal interests.

As we allow our behavior to be driven by negative self-seeking thoughts, emotions and energies, we confine ourselves to the five-sensory world of forms and appearances. To assuage our feelings of loneliness, disconnectedness and isolation, to alleviate our sense of insecurity, vulnerability and unease, we desire the approval, recognition and affection of other people. We desire outward success and material tokens that can offer us feelings of security and certainty. Material achievements accord us with status and power to manage and control the behavior of other people. Such status and power to control others also provides a chimerical sense of security and certainty.

Oblivious of the spiritual dimension of our being, we subscribe to the flatland materialistic worldview. It defines the world in terms of physical laws and processes that are, to a large extent, measurable and quantifiable within the three-dimensional five-sensory world of forms and appearances. This conceptualization provides a sense of security and certainty. By studying and understanding such physical laws, we can control and manipulate events in the world. Such control and manipulation provides a sense of certainty, predictability and power. Thus, the reductionist flatland materialistic worldview caters to our ego-centered conceptual and emotional need for security, certainty, power and control. It becomes our modern palliative.

Nonetheless, without realizing that our thoughts, feelings, emotions, habitual self-seeking energies, physical body and related physiological-chemical processes are not the essence of our being, genuine fulfillment and realization of our deep potential will elude us. Without realizing that our ever-expanding ego-centered conceptual and emotional need for external security and control over others can be deemed a kind of samsaric neurosis and can worsen into a psychological malaise, we would slip deeper into the chasm of afflictive self-centered pursuits. Inner peace will elude us. We are unaware that by experiencing our true essence and nurturing our heart wisdom, we can rise above our ego-

87

centered conceptual and emotional need for external security and control over others, that we can surrender our egoistic grasping and enjoy the present moment. Instead, we will continue to act like the metaphorical beggar, unaware of our inner wealth. We will continue to act like the Persian farmer, fruitlessly seeking external gems and diamonds. We will continue to grasp after meretricious awards, unaware of the refreshing glow of sunlight on our faces.

The Time Is Ripe

Wealth-Creation Secret #16
Creating affluence rests on the discovery of our inner wealth.
The discovery, mining and sharing of our inner wealth rest on
nurturing a healthy mindset that embraces our deep divine
potential. A healthy mindset flows with the natural flow
and sharing of material wealth.

When old words die out on the tongue, new melodies break forth from the heart; and where the old tracks are lost, new country is revealed with its wonders.

Rabindranath Tagore

Whatever selfishness is in our minds, whatever unkindness or insensitivity to other creatures is in our life, is all merely a covering. It is just a thick layer of conditioning that hides our real goodness and kindness..........

Eknath Eswaran

In *Lovingkindness*, Buddhist teacher Sharon Salzberg wrote: "The integrity we develop on a spiritual path comes from being able to distinguish for ourselves the habits and influences in the mind which are skilful and lead to love and awareness, from those which are unskillful and reinforce our false sense of separation." This is congruent with the Buddha's memorable words:

Abandon what is unskillful. One can abandon the unskillful. If it were not possible, I would not ask you to do it. If this abandoning of the unskillful would bring harm and suffering, I would not ask you to abandon it. But as it brings benefit and happiness, therefore I say, abandon what is unskillful.

Cultivate the good. One can cultivate the good. If it were not possible, I would not ask you to do it. If this cultivation were to bring harm and suffering, I would not ask you to do it. But as this cultivation brings benefit and happiness, I say, cultivate the good.

Wherever we are and whatever we are doing, the time is ripe to adopt the skilful mindset. The time is ripe to discover and rejoice in inner abundance. The time is ripe to tap our higher unitary consciousness and touch the ontological Higher Reality. The time is ripe to discover that beneath the veneer of fragmentation, disconnectedness and isolation of our lives, our divine essence is inviolate and wholesome. As reflected in the parable of the prodigal son, when we decide to return home and touch the sanctified source of our being, Divinity would gladly embrace us.

Teach your children that they need nothing exterior to themselves to be happy – – – no person, place, or thing – – – and that true happiness is found within............

Teach them this, and you will have taught them grandly.

Teach your children that failure is a fiction, that every trying is a success, and that every effort is what achieves the victory............

Teach them this, and you will have taught them grandly.

Teach your children that they are deeply connected to all of Life, that they are One with all people, and that they are never separate from God.

Neale Donald Walsch
Communion With God

* * * * * *

Wealth-Creation Wisdom 3
Discovering Inexhaustible Inner Wealth:
The Twelve Gateways To The Perennial Wisdoms

A young monk asked the Master: "How can I ever get emancipated?"

The Master replied: "Who has ever put you in bondage?"

Advaita teaching

An elderly Zen master was meditating when a student walked past him, reading some verses from the Bible: "Ask and it will be given to you; seek and you will find; knock and the door will be opened to you."

The elderly Zen master remarked, "Whoever said that is not far from Buddhahood."

Zen teaching

How do we discover inner wealth? How do we avail ourselves to the gems and pearls of the perennial wisdoms?

It is edifying to trace back to the very beginning, to the awakening of Siddhatha Gautama, the Enlightened One, the immortal teacher embodying the eternal flame that guides us back to our inner Light. What did the Buddha awaken to which made him the exemplar of higher wisdom for two thousand five hundred years? Can we tap his profound wisdom to discover our inner wealth, to heal emotional negativities, to gain a clearer vision of our life purpose?

The truth will set you free.

John 8: 32

Let us continue the Buddha's story of inner transformation.

After experiencing the Four Passing Sights, the young prince was baffled by human finitude and universal suffering. Gradually, he realized that immersing oneself in physical comfort and indulging in sense pleasure could not lead to authentic fulfillment. At the age of twenty-nine, mustering his courage and determination, he left the palace in search of wisdom.

He visited two Hindu masters and learnt much about Hindu philosophy and meditation. For about five years, he devoted himself to traditional spiritual practices. Although he attained profound meditative states, he was still perturbed by inner negativities. Genuine insights into the meaning of universal suffering still eluded him.

Suspecting that it was attachment to physical comfort that was hampering him, he decided to devote himself to ascetic practices. He renounced all physical comfort and subjected his body to austerities, eating "only six grains of rice a day during one of his fasts". As time passed, the Buddha-to-be became emaciated. It was recorded that when he was touching the skin of his stomach, he was actually holding his spine. After months of austere practices, he began to realize that self-mortification could not lead to enlightenment. He decided to nurse himself back to health. However, while on his way from the forest to a village to beg for food, he succumbed to physical weakness and fainted. Fortunately, a village girl named Sujata, who was on her way to give her offering of food to the forest gods, found him lying unconscious. She could discern that Gautama was in need of nourishment and quickly fed him with milk. In *The Feeling Buddha*, David Brazier suggested that Sujata's act of compassion could be considered as the Fifth Legendary Sight.

Awakening from his faint and while recuperating, Gautama was inspired by Sujata's unaffected kindness to contemplate on the innate goodness and altruistic potential of humanity. During one of his reflections, he recalled the tranquility and inner grace which he experienced as a child while sitting under a rose-apple tree in his father's garden. By relaxing into that natural state of wholesomeness and vibrancy, he was already touching the wellspring of mental and spiritual soundness.

Realizing that the seeds of enlightenment was innate in the depths of his being, he began to cherish his body, mind and spirit. He realized there was no need to struggle against his own body and mind, against changing life circumstances. He was intrinsically wholesome. Indulging in sense pleasures and subjecting oneself to austere practices were extremes that should be avoided. Enlightenment consists of treading the Middle Path.

One evening near Gaya in northeast India, feeling that a genuine spiritual breakthrough was approaching, the Buddha-to-be sat down to meditate under a bodhi tree. As the night came, his meditation deepened. His insights into his innate sanctity ripened. When the morning stars glittered in the eastern sky, the Great Awakening dawned on him.

It's too close so we overlook it.
It seems too good to be true so we cannot believe it.
Zen master Dozgchen

93

Twelve Gateways To The Perennial Wisdoms And Inner Wealth

We shall avail ourselves to the gems and pearls of the perennial wisdoms by entering the following gateways.

First Gateway: Self-Understanding Is The Root Of Wisdom

The greatest human quest is to know what one must do in order to become a human being.

Immanuel Kant

What can we gain by sailing to the moon if we are not able to cross the abyss that separates us from ourselves? This is the most important of all voyages of discovery, and without it all the rest are not only useless but disastrous.

Thomas Merton

When you understand one thing through and through, you understand everything. When you try to understand everything, you will not understand anything. The best way is to understand yourself, and then you will understand everything.

Shunryu Suzuki
Zen Mind, Beginner's Mind

If I were asked to summarize the main purpose of cultivating wisdom and positive spiritual qualities, my answer would be: to maintain a healthy perspective of life priorities.

Inner cultivation serves to ground us in authentic fruitful living. Its purposes and aims are therefore practical. However, many of us have misconceived inner cultivation to be arcane, occultist, esoteric and unapproachable. The time is ripe to clarify these basic myths and misconceptions.

There was once a young man named Rajid who was an earnest student of Hinduism. He prayed day and night for many weeks to gain understanding of the ultimate reality, to pierce through the veils of illusion.

One night, his fervent wish came true. While meditating near a river, Rajid experienced a divine light dawning on him. He opened his eyes and was amazed to see Vishnu before him. He briskly prostrated himself before his God and said in a grateful trembling voice, "Thank you, God, for revealing Yourself to me. From this moment onward, I shall devote myself to worshipping you and I shall do anything for you........."

"It is heartening to hear these words. Could you thereby fetch me a small jug of water?" Vishnu replied.

Rajid was astounded by the request. He quickly rushed back to his hut to obtain a small jug and ran to the nearby river whose water was always clear and drinkable.

While he was kneeling down to fill his small jug, he heard the sounds of drums and someone calling, "A beautiful maiden searching for a bridegroom......."

He turned and saw a golden sparkling carriage with six handsome horses and an entourage of guards and servants. The face of an attractive young girl appeared at the window of the carriage. The young girl smiled at Rajid and waved to him. One of the servant promptly approached Rajid and said, "Congratulations. This is the first time that the daughter of our rich master has expressed interest in a young man. You are very lucky. Please come with us. You may become the bridegroom and enjoy immense riches."

Rajid was surprised by these words. By this time, he had already fallen in love with the beautiful girl and went with her to their palatial residence in the city. They were married, had three children and Rajid became a wealthy merchant.

However, Rajid's ambition did not halt. Convinced that his God was secretly helping him, he vowed to become the wealthiest merchant in his country. For the next twenty years, he competed aggressively with many of the city tradesmen. Their rivalries culminated in a sinister plot where a dozen of his bodyguards betrayed Rajid and abducted him.

Rajid found himself imprisoned in a small island. He regretted over his egoistic ambition and greed. While his captors were pondering on how to deal with Rajid, a huge storm swept across the island and everyone, except Rajid, was drowned.

Lying semi-conscious on the beach, Rajid forced himself to meditate which he did not do so for more than twenty years since he last saw Vishnu. Gradually, Rajid experienced a divine light dawning on him. He opened his eyes slowly and saw Vishnu, who said, "Was your heart distracted by the illusory forms and appearances of the world? Did you learn to calm your heart and repose in its natural beauty and sufficiency? Did you succeed in fetching me a small jug of water?"

Sometimes people get the mistaken notion that spirituality is a separate department of life.........But rightly understood, it is a vital awareness that pervades all realms of our being.

Brother David Steindl-Rast

How do we sustain a healthy perspective of life priorities?

The first key to restore our healthy perspective of life priorities and quantum-leap to a higher plane of fruitful living would be to probe into our deep essence. Personal growth and maturation rest on arriving at genuine self-understanding. As observed by Sydney Harris: "Ninety percent of the world's woe comes from people not knowing themselves, their abilities, their frailties, and even their real virtues. Most of us go almost all the way through life as complete strangers to ourselves." This is congruent with Plato's famous words, "The unexamined life is not worth living."

Nevertheless, attaining self-knowledge and self-mastery are not easy. The philosopher Thales once exclaimed, "The most difficult thing in life is to know yourself." which Josh Billings added a humorous twist, "It is not only the most difficult thing to know oneself, but the most inconvenient, too."

Understanding the difficulty of transcending our "small egoistic self", Mahatma Gandhi once said: "I have only three enemies. My favorite enemy, the one most easily influenced for the better, is the British Empire. My second enemy, the Indian people, is far more difficult. But my most formidable opponent is a man named Mohandas K. Gandhi. With him I seem to have very little influence."

Nurturing self-understanding requires us to patiently apply our insightful awareness into the subtle workings of our "small egoistic self". It requires us to dissipate erroneous concepts of an isolated self with its myriad "I-against-others" and "I-against-the-world" ideations and strivings. We can thereby more effectively manage the "crowd" within our "earthly temple":

Within my earthly temple there is a crowd.
There's one of us that's humble; one that's proud.
There's one that's broken-hearted for his sins,
And one who, unrepentant, sits and grins.
There's one who loves his neighbor as himself,
And one who cares for naught but fame and pelf.
From much corroding care would I be free
If once I could determine which is Me.

Edward Sanford Martin

With maturing wisdom, we realize that we are a "bundle of possibilities", endowed with innate autonomy to reinvent ourselves. Harry Emerson Fosdick said, "One must have the adventurous daring to accept oneself as a bundle of possibilities and undertake the most interesting game in the world——making the most of one's best." Greek philosopher Cicero also said, "The precept, "Know thyself", was not solely intended to obviate the pride of mankind, but likewise that we might understand our own worth."

To be convinced that we are a bundle of positive possibilities, we need to be receptive to our innate wholesomeness. We need to patiently nurture a healthy insightful awareness. The rewards of discovering our inner worth and touching the sanctified source of our being are manifold, which exceed the treasures of the world. As beautifully summarized by Lao-Tze, "Knowing others is

98

wisdom; knowing yourself is Enlightenment." In her touching book *Lovingkindness,* Sharon Salzberg depicted that the inherent "reward" of arriving at self-understanding and "breaking the spell of conventional thought" is to recognize that:

No matter how wonderful or terrible our lives have been, no matter how many traumas and scars we may carry from the past, no matter what we have gone through or what we are suffering now, our intrinsic wholeness is always present.........It is as if we were in a small, cramped room on top of a mountain, and all at once the walls have come tumbling down, revealing a panoramic vista.

The Buddha once said, "Playing the flute does not depend solely on practicing the flute. I can play better now because I have found my true self. We cannot reach the higher echelons in our art if we do not first discover the sublime beauty and wisdom in our compassionate heart." Similarly, if we wish to quantum leap to a higher plane of effectiveness and fruitful living in all areas of our life, be it at our homes or workplaces, we need to embark on inner exploration to gain insight into our deep essence.

The true value of a human being is determined primarily by the measure and the sense in which he has attained liberation from the self.

Albert Einstein

To study the Buddha's way is to study the self;
To study the self is to transcend the self.
To transcend the self is to be enlightened by all things.

Zen Master Dogen

Wealth-Creation Secret #17
The depth of our self-understanding and the extent of
our commitment and efforts to step beyond our egoistic mindset
and conditioned behavior reflect the depth of our wisdom.

Second Gateway: Going Beyond The Exhilarating Experiences Of Initial Awakening

Satori is not the end of the path, but the beginning.........it's not the actual enlightenment experience alone that counts, but the living of it, embodying it, stabilizing it, and working out its implications in everyday life. That's what matters.

Lama Surya Das
Awakening To The Sacred

Unbounded freedom and joy, oneness with the Divine, awakening into a state of timeless grace – – – these experiences are more common than you know, and not far away. There is one further truth, however: They don't last.

Dr Jack Kornfield
After The Ecstasy, The Laundry

Like many followers of the spiritual path, my initial awakening in my late twenties was exhilarating. For an entire week, my physical body was so light and porous that I could keenly feel the breezes penetrating and whizzing past the cells of my body. I mistakenly thought that such exhilarating experiences were the climax of enlightenment.

As we continue our spiritual path, with ripening wisdom, it will dawn on us that the delightful sensations and experiences of initial awakening are signposts along our journey. They are not the destination. We should not cling to them. We should not create a new specious spiritual identity and lapse into chasing after and grasping at delightful spiritual states. Such grasping is akin to our yearning for external forms of pleasure, material comfort and security. Instead of liberating us from inner strife and dislocation, it will subtly fuel self-seeking energies. Thus, we should learn to let these spiritual states to naturally arise and pass away. By letting go of subtle grasping at outer and inner forms of security, our deep essence will gradually unveil.

.........*spiritual life is not a process of seeking or gaining some extraordinary condition or special powers. In fact, such seeking can take us away from ourselves. If we are not careful, we can easily find the great failures of our modern society – – – its ambition, materialism, and individual isolation – – repeated in our spiritual life.*

Dr Jack Kornfield
A Path With Heart

As we continue our spiritual path, we will realize the *difference* between the delightful sensations brought about by the techniques of spiritual practice and genuine ripening of wisdom. In many instances, the delightful exhilarating experiences of initial awakening mirror the depth of our bondage to erroneous concepts of self-identity. They mirror the breadth and depth in which we have lost touch with our innate sanctity and life purpose. They mirror the breadth and depth in which we are shackled by spiritual unconsciousness. They mirror the breath and depth of our distorted self-perception and perception of others, of inner conflict and strife.

Thus, the delightful experiences of initial awakening and meditative states need to be integrated with our inner cultivation. Similarly, we need to integrate subsequent doubts and disappointment over our inability to consistently live up to our high expectations as part and parcel of ongoing spiritual practice.

Let the pleasant sensations of initial awakening and spiritual states to naturally arise and pass away. Let them be signposts pointing to our deep essence. Let us go beyond them and heal inner struggle and dislocation, restlessness and unease. Let us apply our insightful awareness to heal egoistic energies.

There was once a king who ordered the arrest of one hundred innocent people. He intended to execute them to satisfy his violent inclinations. Before doing so, he decided to challenge a group of wise men. The king proclaimed, "Within three days, if you can bring me something that can make me happy when I am sad, and make me sad when I am happy, I shall release these people."

The group of wise men immediately discussed among themselves and pondered over the king's challenge.

On the third day, the group of wise men handed a golden ring to the king. Surprised, the king asked whether it was a magical ring that could make him omnipotent and omniscient.

The wise men shook their heads and advised the king to examine closely the words inscribed on it. They read: "This too shall pass."

Akin to ordinary feelings and mental states, the delightful experiences of initial awakening and meditative states will arise and naturally pass away. What does not pass away is deepened insight into the sanctified source of our being.

To cling to these heavens and hells, no matter how beautiful, slows your progress. Not to acknowledge them, or to push them away, is just a more subtle form of clinging. Follow the middle way. As stuff arises in your mind, let it arise, notice it, let it go.

Ram Dass
Journey of Awakening

Although enlightenment includes transcendent states, those states are nothing in themselves if not simultaneously the fountainhead of energetic compassion directed at all beings.

Robert Thurman
Inner Revolution

Wealth-Creation Secret #18
Whenever we become aware that we are slipping into the quagmire of attachment to pleasurable sensations, gently remind ourselves, "This too shall pass." Whenever we become aware that we are entering the labyrinth of pessimistic emotions, also gently remind ourselves, "This too shall pass." We can thereby transform emotional negativities into positive energies and harness them for positive wealth creation.

Third Gateway: Understanding The True Essence Of Our Phenomenal Self

Self-transformation is arduous work, especially at first; but each tiny change brings with it the joyful awareness that your life is gradually becoming a force for peaceful change.

Eknath Easwaran

Abraham Lincoln once remarked that if we were to read the Bible daily and practice its precepts diligently, we will become a "better man".

For beginners of inner cultivation, Lincoln's advice may not be clear. As beginners, we may misconceive that since we contain the divine spark and have awakened to it, we would already be intrinsically "good" and wholesome. Hence, we may misconceive that we cannot be "better" persons since our intrinsic sanctity does not admit of degrees and does not need improvement.

To clarify this confusion, it is useful to differentiate between our phenomenal self and our divine essence. This conceptual framework which is at the level of "relative truth" is useful for beginners. Nevertheless, it should be transcended when our inner cultivation matures. To borrow the Buddha's analogy, this conceptual framework is akin to the raft that carries us across the sea of non-awareness to the radiant shore of awakening. From this perspective of "relative truth", our phenomenal self can be seen to comprise the following dimensions:

- Physical dimension: our physical body, physical appearance and physical attributes
- Cognitive dimension: our ability to think, to conceptualize, to reason and analyze
- Emotive dimension: our capacity to feel and experience a wide range of emotions

- Spiritual dimension: the deep essence and innate wholesomeness of our being

The conventional worldview holds that our phenomenal self is confined to the three-dimensional five-sensory world of forms and appearances, to the natural laws of physical integration and disintegration, of birth, death and decay. Nevertheless, by patiently nurturing wisdom, we can rise above this five-sensory conventional perspective. It will dawn on us that our phenomenal self, like other phenomenal objects, emanates from the divine Nonmanifest Realm. Our phenomenal self has a deep essence that emanates from and partakes of the divine Nonmanifest Realm. It has a spiritual dimension which partakes of Divinity.

With ripening wisdom, it will also dawn on us that our ordinary subjective consciousness is multi-layered and multi-dimensional. It could rise to higher "non-ordinary" unitary levels. To quote the famous words of the American psychologist William James:

Our normal waking consciousness, rational consciousness as we call it, is but one special type of consciousness, whilst all about it, parted from it by the filmiest of screens, there lie potential forms of consciousness entirely different.............No account of the universe in its totality can be final which leaves these other forms of consciousness quite disregarded.

These higher levels of consciousness is *holotrophic* in nature. This term *holotrophic* is coined by Dr Stanislav Grof. It is a composite word (from the Greek *holos* which means "whole" and *trepein* which means "moving toward") which denotes "oriented toward wholeness" or "moving in the direction of wholeness". Thus, our ordinary waking consciousness has a tendency to progress toward a higher form of wholeness, unity and integrity.

We may wonder how could our individuated subjective consciousness partake of cosmic intelligence and expansiveness? We can tap upon the discovery of the holographic principle in the world of science to illuminate this concept, ie. at the level of "relative truth". In his important book *The Holotrophic Mind*, Dr Stanislav Grof explained:

A hologram is produced when a single laser light is split into two separate beams. The first beam is bounced off the object to be photographed, for example, an apple. Then the second beam is allowed to collide with the reflected light of the first beam, and the resulting intereference pattern is recorded on film.............. Unlike normal photographs, every portion of a piece of holographic film contains all the information of the whole. Thus, if a holographic plate is broken into fragments, each piece can still be used to reconstruct the entire image.

Various scientists and philosophers have postulated that our individuated subjective consciousness reflects the holographic principle. It contains and reflects the infinite qualities and potentiality of cosmic consciousness and intelligence. We can seek to experience this higher perspective by undertaking meditations which enable us to raise our individuated subjective consciousness to the higher unitary level. It dawns on us that our insightful awareness emanates from divine Cosmic Consciousness. We touch the higher truth that we are enveloped by Divinity.

Nature is full of genius,
full of the divinity,
so that not a snowflake escapes
its fashioning hand.

Henry David Thoreau

Upon awakening to our spiritual dimension, we realize that our ego is not our true essence. Our ego can be defined as habitual self-centered thoughts and thinking patterns. Our ego is not a fixed and static entity. It is not a static conglomerate of personality traits. Rather, it is our thinking and emotional patterns that evolve under years of negative environmental conditioning.

As our inner cultivation deepens, it will dawn on us that our egoistic self-centered thinking and emotional patterns arise when our physical, cognitive and emotive dimensions of our phenomenal self are not aligned with the deep harmony and wholesomeness of our spiritual dimension. It will also dawn on us that our ego boundary is porous. We have the deep potential to rise above our small egoistic self, to rise above narrow-minded thoughts and thinking patterns.

Your ego is a set of thoughts that define your universe. It's like a familiar room built of thoughts; you see the universe through its windows. You are secure in it, but to the extent that you are afraid to venture outside, it has become a prison.

Ram Dass
Journey of Awakening

Wealth-Creation Secret #19
We are on the threshold of inner affluence by gaining insight into the higher truth that our "ego" is not an inherently substantial entity, but a conceptual delusion that arises from patterns of self-centered thinking.

Patient inner cultivation releases us from the prison of our ego. It enables us to experience that the millions of cells of our body undergo countless changes and transformations every second of our life. Similarly, our thoughts, sensations, feelings and emotions arise and pass away. They are evanescent and fleeting. Our concepts and belief in a static ossified "self" are untenable. As poetically expressed by the Venerable Lama Gendun Rinpoche:

> *Don't believe in the reality*
> *of good and bad experiences;*
> *they are like today's ephemeral weather,*
> *like rainbows in the sky.*

For beginners on the spiritual path, it is useful to understand that the purpose of inner cultivation is to contribute to positive personal growth. Although the spiritual dimension of our being is innately wholesome, the physical, cognitive and emotional aspects of our phenomenal self need to be nurtured and "trained", so as to align them with the deep harmony and constructive potential of our spiritual dimension. In this context, "self-improvement", "self-management", "self-mastery" and "self-healing" are useful conceptual tools at the level of "relative truth", ie. they refer to the ongoing improvement, management, mastery and healing of the physical, cognitive and emotional aspects of our phenomenal self. They facilitate our understanding of and insight into the personal maturation process and our potential to rise to higher planes of holotrophic consciousness.

Fourth Gateway: Understanding The Roots Of Human Suffering

As human beings, it is natural for us to seek happiness and peace of mind. However, owing to negative environmental conditioning, during the process of seeking happiness and peace of mind, we lost touch with our true essence.

Having lost touch with our true essence, we misconceive our thoughts, feelings, emotions, urges, desires, physical body and appearance as constituting an independent "selfhood". Coupled with negative environmental conditioning that emphasizes self-advancement, we sink deeper into existential confusion. Driven by doubts, fear, pride, envy and hostile energies, we erect fortifications around our compassionate heart. We begin to grasp at pleasant sensations and material possessions that we thought could offer us protection and security. However, such grasping could not offer us genuine peace of mind. Instead, it is the root of discontent, frustration and unhappiness. In the Fire Sermon, the Buddha explained:

Everything is burning. The eye is burning and visible sights are burning. The ears and the sounds they hear are burning, the nose, the tongue, the body and mind are burning. With what fires are they burning? With the fires of greed, hatred and ignorance, burning with anxiety, jealousy, loss, decay and grief. Considering this suffering, a follower of the way becomes weary of the fires........... Being weary, one divests oneself of this grasping and by the absence of this grasping one becomes free.

By undertaking inner cultivation, we apply insightful awareness onto our grasping. We gain insight into the origin of our fears and feelings of insecurity. We learn that inner peace cannot be obtained by grasping at pleasant sensations and material possessions, by clinging to ossified concepts of self-identity. Rather, inner peace will dawn on us when we touch our deep essence, when we catch glimpses of the ontological Higher Reality and awaken from our spiritual torpor. Inner peace will dawn on us when we let go of our resistance against the impermanence of phenomenal things and the absence of permanent selfhood, against the flux of life events, against our finitude and mortality.

The cause of suffering is ignorance, a false way of looking at reality. Thinking the impermanent is permanent, that is ignorance. Thinking there is a self when there is not, that is ignorance. From ignorance is born greed, anger, fear, jealousy, and countless other sufferings. The path of liberation is the path of looking deeply at things in order to truly realize the nature of impermanence...............

Thich Nhat Hanh
Old Path, White Clouds

Wealth-Creation Secret #20
The deeper our grasping for external wealth and possessions, the more we become distracted from the inner affluence abiding in the depths of our being.

Fifth Gateway: Clarifying Basic Misconceptions About Inner Cultivation And Understanding That It Is Not A Route To Avoid Suffering

The great enemy of the truth is very often not the lie............but the myth – – – persistent, persuasive, and unrealistic.

John F. Kennedy

The time is ripe to clarify common misconceptions about the aims and purposes of cultivating wisdom and positive spiritual qualities. The time is ripe to dispel basic myths surrounding inner cultivation, so that we do not misperceive that this critical dimension of our life is irrelevant, redundant or a relic of the past.

Misconception 1: Bona fide inner cultivation is reserved for spiritual masters or holy monks and nuns who live in secluded monasteries or remote mountains.

One need not travel to distant lands, seek exotic mystical experiences, master esoteric mantras and treatises, or cultivate extraordinary states of mind in order to experience a radical change of heart and inner transformation. Spiritually speaking, everything that one wants, aspires to, and needs is ever-present, accessible here and now............

Lama Surya Das
Awakening The Buddha Within

...............you only arrive at the other shore when you finally realize that there is no other shore. In other words, we make a journey to the "promised land", the other shore, and we have arrived when we realize that we were there all along.

Chogyam Trungpa

111

This popular misconception about the exclusive or esoteric nature of inner cultivation needs to be clarified. The basic purposes of inner cultivation are not the attainment of transcendental or rapturous spiritual states. Inner cultivation does not seek to provide us with avenues or techniques to avoid suffering, to shun the realities of life or to ignore positive growth. On the contrary, the foremost objectives of inner cultivation are down-to-earth, namely:-

- To contribute to our positive growth and maturation.
- To heal emotional negativities by enabling us to touch our deep essence and innate wholesomeness, the wellspring of our mental, physical, emotional and spiritual soundness;
- To discover our authentic life purpose and constructive potential;
- To free ourselves from attachment to erroneous self-concepts and from the clutches of self-seeking energies;
- To foster and sustain healthy self-esteem, so that we can tap upon our inner wealth to build a sound character, to fulfill our unique talents and to realize worthwhile goals that contribute to the well-being of others.

Thus, the foremost aims and purposes of inner cultivation are not arcane, occultist or esoteric. Instead, they aim to align our thoughts, words and deeds with authentic living that is conducive to manifesting our innate wholesomeness, gifts and talents. Inner cultivation is the foundational activity of fruitful living and personal maturation. It enables us to become better persons, to taste genuine inner peace and fulfillment. It enables us to gain a clearer vision of our authentic life purpose and develop a healthy perspective of life priorities. It fosters a healthy mindset and attitude that aligns our words and deeds with the deep harmony and potential of our spiritual dimension in all areas of our life.

It is therefore critical to dispel the popular misconception that bona fide inner cultivation is restricted to spiritual masters or holy monks and nuns who live in secluded monasteries or remote mountain caves. This misconception of the exclusive, reclusive and esoteric nature of inner cultivation has deterred many of us, lulling us into thinking that nurturing inner wisdom is outmoded and redundant in modern societies, a relic of the past. We are oblivious of the fact that we are being crippled and fettered by spiritual torpor until this malaise brings our lives to a halt.

To understand what "essential" or "pure" being is doesn't require years in monasteries or any advanced degrees. It simply involves getting in touch with your inner sacred core.

Lama Surya Das
Awakening To The Sacred

A man once wrote to me, "I want to make time for more spiritual practices, but I have a wife, three kids, and a full-time job." He hadn't yet realized that his wife and children and work are his spiritual practice – – – a practice far more challenging and rewarding than sitting in a cave and meditating. I know, because I've done both.

Dan Millman
Everyday Enlightenment

Wealth-Creation Secret #21
Inner cultivation does not seek to foster an escapist or
a fatalistic mindset. Rather, it enables us to touch the higher
dimension in our being and enables us to muster
the courage and determination to surmount
the challenges and adversities in our lives.

As we progress along our spiritual path, it will dawn on us that spiritual cultivation has its natural cycle of inner work and participation in the marketplace. Depending on the depth of our spiritual awakening, it is definitely not confined to secluded monasteries or remote mountains. Rather, our inner work serves to unveil our inner resources, to prepare and strengthen us, so that we can participate more constructively in the marketplace. In addition, our daily activities in the marketplace serve to hone our spiritual qualities and deepen our insight into the maturation process. Thus, wherever we are, whether at our homes, workplaces, holiday retreats, meditation centers, at the seaside, or while traveling on the road or trekking in the woods, inner cultivation continues because it is the ground of authentic living. As explained by Ram Dass in his classic *Be Here Now:*

Practice is like a roller coaster. Each new high is usually followed by a new low. Understanding this, it makes it a bit easier to ride with both phases............There is in addition to the up-and-down cycles an in-and-out cycle. That is, there are stages at which you feel pulled into inner work and all you seek is a quiet place to meditate and get on with it, and then there are times when you turn outward and seek to be involved in the marketplace. Both of these parts of the cycle are a part of one's practice, for what happens to you in the marketplace helps in your meditation, and what happens in your meditation helps you to participate in the marketplace...............

Misconception 2: Inner cultivation entails forgoing all our material wealth and possession.

There are many people who concentrate exclusively on developing the material side of their life, while completely ignoring spiritual practice. This is one extreme............there are people who concentrate exclusively on spiritual practice, while ignoring the material conditions that are necessary for supporting a healthy human life. This is another extreme. We need to maintain a middle way that avoids both extremes of materialism and spirituality.

Geshe Kelsang Gyatso
Transform Your Life

Spirituality is not about retreat from life but rather the fullness of life. As Howard Thurman put it, we come into the divine presence not by leaving behind what are usually called earthly things, or by loving them less, but by living more intensely in them, and loving more what is really lovable in them.

Michael Thompson
The Congruent Life

As clarified by the Four Noble Truths of Wealth Creation in Chapter 1, material wealth and possessions are means to an end, and not ends in themselves. They are tools and instruments that can be harnessed for positive or negative purposes.

For example, we could use our material wealth to help the needy, to contribute to the funding of schools, hospitals, orphanages, philanthropic organizations, etc. They are analogous to tools like explosives and medicinal drugs. We can use explosives for positive purposes, like demolishing old dilapidated buildings to make way for new ones or blowing huge boulders into smaller rocks that can be used as building materials. We can also use explosives negatively, by harming or killing innocent people. Similarly, many types of medicinal drugs can be abused that would lead to addiction or they can be used to treat diseases.

By understanding that material wealth is a means to an end, we realize that inner spiritual cultivation need not involve abandoning all efforts at creating external wealth. Rather, guided by inner wisdom, kind intentions and worthwhile objectives, we can tap upon our inner resources to create external wealth to contribute to the well-being of others.

In addition, inner cultivation does not entail forgoing all our material wealth and possessions. Rather, it entails fostering a healthy insight into the true significance of external wealth. It entails nurturing a healthy abundance consciousness that enables us to rise above our "small egoistic self" and narrow-mindedness, so as to dislodge unhealthy attachment to material possessions and sense pleasure that can be bought by external wealth. It enables us to perceive the subtle destructiveness of being driven by self-seeking energies and attachment to external wealth. By dissipating our attachment to material possessions, we understand the meaninglessness of hoarding and amassing external wealth for selfish motives. We learn to identify constructive and creative ways to share our wealth with others and contribute to their positive growth and well-being.

It is not the outer objects that entangle us. It is the inner clinging that entangles us.

Tilopa, a tenth-century yogi

Wealth-Creation Secret #22
When we tap our inner affluence and external wealth
to create value for others, this is the "thusness" route
to inner fulfillment.

Misconception 3: Inner cultivation entails leaving or forsaking our family and friends.

Critics, cynics and skeptics usually quote the example of prince Siddhartha Gautama leaving his palace, parents, wife and son to search for enlightenment. They therefore conclude that inner cultivation entails forsaking our loved ones and friends to live in secluded monastic communities. However, they fail to quote the fact that after the Buddha attained enlightenment six years after he left the palace, he spent the remaining forty-five years of his life to explain the Dharma and higher truths not only to his disciples, but also to his parents, his wife and son, his numerous friends and followers. The Buddha graciously and compassionately reached out and extended his care and affection to everyone who crossed his path, including people who planned to harm him.

Similarly, all great spiritual teachers avail themselves to others, to assist them in their positive growth and maturation. During the initial stages of spiritual cultivation, we may prefer more days of silent contemplation, meditation and inner exploration. With ripening wisdom, it dawns on us that self-isolation, self-absorption and self-preoccupation are antithetical to fostering positive spiritual qualities. It dawns on us that these days of silence and quietness serve to endow us with more vibrancy, freshness and enthusiasm to return to our daily activities and jobs. In turn, performing routine activities and duties and interacting with others are valuable in fostering positive spiritual qualities and broadening our mindfulness practice. Guided by inner wisdom, we learn to re-embrace our loved ones, parents, siblings, neighbors and friends on a higher plane of compassionate understanding, empathy, broad-mindedness and love.

Genuine inner cultivation takes place and bears fruits in a social context. We gain deeper self-understanding from our interactions and relationships with others. We gain deeper understanding of the subtle dynamics of our intentions, emotions, urges and rationalizations from our interactions with others. Our insightful awareness of the subtle intentions and motivations of our words and deeds rises to a higher plane. We can better foster positive spiritual qualities and perceive more deeply our constructive potential by extending our kind understanding and friendly hands to others.

I wish to stress that the true meaning of life is to be discovered in the world rather than within man or his own psyche, as though it were a closed system.........The more one forgets himself— — by giving himself to a cause to serve or another person to love — — the more human he is and the more he actualizes himself. What is called self-actualization is not an attainable aim at all, for the simple reason that the more one would strive for it, the more he would miss it. In other words, self-actualization is possible only as a side-effect of self-transcendence.

Viktor Frankl
Man's Search For Meaning

Service is both a means and an end, for in giving to others, you open yourself to love, abundance, and inner peace. You cannot serve others without uplifting yourself.

Dan Millman

Wealth-Creation Secret #23
Inner fulfillment and affluence can blossom
only when we connect ourselves with the oneness of humanity,
which includes our loved ones and friends, as well as our
opponents and rivals.

Misconception 4: Inner cultivation is for the cowardly and faint-hearted, an avenue to escape the harsh realities and suffering of life.

The lotus of enlightenment will not take root on the high plateaus of abstraction, nor in the rarefied atmosphere of the cloistered retreats. It grows in the swamp of everyday living.......

Taitetsu Unno

...........work and the work environment are fertile soil for spiritual growth and maturity. There is no place in our lives that more exposes our weaknesses or stretches our limits, teaching us about who we truly are. We are thrown together with people who are often very different from ourselves, forcing us to appreciate both their value and our own.

Michael Thompson

Inner cultivation is not an escape route. It seeks to strengthen our resilience, emotional maturity and capacity to endure adversities and the uncertainties of life. It enables us to gain insight into the true significance of suffering. It enables us to more effectively manage the practical difficulties of life, to courageously face its flux and uncertainties, to extend our sympathy and sincere assistance to the needy. We learn to appreciate reality with broadmindedness and be receptive to trying moments without cynicism or despair. It dawns on us that without learning to accept suffering and endure pain, our growth will stagnate and become stunted. Without learning to accept suffering and the imperfections of the phenomenal world, genuine broadmindedness will elude us.

Without suffering, you cannot grow. Without suffering, you cannot get the peace and joy you deserve. Please don't run away from your suffering. Embrace it and cherish it...............With understanding and compassion, you will be able to heal the wounds in your heart, and the wounds in the world. The Buddha called suffering a Holy Truth, because our suffering has the capacity of showing us the path to liberation.

Thich Nhat Hanh
The Heart of the Buddha's Teaching

How much digging do you do in your life? When something unpleasant happens, do you look inside to see what you can learn? When a tragedy happens, like the death of a child, do you try to see what this painful experience means? Digging in your life means looking for what you can learn about yourself when you are feeling angry, sad, or frightened. If you don't look for what you can learn about yourself when you feel these things, you aren't digging. If you don't dig, you won't find the gold.......... Everything – – – even things that are painful – – happens for a reason. That reason is to help you grow spiritually.

Gary Zukav
Soul Stories

The higher truth is that we can fruitfully nurture a healthy insightful awareness in daily activities, at our homes with parental and filial duties, at our workplaces with taxing workload and demanding bosses and customers, at any situations that strain our patience and require further opening and maturation of our compassionate heart. Gradually, we learn to appreciate these difficult and taxing moments as valuable opportunities for deeper awakening, for strengthening our character and resilience. They emerge as the fire of baptism for genuine growth.

When we stop discussing things and begin to realize the teachings in our own life, a moment comes when we realize that our life is the path...............We do not have to transcend the "world of dust" (saha) in order to go to some dust-free world called nirvana. Suffering and nirvana are of the same substance. If we throw away the world of dust, we will have no nirvana.

Thich Nhat Hanh
The Heart of the Buddha's Teaching

To stay with that shakiness — — to stay with a broken heart, with a rumbling stomach, with the feeling of hopelessness and wanting to get revenge — — that is the path of true awakening. Sticking with that uncertainty, getting the knack of relaxing in the midst of chaos, learning not to panic — — this is the spiritual path.

Pema Chodron
When Things Fall Apart

There was once a devoted Zen student ardently seeking spiritual awakening. Nevertheless, after months of intense practice, satori eluded him. He understood from his teachers that there lived an enlightened wood-cutter in a nearby mountain. He decided to visit him for guidance.

As the Zen student was hiking up the mountain, he met the wood-cutter who was coming down and carrying a load of freshly cut woods. The Zen student sincerely bowed at the wood-cutter whose countenance radiated with wisdom, vibrancy and compassion. The Zen student seized the opportunity to enquire how he could attain enlightenment.

Thereupon, the wood-cutter briskly released the load that he was carrying which hit the ground with a loud noise. At that instant, the Zen student experienced his initial awakening.

The old wood-cutter gently patted the Zen student on his back. Thereafter, he picked up the load, heaved it over his shoulders and, once again, patiently and mindfully carried it down to the mountain.

You're part of society, you're part of a family, you're part of all sorts of groups. Do what you must to meet your responsibilities, but do it as an exercise that furthers your own liberation as well. The true freedom of awareness that you seek is possible only when you acknowledge and fulfill honorably all aspects of the dance of life.

Ram Dass

............one could say that the post-meditation periods are the real test of the strength of your practice. During formal meditation, in a sense you are recharging your batteries, so that when you come out of the session you are better equipped to deal with the demands of your everyday life.

The Dalai Lama

As we continue our inner cultivation, we realize that there is no basic difference between mindful daily living and enlightened living. Inner cultivation should not be misconceived as a license or a route to flee from the difficulties, suffering and obligations of daily living. Rather, it nurtures a positive life-affirming mindset that enables us to fulfill our daily duties and obligations under the guidance of inner Light. We gain deeper insight into the indelible words of Dr Viktor Frankl who recorded his traumatic experiences at a Nazis concentration camp in his classic *Man's Search For Meaning:-*

Suffering is an ineradicable part of life............Without suffering and death, human life cannot be complete............The way in which a man accepts his fate and all the suffering it entails, the way in which he takes up his cross, gives him ample opportunity — even under the most difficult circumstances — to add a deeper meaning to his life............

Misconception 5: Inner cultivation entails denying our physical and emotional needs and forgoing our normal reasoning capacity, so that we sacrifice ourselves to help others.

People who misinterpret the Buddha's teachings often worry that if they rid themselves of craving, they will no longer be able to love or live with passion. Quite the opposite is true. We will still have our healthy desires, but now they won't be contaminated and misdirected by insatiable craving. The Buddha never taught we shouldn't feel love. In fact, he preached universal love and compassion.

Lama Surya Das
Awakening The Buddha Within

The first step in the process of actually countering our negative thoughts and emotions is to avoid those situations and activities which would normally give rise to them. If, for example, we find we become angry whenever we meet with a particular person, it may be best to keep away from them until we develop our internal resources more.

Dalai Lama
Ancient Wisdom, Modern World

> *Hungers and appetites – – for sexual release, for food, for life –*
> *– – are as natural to you as clouds are to the sky or waves to the*
> *sea............Life is not a matter of indulging or denying the*
> *energies of life, but observing, accepting, and wisely channeling*
> *them. Embracing your sexuality celebrates your humanity.*
>
>

Dan Millman
Everyday Enlightenment

Once again, the Buddha's search for enlightenment serves to dispel this misconception. Self-mortification, self-denial, repression and suppression of our basic physical and emotional needs are extremes to be avoided. Genuine spiritual cultivation honors our natural physical and emotional needs by fostering a higher form of healthiness whereby we develop an insightful awareness of our intrinsic sanctity and wholesomeness. We also learn to loosen our attachment to pleasant sensations and feelings. We gain insight into their evanescent and transitory nature. This is tersely highlighted by Shunryu Suzuki Roshi with a dose of humor in the following anecdote:

> *When a student asked, "You teach us to just sit when we sit, just eat when we eat; could a Zen master be just angry in the same way?"*

> *Suzuki Roshi replied, "You mean to just get angry like a thunderstorm and be done when it passes? Ahh, I wish I could do that."*

Undertaking inner cultivation enables us to catch glimpses of our innate wholesomeness. We thereby do not erroneously view our physical bodies as "shameful" or "sinful". Rather, we learn to treasure our physical body as a sacred vessel with immense potential to manifest our innate sanctity, to contribute to the well-being of others and to assist others to gain insight into their higher dimension. We learn to appreciate the subtle positive and negative urges and impulses that course through our thinking mind and how they arise due to environmental conditioning. We foster a healthy skilful mindset whereby we attune our healthy intentions, feelings, words and deeds to the deep harmony and potential of our deep essence. We learn to dissipate and heal self-seeking thoughts and desires, to meaningfully experience our feelings and let them arise and pass away. By nurturing a flexible receptive mindset that responds vibrantly to the flux and uncertainties of life, we do not squelch ourselves into a rigid pseudo-spiritual persona that seeks to shun or become oblivious to the harsher aspects of life.

Moreover, we learn to derive intrinsic fulfillment and joy from participating in constructive daily activities, from creating value for others. As observed by Ralph Waldo Emerson, "It is one of the most beautiful compensations of life that no one can sincerely try to help another without helping himself." When we carry a flaming torch to light the way for others, we are also bringing light to our own path.

Enlightened people have preferences. I don't know if you know any people who you believe are enlightened. I have known a few, and they all have their own likes and dislikes, their own individual, personal style. This tells us that enlightenment, freedom, Buddha-nature, lives and expresses itself through each personality. Each of us is different, thank God, not uniformly bland like some kind of fake dessert topping.

Lama Surya Das
Awakening The Buddha Within

125

It is not that you erase all of your individuality, for even an enlightened being has a personality marked by all sorts of idiosyncrasies. An enlightened being doesn't necessarily have beautiful hair, sparkling teeth, a young body, or a nice disposition. His or her body has its blemishes; it ages and dies. The difference is that such a being no longer identifies with that body and personality.

> Ram Dass
> *Journey of Awakening*

Inner cultivation does not entail giving up healthy feelings, emotions and experiences. Rather, we embrace them mindfully, nurturing the "skilful mindset" to distinguish egoistic feelings and cravings from altruistic intentions. Inner cultivation does not entail giving up healthy activities, hobbies and preferences. It does not entail forgoing healthy sexual activity with our life partner or soul-mate. However, spiritual cultivation does entail releasing selfish thoughts and egoistic desires. It does entail giving up self-centered thinking and emotional patterns that could harm others. It does entail cultivating discipline by eliminating unhealthy habits and addictions, by giving up sexually irresponsible conduct and unethical motives. It does entail cultivating commitment to a life partner, to fulfilling our parental and filial duties, to worthwhile life goals that are conducive to our personal growth and the well-being of others.

Furthermore, inner cultivation does not hold that we forgo the conceptual mode of knowing or abandon our reasoning ability. Rather, we appreciate our reasoning capacity, for it is a God-given ability that enables us to understand relative truths of good and bad, right and wrong, just and unjust, kindness and maliciousness, honesty and deceit, wisdom and gullibility. Our logical-rational thinking and conceptual-symbolic knowledge enable us to function effectively in daily practical living as well as facilitate understanding of the maturation process, serving as a bridge to higher ethical vision and spiritual maturity.

Thus, in undertaking spiritual cultivation, we are not reverting to childish gullibility. Rather, we are cultivating an insightful compassion, not mawkishness or immature sentimentality. We are fostering a healthy insightful awareness to better understand the subtle intentions and motivations of our words and deeds as well as those of others. We learn to value ourselves as constructive members of our families, organizations and society. Although we learn to extend kind understanding, broadmindedness and forgiveness to the spiritually unconscious words and deeds of others, we do not foolishly expose ourselves to physical, emotional or sexual mistreatment and abuse. We learn to appreciate our phenomenal selves as sacred vessels with immense potential to contribute to the well-being of others. We therefore engage in constructive activities conducive to our personal growth. We also engage in activities that prevent others from doing harm to innocent people. For example, if we know that some of our neighbors are planning terrorist activities, we should quickly inform the police.

Above all, inner cultivation does not entail that we indiscriminately comply with the wishes of others to satisfy their self-centered desires. It does not entail that we indiscriminately participate in deeds or sacrifice ourselves to meet the selfish craving of others. If we do so, we are being unwise since we are hindering others in their positive growth and maturation.

127

The Buddha once told the following story about a cunning and deceitful heron.

Once upon a time, there lived a group of small shrimps and fish in a small lotus pond. A heron, which flew past the pond, saw the crowded condition of the small pond. It began to hatch a plan on how to trick the shrimps and fish into migrating to another larger pond.

A few days later, the heron thought of a wonderful plan. It flew to the edge of the small pond and pretended to be sympathetic to the inhabitants of the small pond.

The small shrimps and fish asked with a mixture of fear and curiosity, "Mister Heron, why do you look so sad and forlorn."

The Heron replied, "I am sympathizing with your poor lot in life. Your small pond is so crowded. I was thinking whether I could assist you to migrate to a larger and more luxuriant pond where your children can grow up more comfortably."

The group of small shrimps and fish were surprised by these words. However, they were suspicious of the kind intentions of the Heron.

"Perhaps you are doubtful of my sincerity. There really is a much larger and cleaner lotus pond some distance away. I can bring one of you to that larger pond to witness it and validate my words," said the Heron.

After much discussion, one of the elder fish volunteered to be carried by the beak of the Heron to the larger lotus pond. The Heron briskly picked up the elder fish and flew it to a larger lotus pond some distance away. It dropped the elder fish into the larger pond and allowed it to relish the clear fresh water. Thereafter, the Heron picked up the elder fish and flew it back to the small lotus pond. The elder fish excitedly reported all that it had seen and experienced.

All the other shrimps and fish were enthusiastic and were willing to migrate to the larger pond. One by one, the Heron picked up the shrimps and fish and flew them toward the direction of the larger pond. However, instead of dropping them into the larger pond, it would land near a plumeria tree where it would rip off the flesh of the shrimps or fish and devour them.

Therefore be as wise as serpents and harmless as doves.
Matthew 10: 16

In undertaking spiritual cultivation, we also learn to cultivate a practical form of higher wisdom whereby we develop an insightful awareness to perceive the subtle intentions and motivations of our words and deeds as well as those of others. We are not exposing ourselves to charlatans, quacks and cheats. Instead, we understand more deeply their negative motives and spiritual torpor. Depending on the circumstances and the depth of our spiritual and emotional maturity, we can either avoid them or advise them to give up their negative motives and harmful deeds.

Sri Ramakrishna once told a delightful story which contains a profound lesson on how we should practice insightful kindness, compassion and altruism in daily living which is filled with spiritually unconscious and difficult people.

One day, a spiritual teacher was passing through a village and saw some children chasing and attacking a huge snake with sticks and stones. The teacher sympathized with the suffering of the snake and he persuaded the children to go away.

The spiritual teacher told the snake, "I can discern that these children hated you and are seeking to hurt you because you have previously bitten one of them. Hence, do not try to bite these children." The teacher thereafter departed.

A few weeks later, the spiritual teacher returned and was astonished to find the same snake in an emaciated and dying condition. The snake said, "I listened to your advice not to bite the children, but they kept tormenting me. Now, my entire body is wounded by their repeated assaults."

The teacher replied, "Oh no, I have erroneously assumed that you are a wise snake. Yes, I have advised you not to bite these children. But you should have continued hissing and scaring them away.............."

As we continue our spiritual path, we will be exposed to the condition of "mature vulnerability", whereby spiritually unconscious, egoistic and shrewd individuals will seek to take advantage of our kindness and compassion. Thus, to function effectively in the modern society which is filled with aggressive, covetous, self-indulgent and arrogant people, we need to practice compassionate "hissing" whenever appropriate. This means that we maintain a moderate level of aloofness and sternness toward spiritually unconscious people, so as to ensure that they do not abuse us and encroach upon our basic rights. Nevertheless, in practicing compassionate "hissing", we sustain a healthy awareness of our altruistic intentions and, whenever appropriate, we should participate in activities that contribute to the positive growth of others.

Misconception 6: Inner cultivation entails adherence to outdated religious tenets and doctrines.

I believe that the practice of compassion and love − − a genuine sense of brotherhood and sisterhood − − is the universal religion. It does not matter whether you are Buddhist or Christian, Moslem or Hindu, or whether you practice religion at all. What matters is your feeling of oneness with humankind.

The Dalai Lama

The important point to keep in mind is that ultimately the whole purpose of religion is to facilitate love and compassion, patience, tolerance, humility, forgiveness............even if we are fervent believers in our own faith, it will avail us nothing if we neglect to implement these qualities in our daily lives.

Dalai Lama

God, unlike some organized religions, does not discriminate. As long as you reach out to Her, She will go the better part of the way to meet you.

Dr M Scott Peck

Inner cultivation is distinct from participating in religious activities, practices or worship. Inner cultivation involves inner exploration and discovery of our deep essence. By touching the sanctified source of our being, we can better understand and appreciate the true significance of traditional religious tenets.

131

Many useful time-honored religious concepts and practices can assist inner cultivation. However, inner cultivation essentially involves elevating our subjective consciousness and mental horizon to a higher plane of authentic living. By fostering an insightful awareness of our higher dimension, it enables us to realize that genuine religious concepts, tenets and practices also aim to enable us to touch our deep essence and higher dimension. As explained by the Buddha, they are akin to the raft that carries us over the sea of samsaric ignorance to the shore of awakening.

Thus, inner cultivation does not require us to adhere or become attached to certain religious tenets or teachings. Rather, it enables us to foster a flexible and receptive mindset, and broadens our mental and spiritual horizon. Guided by inner wisdom, we can better appreciate the natural boundary and limitations of religious concepts and notions since they subsist at the level of "relative truth". We realize that religious concepts and tenets can be subject to positive and negative interpretations by their followers and supporters. Inner cultivation fosters a higher form of discernment and acumen whereby we can distinguish the positive and negative aspects of traditional religious tenets and doctrines. We learn to appreciate which of these aspects are relatively outmoded in the contemporary context of collective awakening and social progress.

Inner cultivation therefore does not entail rigid adherence to traditional religious tenets and doctrines. Rather, it fosters a deep understanding of the common aspirations and vision that inspire humankind to formulate these religious tenets and doctrines. We learn to develop an insightful awareness to understand which aspects of traditional religious tenets and doctrines are healthy and useful and arise from kind and compassionate intentions, and which aspects stem from narrow-mindedness and a parochial vision that do not contribute to the fulfillment of our deep potential or hinders social harmony and progress. We learn to guard against subscribing to divisive narrow-minded tenets and doctrines.

Do not believe in anything simply because you have heard it.

Do not believe in traditions because they have been handed down for many generations.

Do not believe in anything because it is spoken and rumored by many.

Do not believe in anything simply because it is found written in your religious books.

Do not believe in anything merely on the authority of your teachers and elders.

But after observation and analysis, when you find that anything agrees with higher understanding, and is conducive to the good and benefit of one and all, then accept it and live up to it.

The Buddha

............I believe there is an important distinction to be made between religion and spirituality. Religion I take to be concerned with faith in the claims to salvation of one faith tradition or another.........Spirituality I take to be concerned with those qualities of the human spirit – – – such as love and compassion, patience, tolerance, forgiveness, contentment, a sense of responsibility, a sense of harmony – – – which bring happiness to both self and others. While ritual and prayer, along with questions of nirvana and salvation, are directly connected with religious faith, these inner qualities need not be............This is why I sometimes say that religion is something we can perhaps do

without. What we cannot do without are these basic spiritual qualities.

Dalai Lama
Ancient Wisdom, Modern World

Misconception 7: Inner cultivation entails whole-hearted unswerving loyalty to a spiritual master.

Rely on the message of the teacher, not on his personality.
Rely on the meanings, not just on the words.
Rely on the real meaning, not on the provisional one.
Rely on your wisdom mind, not on your ordinary, judgmental mind.

The Buddha

...........enlightenment is alive, like a tree. If it does not continue to grow, it will die. The enlightenment of the Buddha, the compassion and loving-kindness of Jesus, grow every day. We ourselves are responsible for their growth.

Thich Nhat Hanh
Living Buddha, Living Christ

The misconception that inner cultivation entails unswerving loyalty to a spiritual master has deterred many of us from undertaking inner cultivation and from finding sincere spiritual friends who can assist us in our path toward positive growth and maturation. This is understandable since there were many shocking reports in the past about the deceptions and abuses of powers perpetrated by well-known spiritual teachers.

Nevertheless, we need to be receptive to the truth that inner cultivation is the time-honored path that serves to raise our insightful awareness of the subtle intentions of our deeds as well as those of others. By cultivating higher wisdom, we can better understand and perceive the subtle motives of others. We can better appreciate human sincerity or discern the pretense and hypocrisy of charlatans. To quote the golden advice of Dr Jack Kornfield in A Path With Heart:

In seeking a teacher, we must listen to our heart, and we must look at ourselves with honesty. What are we really seeking? Is this what is offered by this teacher and by this way of practice? What draws us to this teacher? Does this teacher and way of practice fit my temperament and serve me, or conversely, does it reinforce my fears and neuroses?

Sincere spiritual friends and teachers can assist us to better understand various difficult aspects of our spiritual practice. They can create the sacred opportunity and environment for us to experience spiritual rejuvenation and awakening. However, nobody can undertake inner exploration on our behalf. Nobody can make the decision on our behalf to sustain the commitment to post-awakening spiritual cultivation. Only we can touch our innate sanctity and wholesomeness. Only we can commit ourselves to ongoing post-awakening inner cultivation. Only when we rise to the higher plane of a holistic worldview of the interwoven nature of life can we awaken from our spiritual slumber.

Sincere spiritual friends and teachers are helpful as they have traversed the spiritual path and can provide us with useful pointers on pitfalls that we should avoid. A genuine spiritual teacher is not only a master of the tradition which he practices. He is also a highly compassionate and empathetic individual who can pierce through the difficulties of his students and offer appropriate advice and counsel. For example, in a famous dialogue, the Buddha introduced his visitor on the different types of teachers residing in his forest monastery: "Students who have an interest in inquiry are gathered there with my wisest disciple, Sariputtra, and those who are inspired by the practice of monastic discipline are there with Upali, the exemplary practitioner of monastic life. Those who are attracted by psychic development are with the great psychic Mogallana, and others who are naturally drawn to mental concentration and meditation are over there with Mahakassapa."

Teachers and teachings are forms, and ultimately you must go beyond forms. If you are true to your own inner voice, as it gets subtler and subtler it brings you to the moment beyond separateness of seeker and guide. Then you have served your teacher well.

Ram Dass

Some of you may have the impression that the Dalai Lama is somehow different. That is absolutely wrong. I am a human being like all of you. We have the same potential.

The Dalai Lama

A genuine spiritual teacher is also able to instill healthy spiritual balance and mental perspective in his students. Sometimes, he is seen to offer seemingly contradictory advice to different students. This may be best explained in the words of the venerable Buddhist master Achaan Chan, as recorded by Dr Jack Kornfield in *A Path With Heart*: "The way I teach is more like this: I look down a path which I know well, but it may be dark or foggy, and the student in front of me is about to fall off in a ditch on the right-hand side or get lost in a side track to the right. So I call out to them, "Go to the left, go to the left." Then some time later, the same student or another following the foggy path may be ready to fall in a ditch on the left-hand side to get lost on a side track in that direction. Again I call out, "Go to the right, go to the right." I remind them whenever they get off the path. In a way, that is all I do."

As we continue our inner cultivation, it will gradually dawn on us that we do not need to declare unswerving loyalty to a particular spiritual mentor. A genuine spiritual teacher will not demand rigid loyalty. On the contrary, he or she will embody healthy flexibility and adaptiveness as well as vibrant open-mindedness. He or she will be most pleased if we touch the innate freedom, flexibility, spaciousness and expansiveness of our deep essence. It will also dawn on us that inner cultivation endows us with the discernment to appreciate the good points and weaknesses of our spiritual friends and teachers, for we all have some shadow aspects that require the constant guidance and healing of our insightful awareness. Thus, in finding spiritual friends and mentors, we should maintain a healthy vigilance and, as appropriate, we closely perceive and examine their intentions and behavior. We can thereby learn from their honest words and virtuous deeds, and avoid falling prey to pretense and egoistic motives. Once again, let us remember the golden words of Dr Jack Kornfield in *A Path With Heart*:

Some teachers are rascals and coyotes who trick and surprise their students; some are harsh taskmasters trying to whittle down ego and pride; others teach through honoring and encouragement, nurturing the best in a student; some teachers lecture like a professor; others can melt us open with their love and compassion. The greatest and simplest power of a teacher is the environment of their own freedom and joy.

Sixth Gateway: Taming Our Roaming Mind And Healing Inner Negativities Are Part And Parcel Of The Ripening Of Wisdom

> *Our capacity to make peace with another person and with the world depends very much on our capacity to make peace with ourselves. If we are at war with our parents, our family, our society, or our church, there is probably a war going on inside us also, so the most basic work for peace is to return to ourselves and create harmony among the elements within us – – – our feelings, our perceptions, and our mental states.*
>
> > *Thich Nhat Hanh*
> > *Living Buddha, Living Christ*

As will be discussed in chapters 4, 5 and 6, training our roaming mind, awakening to our genuine life purpose, and healing negative emotions are part and parcel of nurturing wisdom. As we have been subject to years of negative environmental conditioning, mind training and healing inner negativities are continuous and ongoing. They foster healthy self-acceptance and understanding of the porous nature of our ego. They enable us to dissipate rigid erroneous beliefs in an independent self. Restoring our emotional and spiritual health, they enable us to develop a clearer vision of our authentic life purpose and to tap upon our innate freewill and deep potential to positively recreate ourselves. We learn to let go of our scarcity mindset by understanding that we need not be the center of the world to enjoy inner peace, that the intrinsic sanctity of our being is the wellspring of deep fulfillment.

............if we wish to pick flowers from a tree, we must first cultivate the roots and trunk, which means that we must work with our fears, frustrations, disappointments and irritations, the painful aspects of life.

Chogyam Trungpa

Seventh Gateway: Self-forgiveness Is The Royal Road To Wisdom

Guided by inner wisdom, inner cultivation is an ongoing process of forgiving and accepting our imperfections as well as the imperfections of others.

For most of us, inner strife, discontent, frustration and unease arise from our inability to forgive ourselves. We could not forgive ourselves for not meeting our high expectations and perfectionist standards. We could not forgive ourselves for not meeting the expectations and demands of our parents, spouses, children, siblings, bosses and colleagues. We could not forgive ourselves for not being as wealthy as our neighbors. We could not forgive ourselves for not meeting the sales targets. We could not forgive ourselves for not being able to afford a decent overseas holiday for our family. We could not forgive ourselves for not being able to afford a splendid necklace for our spouse during her recent birthday. We could not forgive ourselves for not being able to afford a more luxurious car.......... and the list goes on............

The time is ripe to lessen self-criticism and self-flagellation. Many of us have been too harsh and demanding on ourselves. Owing to years of negative environmental conditioning, we have become unreasonably perfectionist.

In order to relax and touch our innate wholesomeness, we need to continuously befriend and forgive ourselves. We need to learn to release our harshness and high expectations. We need to set more realistic standards and learn to continuously compliment ourselves whenever we attain them. With ripening wisdom, it will dawn on us that, regardless of external achievements and failures, regardless of life events and circumstances, we are wholesome in the depths of our being. We gradually rise to a higher form of healthy self-esteem that imbues us with vibrant confidence and commitment to engage in activities that contribute to the positive growth of others.

Guided by heart wisdom, we learn to forgive ourselves, our shortcomings and imperfections. By engaging in spiritual practice, we gradually heal and dissipate self-seeking energies and inner strife. Similarly, we learn to forgive and accept the shortcomings and imperfections of others. We learn to renounce unrealistic expectations and standards, to appreciate our strengths and unique talents.

Whenever I have been too harsh and demanding on myself, I will reread the following account in Dr Gerald Jampolsky's illuminating book *Forgiveness*. Its condensed version is below:-

Whenever a person acted wrongly or irresponsibly in the Babemba tribe in South Africa, he would be placed in the center of the village.

Everyone in the village stopped working and gathered in a circle around that accused person. Each of the villagers would sincerely tell the person and the other villagers about the good things that he performed in the past. All that person's positive attributes, good deeds, strengths and kindnesses are clarified for everyone to hear.

The ceremony continued for several days until every villager had spoken on how they valued and appreciated that person as a member of the village. At the end of the ceremony, the tribe broke the circle which was followed by a joyous celebration, welcoming the person back into the tribe.

Although we rarely encounter such magnanimity and broad-mindedness in our society, we should be magnanimous and broadminded with ourselves. When we have committed a mistake, we repent promptly and forgive ourselves. We retouch our innate sanctity, gently remind ourselves of our strengths and innate goodness, offer sincere apologies and make amends as appropriate. We learn from our mistake and constantly apply mindfulness in our future words and deeds, so as not to commit the same mistake.

Wealth-Creation Secret #24
Self-forgiveness and forgiveness of others
are the gates to inner well-being.

Eighth Gateway: Discovering Our Compassionate Heart And Innate Autonomy For Positive Self-Creation

Look at every path closely and deliberately. Try it as many times as you think necessary. Then ask yourself, and yourself alone, one question………. Does this path have a heart? If it does, the path is good; if it doesn't, it is of no use.

Carlos Castaneda
The Teachings of Don Juan

Mencius, the great Chinese philosopher, said that all human beings have a compassionate heart. For example, if we suddenly saw a child falling into a well, our natural response would be shock and unease, and an instinctive desire to help that child.

Nevertheless, years of negative environmental conditioning and conditioning by self-seeking energies have barricaded our compassionate heart. We become distrustful of our kind intention. This is tragic. To fulfill our deep potential, we need to rediscover our innate capacity to sprinkle kind intentions into our thoughts, words and deeds.

Let us share a traditional Swedish story.

There was once a ferocious dragon which vowed to destroy the entire country if a beautiful young princess named Aris was not married to it. With much grief and reluctance, the king decided to comply with the dragon's desire.

Aris was frightened and in anguish. Nevertheless, to save her country from ruination by the ferocious dragon, she agreed to the marriage. Fortunately, a wise woman taught Aries a plan that could outwit the dragon.

On the night of the wedding, Aries put on ten gowns. After the wedding feast, the dragon accompanied her to the bedchamber. Thereupon, Aries said to the dragon, "If you wish to make love to me, as I take off my gowns, you too must remove a layer of your scales."

The dragon complied with Aries' request. As she removed her gown one piece at a time, the dragon also shed a layer of its scales. With each shedding of its scaly armor, the dragon's skin became more tender. Finally, when Aries removed her tenth gown, the dragon emerged as a handsome young prince.

If we quiet down and listen to our heart wisdom, we can gradually dissipate aggressive and hostile energies. We can gradually dismantle the fortifications erected around our compassionate heart. We discover that our skepticism, cynicism and distrust of our innate goodness and kind intentions arise from losing touch with our deep essence.

We realize that genuine self-deception consists of lulling ourselves into thinking that we are only a bundle of animal instincts and urges, without a higher spiritual dimension. By discovering the intrinsic joy and fulfillment of leading a life more oriented toward helping others, we allow our compassionate heart to breathe again. We experience the vibrancy and lightheartedness by forgoing inner fortifications. Once again, we can feel our altruistic impulses. We also begin to feel the fortifications and barricades that other people have built around their hearts. It dawns on us that kind understanding and empathy are crucial ingredients in nurturing positive relationship with ourselves and others.

By forgoing unhealthy inner fortifications, inner Light would pervade our being. Our capacity to sprinkle seeds of kind intention into our thoughts, words and deeds unveils. We realize that sprinkling these seeds of kind intentions are part and parcel of positive self-creation. It is an integral part of the process of nurturing a healthy insightful awareness, of aligning our thoughts, words and deeds with the natural laws of abundance.

By sprinkling seeds of kind intentions into our thoughts, words and deeds, we gradually heal self-rejection and inner strife. We learn to positively redefine our worldview, value and belief systems, and life goals. Our authentic ability to make constructive choices that enable us to become positive members of our family, organization and society unveils. It dawns on us that we are endowed with the following precious inner assets:-

- The capacity to gain insight into our divine essence and to awaken to our authentic life purpose.
- The capacity to touch and relax into the embrace of inner spaciousness and deep peace, to discover Divinity and the holiness of the higher reality in the gaps and spaciousness between our thoughts, sensations and feelings.
- The capacity to tap on our heart wisdom to tame and train our roaming thinking mind, to dislodge erroneous concepts of self-identity and beliefs in an independent self, to heal emotional negativities and inner strife.
- The capacity to nurture healthy insightful awareness and insightful compassion, and align our words and deeds with inner wisdom.
- The capacity to forgive ourselves and others, to emphathise with and be receptive to the suffering of others.
- The capacity to be guided by heart wisdom and to sprinkle kind intentions into our thoughts, words and deeds.
- The capacity to positively re-create ourselves and align our worldview, our belief and value systems with the natural laws of abundance.

- The capacity to tap upon our heart wisdom to nurture healthy habits, positive thinking and emotional patterns, and a resilient character.
- The capacity to tap upon our inner wisdom to creatively and effectively solve practical daily problems.
- The capacity to commit ourselves to worthwhile life goals and activities that are conducive to our positive growth and to the well-being of others.

I always marvel that we can positively tap upon these inner assets to fulfill our deep potential and unique talents, to create external wealth for worthwhile purposes, to become co-creative partners of Divinity.

Wealth-Creation Secret #25
When we have developed a skilful mindset
to tap our bountiful inner assets to attain worthwhile ends,
external wealth emerges as a natural by-product.

Ninth Gateway: Building A Sound Character

I hope I shall always possess firmness and virtue enough to maintain what I consider the most valuable of all titles, the character of an honest man.

George Washington

It is recognized throughout the ages that having a sound character is essential to achieving success. Essentially, character formation depends on our habits, daily conduct, thinking and behavioral patterns, belief and value systems.

Thus, how do we ensure that our habits, daily thinking and behavior, belief and value systems are not driven by unhealthy self-seeking energies? How do we ensure that the formation of our character is guided by salutary insights into the genuine meaning of Life?

With ripening wisdom, we realize that there is an indelible linkage between inner cultivation and the formation of a sound character. Nurturing wisdom and spiritual qualities enables us to touch our innate wholesomeness and to gain a clearer vision of our life purpose. We can thereby align our life goals, belief and value systems, habits, thinking and behavioral patterns with our authentic life purpose. When our wisdom and compassion ripen, a sound character is the fruit. As explained later in Chapter 8, by aligning our words, deeds and habits with the time-honored principles of "wise view, wise intentions, wise speech, wise action, wise livelihood, wise effort, wise mindfulness and wise concentration", we can cultivate a healthy and resilient character.

Tenth Gateway: Attaining The Higher Perspective

There is no Nirvana except where there is Samsara; there is no Samsara except when there is Nirvana; for the condition of existence is not of a mutually exclusive character. Therefore it is said that all things are non-dual as are Nirvana and Samsara.

Lankavatara Sutra

...........mistaking words for reality. When we are unaware that words and concepts are arbitrary constructs, interwoven into dualistic thinking, we cling to them as if they are real. When our emotional life becomes caught up with these words and concepts, we plunge deeper into samsara.

Taitetsu Unno
River of Fire, River of Water

You can touch the ultimate dimension right now by breathing, walking, and drinking your tea in mindfulness. Everything and everyone is dwelling in nirvana, in the Kingdom of God.

Thich Nhat Hanh
Living Buddha, Living Christ

The Buddha once told the following story.

A group of children was playing on a beach. Each of them brought along simple tools to build separate beautiful sandcastles of various designs, shapes and sizes.

After an hour or so, each of the children proudly declared his separate sandcastle to be his sole possession and would not allow other people to trespass on it. Thereafter, they began playing chasing games and one of the children accidentally stepped upon the sandcastle of another child and partially demolished it.

The sandcastle's owner was infuriated and shouted at the top of his voice, "You destroy my sandcastle. I shall also destroy yours." In a revengeful manner, he promptly jumped upon the castle of his trespasser and kicked at it angrily. Soon the two children were fighting with each other. They clamped around each other and rolled on the beach. The other children watched and laughed, with the mischievous ones cheering them on. The more mature children intervened and mediated between them until they reconciled and began to continue their chasing game.

When night came, the children realized that it was time to return home. In their rush to go home, they stepped upon each other's sandcastles and ignored their "sole possession" status. Everyone was too busy returning home to defend his or her separate sandcastle.

Did we sometimes lose our perspective of the higher reality and bigger picture, and become fervently embroiled in defending our separate sandcastles? Did we sometimes become preoccupied with relative notions of "yours" and "mine", with erroneous concepts of a separate self that needs constant defense and protection? Did we sometimes mistake the relative truths as the higher reality, and lose sight of our life priorities?

In undertaking inner cultivation, it is important to remind ourselves not to be mesmerized and imprisoned by the conceptual-analytical functions and capacity of our normal thinking mind. The analytical, deductive, inductive, classifying and generalizing abilities of our thinking mind enable us to function normally and healthily in the phenomenal world. For example, they enable us to understand the natural physical laws governing this cosmos, endowing us with the conceptual knowledge to build houses, roads, bridges, automobiles, trains, planes, computers, rockets and space shuttles. They enable us to investigate the microcosmic world of germs and viruses, which endow us with the knowledge to discover cures for many diseases. They enable us to study human behavior and create laws and institutions to guide human behavior, to protect basic human rights, to implement democratic principles of government, freedom of conscience, freedom of speech, freedom of the press, freedom of assembly, religious tolerance, equal opportunity and meritocracy, etc.

However, we should awaken to the instrumental value of the analytical, reasoning and classifying functions of the thinking mind. They should not be mistaken as the only guideposts to the higher truths. If we do not awaken to their instrumental value and the natural boundary and limitations of conceptual knowledge, we would mire ourselves in over-conceptualizations, over-analysis and over-rationalizations. We would become entangled in the immense classifying, categorizing and rationalizing capacity of our thinking mind, trapped by its false sense of security provided by its dualistic concepts and dichotomous thinking patterns, by its numerous intricate notions of "yours and mine", by its relative concepts of the separateness of phenomenal things. Our lives would be marked by unending efforts to defend and protect our "separate sandcastles", our separate territories of external possessions and achievements.

Thus, in undertaking inner cultivation, it is useful to distinguish between "relative or conditional truths" and the "Higher Truth". Broadly speaking, the validity and meaningfulness of "relative or conditional truths" depend on the preconditions that underpin the existence of this cosmos and countless prior causative events. These preconditions comprise the basic features of this cosmos, like the fundamental characteristics of the elementary particles, atoms and molecules that make up both sentient beings and inanimate objects. They comprise the many natural physical laws and processes that characterize this cosmos. If there are fundamental changes to these preconditions, the phenomenal realm of forms and appearances would undergo changes. In turn, many of our conditional truths would change.

From this perspective, the everyday empirical observations and truths that give rise to the principles of the physical and social sciences are conditional truths.

For example, under normal circumstances, we can confidently say that the apple falls to the ground when ripe. However, if the Milky Way suddenly underwent a transformation and the gravitational pull of planet Earth is neutralized, the ordinary empirical truth about the ripe apple falling to the ground is no longer tenable.

Under normal circumstances, it is correct to assert that the sun rises in the east. However, assume that a giant celestial body crashed into our sun and severely affected its gravitational pull. In turn, the rotational axis of planet Earth underwent a radical change that rendered meaningless the conventional concepts of "North, South, East and West". The proposition that "the sun rises in the east" would thereby lose its validity.

Under normal circumstances, natural scientists observe that the green leaves of the trees undergo photosynthesis to transform carbon dioxide into oxygen. However, if the sun suddenly underwent a transformation and began to radiate rays that disrupted the process of photosynthesis, scientific observations relating to photosynthesis would need to be restudied.

Under normal circumstances, social scientists observe that generally, human beings purchase more of an item if its price decreases. However, if most of us suddenly adopted an enlightened way of life that embraces simplicity and discards greed, this economic law would lose its general applicability.

Our everyday dualistic, "subject-object" and "cause-and-effect" thinking, conceptualizations and reasoning are at the level of "relative truth". They give rise to conceptual-symbolic knowledge that can be described in dualistic language. These conceptual-symbolic knowledge are signs or symbols which "represent" certain phenomenal events or processes. They are akin to the map of a territory, and not the territory itself. As we progress in our spiritual path, we awaken to the ontological Higher Truth, namely (i) the Phenomenal Realm of forms and appearances emanates from the Nonmanifest Realm and (ii) the Phenomenal Realm and the Nonmanifest Realm are two aspects of the same Ultimate Reality. Mahayana Buddhism aptly describes ultimate reality as "thusness", ie. "just as they are". Guided by this higher perspective, we perceive more clearly the boundary and limitations of dualistic concepts, cause-and-effect thinking and conceptual-symbolic knowledge. We realize that to fulfill our deep potential and reinvent ourselves, we need to tap upon the intuitive mode of knowing and rise to the higher trans-conceptual trans-dualistic perspective.

To practice is to go beyond ideas, so you can arrive at the suchness of things.

Thich Nhat Hanh

Nevertheless, attaining this higher perspective does not entail forgoing dualistic concepts and conventional scientific truths. It does not entail denigrating or renouncing logical-rational thinking and moral reasoning. It does not mean that we are espousing an anti-conceptual, anti-logical or anti-rational stance. It also does not mean that we are reverting to the pre-conceptual pre-rational "blissful" state of an infant. Rather, it means that we become more aware of the limitations of the conceptual mode of knowing. We become alert to the higher truth that solely relying on the study and acquisition of conditional or empirical truths could not lead

151

us to a clearer vision of our life purpose. To gain deeper understanding of the interwoven fabric of life, to touch our divine essence and rise above the fixation on a solidified independent self, we need to avail ourselves to the intuitive mode of knowing. This subject is further explored in chapter 4.

Wealth-Creation Secret #26
When we arrive at the "thusness" of reality,
the myriad miracles of being alive unfold before our eyes.

Eleventh Gateway: Practicing Trans-Dualistic Wisdom And Embracing The Good And Bad

Master Tung Kwo asked Chuang Tzu: "Show me where the Tao is to be found."
Chuang Tzu replied: "There is nowhere it is not to be found."
The Way of Chuang Tzu

The significant problems we face cannot be resolved at the same level of thinking we were at when we created them.
Albert Einstein

With maturing wisdom, we learn to fully appreciate our strengths, talents and innate goodness. We learn not to flee from our shadow aspects and the darker side of our personality. They may include unhealthy desire for sense enjoyment, yearning for fame, fortune, status and power to satisfy egoistic urges or seeking spiritual comfort to avoid household or parental responsibilities. Seeking to gain deeper insight into their origin, we discover that they arose from losing touch with our innate wholesomeness, from years of unhealthy environmental conditioning, from negative thinking and emotional patterns.

By extending insightful awareness to our egoistic urges, it dawns on us that they are neither solid entities nor ingrained components of our being. Rather, they reveal themselves as thinking and emotional patterns. By extending healthy mindfulness and kind understanding to them, their grip on us will loosen and dissipate over time.

Similarly, as our wisdom and compassionate heart ripen, we learn not to resist and struggle against external events, adversities and difficult people. We learn to patiently accept them as part and parcel of inner cultivation, as grist to the mill, as valuable opportunities to deepen our insight into the misery, fear and insecurity of other people and how their aggressive words and behavior are subtly crying out for our affection. We learn to patiently accept adversities and difficult people as spiritual bricks and mortar to build a resilient character.

Every spiritual life entails a succession of difficulties because every ordinary life also involves a succession of difficulties, what the Buddha described as the inevitable sufferings of existence. In a spiritually informed life, however, these inevitable difficulties can be the source of our awakening, of deepening wisdom, patience, balance, and compassion. Without this perspective, we simply bear our sufferings like an ox or a foot soldier under a heavy load.

Dr Jack Kornfield
A Path With Heart

Touching our divine essence requires us to loosen the grip of dualistic concepts and dichotomous thinking patterns. Nevertheless, in the beginning, we may rely on the notions and concepts of the wisdom traditions to loosen our rigid conventional worldview and dualistic mindset, our scarcity consciousness and distorted concepts of self-identity. With ripening wisdom, we understand that the notions and concepts of the wisdom traditions need to be transcended, so as to attain a trans-conceptual awakening to the Ultimate Reality. The notions and concepts of the wisdom traditions are signposts pointing to the Ultimate Reality. They themselves are not the Ultimate Reality. In his classic *Living Buddha, Living Christ*, Thich Nhat Hanh explained:

In the beginning, we sometimes use new notions and concepts to neutralize our old ones and lead us to direct experience of reality. The notion of emptiness (sunyata), for example, can liberate us from the belief in a self. But then, if we are not vigilant, we can get caught in the notion of emptiness, which is even a bigger problem. To give us a second chance, the Buddha offered the notion of non-emptiness (asunyata). If we are able to see that emptiness and non-emptiness point to the same reality, both notions will be transcended and we will touch the world that is free from notions and concepts.

With deepening insight into our true essence, we will realize that from the very beginning, our partaking of Divinity is guaranteed. From the very beginning, we are enveloped and embraced by Divinity. This is the miraculous truth.

And this new awareness begins to become vivid and almost unbroken, there occurs what the Upanishads call 'a turning about in the seat of consciousness', a personal, utterly non-conceptual revelation of what we are, why we are here, and how we should act, 'which amounts in the end to nothing less than a new life, a new birth, you could say a resurrection.

Sogyal Rinpoche
The Tibetan Book of Living and Dying

Fostering this trans-dualistic awareness and perspective broadens our wisdom and deepen our awareness of the natural boundary and limitations of the symbolism of human language, of ordinary dualistic notions and concepts, of analytical-logical thinking. We learn to accept the absence of an independent selfhood. We learn to avail ourselves to the higher truth of the interconnected interwoven fabric of life and the impermanence of all phenomenal things. We embrace the higher truth that everyday reality is suffused with divinity; that adversities and external failures cannot diminish our innate wholesomeness; that the depths of our being are resting in the arms of Divinity.

Some waves on the ocean are high and some are low. Waves appear to be born and to die. But if we look more deeply, we see that the wave, although coming and going, are also water, which is always there. Notions like high and low, birth and death can be applied to waves, but water is free of such distinctions. Enlightenment for a wave is the moment the wave realizes that it is water..............If you practice deeply, one day you will realize that you are free from birth and death...............you will understand that you do not have to abandon this world in order to be free. You will know that nirvana, the Kingdom of Heaven, is available here and now.

Thich Nhat Hanh
Living Buddha, Living Christ

A Buddha is a Tathagata, a "thus-goer", because he is awakened to this primary, nonconceptual world which no words can convey, and does not confuse it with such ideas as being or non-being, good or bad, past or future, here or there, moving or still, permanent or impermanent.

Alan Watts
The Way of Zen

Twelfth Gateway: Post-Awakening Mindfulness Practice Is The Wellspring Of Enlightenment

Little by little, wean yourself.
This is the gist of what I have to say.
From an embryo, whose nourishment comes in the blood,
move to an infant drinking milk,
to a child on solid food,
to a searcher after wisdom,
to a hunter of more invisible game.

Rumi

To be enlightened about delusion is to be a Buddha. To be deluded in the midst of enlightenment is to be an ordinary person.

Zen Master Dogen

At fifteen, I set my heart upon learning.
At thirty, I had planted my feet firm upon the ground.
At forty, I no longer suffered from perplexities.
At fifty, I knew what were the biddings of Heaven.
At sixty, I heard them with a docile ear.
At seventy, I could follow the dictates of my own heart; for what I desired no longer overstepped the boundaries of right.

Confucius

Adult personal growth can be generalized into various stages. We shall discuss two useful frameworks on adult development to deepen our understanding of the maturation process and the general characteristics of our psychological-emotional-spiritual growth. It is useful to bear in mind that our thinking, emotional and behavioral patterns do not fall rigidly and inflexibly into distinct developmental stages all the time. Silent meditation exercises would readily reveal the evanescent feelings and mental states that we can experience within a short span of time.

Nevertheless, broadly speaking, without committing ourselves to inner cultivation, our mindset or "frame of mind" exhibits certain thinking, emotional and behavioral patterns and habits. In this regard, our habitual thinking and behavior can thereby be subsumed into a particular stage of adult development or psychological-spiritual growth. Gaining insight into the particular developmental stage that we broadly fall into is conducive to deeper understanding of our mental-emotional dynamics, of the state and progress of our maturation. It is also conducive to attuning the physical, cognitive and emotive dimensions of our phenomenal self to the harmony and potential of our deep essence. As observed by Michael Thompson in *The Congruent Life*:

Human development is a dynamic process that follows a unique course within each individual. It is anything but predictable, subject to life situations and traumas that can arrest the process as well as graced moments of insight that can accelerate it............That said, it is still possible to make generalized statements about the differences between people at various levels of development............

We shall now examine the stages of spiritual growth as presented in Dr M. Scott Peck's bestseller *Further Along The Road Less Travelled* where he refined Professor James Fowler's "stages of faith" into four stages of spiritual growth. I have rephrased and condensed it in the following paragraphs, aligning it to match our need for a broad, open-minded and discerning understanding of the common characteristics and phases of psychological-spiritual growth.

Stage One is labeled as the "chaotic/antisocial" stage. It was estimated that about twenty percent of the American population would fall into this category. Broadly speaking, people under this stage are spiritually unconscious. Their words and deeds are not guided by any stable spiritual-ethical values and principles. Instead, they are overtly or covertly manipulative and seek to exploit others for personal gain. They are inwardly "chaotic", lacking an inner moral compass. The profound significance of practicing "sincerity", "integrity" and "kind intentions" eludes them. They also display a subtle "antisocial" proclivity in the sense that their behavior is driven by surreptitious or patent self-seeking urges where sincere concern for the well-being of others is minimal. Their self-centered and self-preoccupied behavior tends to undermine and disrupt the basic consonance of human relationships. Some of them may also display subtle suaveness and tactfulness and are capable of "pretending" to be caring. Nonetheless, if they engage in inner exploration, they will discover that their deeds are subtly driven by egocentricity and self-interest.

Stage Two is labeled as "formal/institutional". People under this category are "dependent upon an institution for their governance". The institution may be a business corporation, a religious organization, the church, the military or even a law enforcement institution like the prison. These people are "formal" in the sense that they are attached to the "outward forms and rituals" as dictated by the institution. They become very "disturbed and upset" if other people slighted or opposed such "forms and rituals". In addition, people under this stage perceive God mainly as an "external being". They have little insight into the divine spark immanent in them, oblivious of the "dwelling divinity within the human spirit". They mostly perceive God as "up there" and "out there", as omnipotent and paternalistic, and quite willing to use force and "punitive power" on those who have violated the official doctrines of their institution.

Stage Three is labeled as "skeptic/individual". People in this category are ahead of people in Stage Two in their spiritual growth. Being committed truth-seekers, they are "rational, moral and humane", displaying self-reliance and self-confidence in their quest for deeper self-understanding and a more mature perspective of life. They are rational and objective in showing concern for the needy, the vulnerable and the underprivileged members of society. Many of the people under this stage are scientists where they are individualistic and scientific-minded in their search for the truths. However, their worldview is still primarily three-dimensional and five-sensory in nature, dominated by the conceptual mode of knowing, analytical-logical thinking and rationalizations. They distrust the intuitive mode of knowing and the human capacity to gain insight into the higher truths. They are skeptical or dismissive of phenomena which, in their five-sensory worldview, cannot be scientifically proven and verified. Thus, they are skeptical toward spiritual matters and are wary of people in Stage Four, the "mystics". In their quest for the truth, people in Stage Three have yet to rise above their conviction in the supremacy of conceptual-logical thinking and the resultant conceptual-symbolic knowledge, which excludes the validity and meaningfulness of tapping upon our higher unitary holotrophic consciousness to touch our deep essence. They harbor doubts about the veracity of higher intuitive-experiential understanding. They have yet to rise to the higher plane of holistic trans-conceptual trans-rational understanding.

People in Stage Four, who are labeled as "mystics/communal", have "seen a cohesion beneath the surface of things". They have caught glimpses of the higher reality and discovered their deep potential to rise above their parochial ego-centered perspective. Genuine mystics of all cultures and religions perceive the "unity" and interconnected nature of all phenomena and their spiritual foundation. Their mindset moves toward a unified vision of life, rather than mainly conceptualizing and analyzing the "separateness" and distinct properties of different things and phenomena. They are able to attune their daily words and deeds with a higher perspective of the interwoven nature of life. With deepening wisdom, people at Stage Four realize the importance of practicing compassion, empathy, altruism and reverence for life. Thus, they display a healthy "communal" and other-oriented behavior where they sincerely seek to contribute to the well-being of others.

In *Manifest Your Destiny*, Dr Wayne Dyer reinterpreted Carl Jung's stages of adult development, categorizing them into four main stages. Similarly, I have rephrased and condensed it here.

The first stage is called the "athlete". This term is not meant to belittle healthy athletic behavior and activities. Rather, it means that the "primary identification" and self-identity of a person at this stage of adult development is his physical body, physical appearance and physical abilities. To a large extent, his sense of self-worth and happiness depends on the way he perceives the attractiveness and abilities of his physical body. The athlete also requires a "stream of external approval" and commendation to bolster his sense of security. External achievements and recognition are his overriding concern. His daily activities "revolve around" or are fixated on a "predetermined standard of performance and appearance". Covertly or overtly, he resists the impermanence of all things and the flux of life as he subtly yearns for a kind of immortal youth and physical attractiveness. To tap our deep potential and inner resources, we need to move beyond the stage of the athlete, the over-identification with the physical self and body as the primary reality.

The next stage is the "warrior", who is ego-driven and ego-dominated. He experiences a persistent compulsiveness to display his superiority, to "subdue others and conquer the world". Driven by an unhealthy attachment to his physical self and limited to the five-sensory worldview, the warrior regards others as "separate entities" to be defeated and subjugated. "Winning is everything" becomes his motto. He leads an anxiety-ridden competition-driven existence where external success, status and accomplishments are his subtle preoccupations. As time passes, the warrior experiences inner dislocation, oblivious of his spiritual dimension and inner affluence.

The next stage of adult development is the "statesman" stage. This is a healthy and mature plane of adult growth whereby a person begins to gain deeper understanding of the meaning of life. He begins to pierce through the inadequacies and limitations of an ego-driven impulsive existence. Perceiving the inter-related nature of all things, he begins to be concerned about improving the welfare of others and begins to participate in activities that assist the needy. As time passes, "service to all" emerges as his motto. Gradually, the primary motivation of the maturing individual is no longer self-aggrandizement and external commendation. Rather, he has taken a leap to a higher level of personal growth whereby he becomes receptive to and experiences inner fulfillment, peace and joy in contributing to the well-being of others.

The next higher stage is the stage of the "spirit" wherein we become more clearly and vibrantly aware of our divine essence and capacity, that we are "an infinite, limitless, immortal, universal and eternal energy temporarily residing in a body". Through patiently undertaking spiritual exercises, cultivating positive inner qualities and practicing compassion and altruism to others, we gain deeper insight into our immanent sanctity. We touch the higher dimension of our life and perceive that its incessant flux and changes occur within the ambit of the nonmanifest divine realm. By undergoing healthy emotional-spiritual healing and rejuvenation, we undertake our daily activities with a vibrant understanding of our authentic life purpose, manifesting our deep potential to live to the full measure of our humanity.

The above two frameworks of adult development are useful in broadening our understanding of the maturation process. Without awakening to our deep essence and by adhering to an ego-dominated, compulsive and impulsive existence, we would stagnate at the stage of the athlete or the warrior. The deep significance of attaining a quantum leap to a higher plane of authentic living and ethical vision would elude us.

On the contrary, by committing ourselves to inner cultivation, we realize that it is the royal road to positive maturation. With ripening wisdom, it will also dawn on us that post-awakening practice is an ongoing lifelong process. It is a year-by-year, month-by-month, day-by-day, moment-by-moment nurturing and maturing process. Unending post-awakening practice is the foundation and wellspring of enlightenment.

Whether you practice zazen or not, you have Buddha nature. Because you have Buddha nature, there is enlightenment in your practice.

Suzuki Roshi

As we continue our inner cultivation and rise to the statesman-mystical-communal stage of adult maturation, we should be vigilant and wary of slipping into spiritual unconsciousness, of slipping into the warrior-like ego-dominated mental state. Owing to years of negative environmental conditioning, although inner cultivation can enhance our spiritual-emotional maturity, we can still lapse into spiritually unconscious thinking and behavior. It is also relatively common that as we continue our inner cultivation, we will be assailed by doubts, anxiety, uncertainty and disappointment over our imperfections and seeming inability to consistently uphold compassionate intentions. Nevertheless, do not be discouraged. This is part and parcel of post-awakening practice, of the lifelong process of cultivating wisdom.

It's more that through years and years of gentle training and honest, intelligent inquiry, we begin to trust our basic wisdom mind.

Pema Chodron
When Things Fall Apart

As we continue our spiritual path, it is useful to constantly remind ourselves that although we have caught glimpses of our innate sanctity and the ontological Higher Reality, post-awakening practice is even more important.

The crux of post-awakening practice is to continue to nurture and sustain a healthy insightful awareness in our daily living, to foster a healthy commitment to catch ourselves slipping into egoistic thinking and self-seeking behavior, to catch ourselves slipping into doubts, confusion, non-mindfulness, disappointment, despair, fear and anxiety. Such catching is itself of momentous significance. It is an important signpost of deeper awakening. Alertness to our slippage into spiritually unconscious thinking and behavior points to the ripening of wisdom. It initiates a virtuous pattern of insightful awareness over subtle negative urges and energies. It initiates a virtuous cycle of generating compassionate intentions toward ourselves and others.

As we continue our inner cultivation, such catching and alertness will ripen, becoming more natural and proficient over time. It will dawn on us that owing to years of negative environmental conditioning, we are always at risk of regressing and slipping into egoistic thinking and behavior. It is therefore imperative to be mindful at all times, so as to minimize such slippage and the emergence of unkind behavior.

Post-awakening practice also involves the healing of emotional negativities and inner strife. No spiritual teachers or mentors can undertake this process on our behalf. By undergoing this self-healing process, we learn to stop clinging to the past and worrying about the future, to cease clinging to an ossified self-identity. We learn to relish the immediacy of our experiences, the immense healing potential of our innate spaciousness and broadmindedness. Our basic conscience and compassionate awareness will emerge to guide our daily words and deeds. In the words of the Buddha, we become "a lamp unto ourselves".

Many of us heard about the unpredictable and haphazard nature of spiritual awakening. With ripening wisdom, it will dawn on us that the royal road to deep awakening is patient, constant and ongoing mindfulness practice.

Spiritual transformation is a profound process that doesn't happen by accident. We need a repeated discipline, a genuine training, in order to let go of our old habits of mind and to find and sustain a new way of seeing. To mature on the spiritual path we need to commit ourselves in a systematic way.

Dr Jack Kornfield
A Path With Heart,

Post-awakening cultivation of wisdom and spiritual qualities are neither random nor haphazard. It hinges on systematic and continuous inner cultivation whereby at all times and at all places, we can patiently nurture wisdom and spiritual qualities, whether at the churches or monasteries, at meditation retreats, at holiday resorts, at our homes with rowdy children, at our workplaces with demanding bosses and customers, or even while traveling on a plane, a train or a congested bus. Our ripened heart can graciously accept all these places as unique opportunities for bravely facing disagreeable or adverse circumstances, for extending an insightful awareness to subtle egoistic energies.

Just as a garden needs to be protected, tended, and cared for, so do ethical integrity, focused awareness, and understanding. No matter how deep our insight into the empty and contingent nature of things, that alone will do little to cultivate these qualities. Each of these areas in life becomes a challenge, an injunction to act. There is no room for complacency, for they all bear a tag that declares: "Cultivate Me."

Stephen Batchelor
Buddhism Without Beliefs

We say, "Pulling out the weeds we give nourishment to the plant." We pull the weeds and bury them near the plant to give it nourishment. So even though you have some difficulty in you practice, even though you have some waves while you are sitting, those waves themselves will help you............If you have some experience of how the weeds in your mind change into mental nourishment, your practice will make remarkable progress.

Suzuki Roshi

............not only does personal spiritual growth foster qualities and traits that both adult developmental theory and depth psychology have identified with the highest stages of human development, but these are just the qualities and traits most needed for life and leadership in the workplace of the twenty-first century.

Michael Thompson
The Congruent Life

As time passes, it dawns on us that daily living is the fertile ground for planting and cultivating insightful awareness. Daily living can be naturally transformed into mindful and enlightened living. As time passes, we awaken to the higher truth that enlightened living is the naturally healthy, liberating, joyful and vibrant way of living. In contrast, unenlightened living whereby we are driven by self-seeking energies and urges are not only crippling and destructive, but fundamentally unnatural. They corrode our natural sense of peace, afflicting us with restlessness, anxiety and inner strife.

With ripening wisdom, we realize that enlightenment is not a static immutable achievement. Instead, it is a day-by-day, hour-by-hour and moment-by-moment affair wherein our words and deeds are aligned with the deep harmony and potential of our divine essence. Enlightenment is grounded on committed, patient and compassionate post-awakening practice. It is grounded on and arises from the ongoing non-idealistic non-romantic practice of sustaining mindfulness in every word and deed, of avoiding slippage into spiritually unconscious thinking and behavior. It is grounded on and arises from sustaining a healthy insightful awareness over subtle egoistic cravings and urges, so as to heal and dissipate them. Enlightenment arises from moment-to-moment acceptance of the present, of relaxing into our inner wealth and wholesomeness, of sharing St Luke's insight that "The Kingdom of God is within". Enlightenment arises from moment-by-moment mindfulness over our basic unity with the Ultimate Reality, with Divine Consciousness and Intelligence. To quote the memorable words of Suzuki Roshi: "Strictly speaking, there are no enlightened people, there is only enlightened activity......What we are speaking about is moment-to-moment enlightenment......."

Wealth-Creation Secret #27
Enlightenment is the continuous awakening of
the human mind to the holiness of our deep essence,
despite our foibles, inadequacies and idiosyncrasies.
Only the committed and resolute practice of compassion
and broadmindedness can bring about such continuous
awakening.

Having entered the Stream of Dharma, the practitioner regularly examines his own heart. He constantly reminds himself, "These are the freedoms thus won and these are the fetters, the entanglements yet to be released in me."

The Buddha

167

As far as Buddha Nature is concerned, there is no difference between sinner and sage..........One enlightened thought and one is a Buddha, one foolish thought and one is an ordinary person.

Hui Neng, Zen Patriarch

After you have practiced for a while, you will realize that it is not possible to make rapid, extraordinary progress. Even though you try very hard, the progress you make is always little by little.

Shunryu Suzuki
Zen Mind, Beginner's Mind

Read the great spiritual books of all the traditions, come to some understanding of what the masters might mean by liberation and enlightenment, and find out which approach to absolute reality really attracts and suits you most. Exercise in your search as much discernment as you can; the spiritual path demands more intelligence, more sober understanding, more subtle powers of discrimination than any other discipline, because the highest truth is at stake.

Sogyal Rinpoche
The Tibetan Book Of Living And Dying

With ripening wisdom, the key message will dawn on us: Upon awakening to our deep essence, we need to patiently nurture a healthy insightful awareness. We need to be vigilant against slipping into spiritually unconscious words and deeds. Whenever we slip, do not be discouraged. Quickly pick ourselves up and practice again. Do not give up. Do not despair. Do not flee. It is human to slip. But it is divine to muster our courage and innate goodwill to pick ourselves up and try again with a pure heart. It is divine to remind ourselves that the only way to practice enlightened living is through daily living. By extending indomitable kind intentions toward ourselves, through commitment and determination, we become attuned to our authentic life purpose, deepening our insight that we are destined to awaken to our inner Light and to be guided by it.

The spiritual journey is one of continually falling on your face, getting up, brushing yourself off, looking sheepishly at God, and taking another step.

Aurobindo

Mature spirituality is not based on seeking perfection, on achieving some imaginary sense of purity. It is based simply on the capacity to let go and to love, to open the heart to all that is. Without ideals, the heart can turn suffering and imperfections we encounter into the path of compassion.

Dr Jack Kornfield
A Path With Heart

The well is within us. If we dig deeply in the present moment, the water will spring forth.

Thich Nhat Hanh
Living Buddha, Living Christ

* * * * * *

Emerson Lee

PART II

Recreating Our Phenomenal Self To Harvest External

Affluence

Emerson Lee

Wealth-Creation Wisdom 4
Taming, Training & Remolding The Galloping Mind

When water is still, it is like a mirror.......
And if water thus derives lucidity from stillness,
how much more the faculties of mind?
The mind of the sage being in repose
becomes the mirror of the universe.

Chuang Tzu

If your mind is not clouded by unnecessary things,
This is the best season of your life.

Chinese poem

The gift of learning to meditate is the greatest gift you can give
yourself in this life. For it is only through meditation that you can
undertake the journey to discover your true nature, and so find the
stability and confidence you will need to live, and die, well.

Sogyal Rinpoche
The Tibetan Book of Living And Dying

Jack Canfield, who developed the Chicken Soup series with Mark Victor Hansen, once told the following story:

An elderly monk was instructing a young monk on the importance and difficulty of mental concentration. The young monk was impatient and did not believe the elderly monk's words. He was confident that he could easily steady and focus his mind.

The elderly monk decided to pose a challenge to him and said, "If you can recite The Lord's Prayer from beginning to end without an interruption, I will give you the finest horse kept in this monastery."

The young monk grinned broadly and exclaimed, "I will definitely win.............." He took a deep breath and began, "Our Father in Heaven, Hallowed be Thy name, Thy kingdom cometh, Thy will be done on earth as it is in Heaven, Giveth us this day our daily bread...........and does that include the saddle............?"

Let us share another interesting Zen story about a man riding a robust and energetic horse. He was seen galloping at furious speed in various directions. When the horse was finally exhausted and slowed down, his friends were curious and enquired where was he going. He replied, "I don't know. Please ask my precious horse..........."

Since you cannot tame the minds of others until you have tamed your own, begin by taming your own mind.

Venerable Atisha

Meditation is, first of all, a tool for surveying our own territory so we can know what is going on. With the energy of mindfulness, we can calm things down, understand them, and bring harmony back to the conflicting elements inside us. If we can learn ways to touch the peace, joy, and happiness that are already there, we will become healthy and strong, and a resource for others.

Thich Nhat Hanh
Living Buddha, Living Christ

Wealth-Creation Secret #28
Discovering and patiently learning the art and science of mind training is to inherit the essence of the perennial wisdom.

Without patiently taming, training and disciplining our galloping mind, it is equivalent to riding on a robust horse but not knowing where we are heading. Mesmerized by its erratic streams of frenzied thoughts and plans, internal dialogues, argumentation and soliloquies, desultory imaginations and fantasies, we lose touch with the inner wellspring of serenity. The cultivation of wisdom is thereby impeded.

Thus, taming and training the galloping mind is the first key step toward positive self-creation, toward attuning the physical, mental and emotional aspects of our being to the harmony and creative potential of our deep essence. By remolding the galloping mind, we can transform it into a prized asset for attaining inner and outer success.

You shine the light of mindfulness on the object of your attention, and at the same time you shine the light of mindfulness on yourself. You observe the object of your attention and you also see your own storehouse full of precious gems.

Thich Nhat Hanh
The Heart of The Buddha's Teaching

More than those who hate you,
More than all your enemies,
An untrained mind does greater harm.
More than your mother,
More than your father,
More than all your family,
A well-trained mind does greater good.

The Buddha

175

The Four Pitfalls Of An Untrained Mind

(1) *The Untrained Galloping Mind Afflicts Us With "Attention Deficit Disorder".*

All of humanity's problems stem from man's inability to sit quietly in a room alone.

Pascal

An untrained mind has short and erratic attention span. Its concentration power is limited. Psychiatrists, psychologists and social scientists have discovered that a significant number of juvenile delinquents and maladjusted adults in modern societies suffer from short attention spans and low concentration ability. In his classic *Essential Spirituality* Dr Roger Walsh wrote:

Psyhiatrists identified ADD (Attention Deficit Disorder) only recently. Now it is apparent that it is a common disorder, affecting some 3 percent of children and many adults, exacerbated by our frenetic, deadline-driven, sound-bite culture and exacting enormous individual and social costs............

Two thousand years earlier, the great religions came to a similar, though more profound diagnosis. With the aid of the mental microscope of meditation, they were able to observe the mind and its wandering attention in minute detail. Their arresting conclusion was that we all suffer from attention deficit disorder. All of us suffer from a hyperactive attention which, while not as frenetic as in people with a clinically severe disorder, still careens uncontrollably from one object to another............

A group of students visited their senile Zen master who was dying. The students hoped to receive some final words of advice and inspiration from him. As the Zen master could no longer speak audibly, the most senior student handed a sheet of white paper for him to write down his final counsel.

When the sheet of paper was returned to the senior student, he was amazed to find only one word: "Attention." He wondered whether the Zen master's intellect was impaired and beseeched him a second time for some final words of inspiration. Again the Zen master scribbled the word "Attention" on the white sheet of paper.

The senior student and his companions were surprised. Could the final secret to enlightenment be summarized into a single word?

Undeterred, the group of students handed another fresh sheet of white paper to the dying Zen master and sincerely requested for some final words of inspiration. This time, the Zen master scribbled three words: "Attention. Attention. Attention."

The stream of thoughts surges through the mind of an ordinary person. Often called "black diffusion", this state is an unwholesome pattern of dissipation in which there is no knowledge whatsoever about who is thinking, where the thought comes from, and where the thought disappears. One has not even caught the "scent" of awareness; there are only unwholesome thought patterns operating, so that one is totally and mindlessly carried away by one thought after another. That is definitely not the path of liberation.

Tulku Urgyen Rinpoche

Students of meditation understand how difficult it is to sustain attention and concentration. Hence, it should not astound us to learn that sustaining present-moment awareness is the key to enlightened living. In *Peace Is Every*

Step, Thich Nhat Hanh reiterated, "Our appointment with life is in the present moment. If we do not have peace and joy right now, when will we have peace and joy — — tomorrow, or after tomorrow?" Many Buddhist and Zen teachers also use the memorable analogy of "a dog chasing after a bone" to depict the vicious cycle of being enslaved by our seemingly endless torrents of thoughts. In this analogy, the dog signifies our hyperactive attention, while the bone refers to any thought that comes to our mind. We are prone to chase after our thoughts and chew on them. Such chasing enervates us. Such chasing hinders us from appreciating the nowness of the present moment and impedes us from touching our deep essence. By undertaking meditation, we discover our ability to generalize and extend the meditative state to our normal waking hours, whereby we learn not to chase after the bones. We allow egoistic, unwholesome, mean-spirited and afflictive thoughts to arise and pass away naturally.

In *The Power Of Now* Eckhart Tolle described that a basic dysfunction of the modern mind is its "attachment to past and future and denial of the Now". He wrote:

All negativity is caused by an accumulation of psychological time and denial of the present. Unease, anxiety, tension, stress, worry – all forms of fear – are caused by too much future, and not enough presence. Guilt, regret, resentment, grievances, sadness, bitterness, and all forms of nonforgiveness are caused by too much past, and not enough presence.

How do we heal inner negativities that are spawned by our attachment to the past and overwhelming anxiety about the future? How do we tame the galloping mind and refocus it on the miraculous present moment?

Meditation and silent contemplation can nurture healthy attention span, ameliorate energy-wasting anxieties and lessen aimless mental roaming that distracts us from present-moment experiences. Cultivating present-moment awareness alerts us to the mental, emotional, physical and spiritual imbalances of a frenzied life that is dominated by urges to achieve future goals and satisfy future expectations. Rabbi Nachman said: "A person who does not meditate cannot have wisdom. He may occasionally be able to concentrate, but not for any length of time. His power of concentration remains weak and cannot be maintained."

Breathing in, I calm my body.
Breathing out, I smile.
Dwelling in the present moment,
I know this is a wonderful moment.

Thich Nhat Hanh
Peace Is Every Step

Wealth-Creation Secret #29
Nurturing a healthy attention enables us to foresee more clearly
the likely consequences of our words and deeds,
as well as the immense inner freedom that we have
to channel our words and deeds to worthwhile ends.

---

(2) *The Untrained Galloping Mind Loses Touch With Its Divine Essence*

We are all prisoners of our minds. This realization is the first step on the journey to freedom.

Ram Dass

Most of us use our thinking as ammunition against ourselves many times a day, without even knowing it. We think like victims or we think ourselves into a corner. We blow things out of proportion and make a big deal out of little things.

Dr Richard Carlson,

Why are you unhappy?
Because 99.9 percent,
Of everything you think, and
Of everything you do,
Is for yourself— — —
And there isn't one.

Wei Wu Wei

As elaborated in Chapter 2, growing up in materialistic societies has negatively conditioned our minds. We are being constantly bombarded by negative stimuli and erroneous messages echoing that happiness and personal success depend on external achievements, material acquisitions and social status. Without patiently training the galloping mind, it will internalize and recycle these erroneous messages. Running amok like a wild horse, self-gratification and self-advancement become its primary urges and motivations.

As time passes, the robust energy of the galloping mind generates a gamut of inner negativities in response to external events that hinder its quest for self-advancement. Fixated on the physical-emotional dimensions of the phenomenal self but oblivious to its deep essence, the galloping mind misconceives that only the satisfaction of self-seeking urges would bring fulfillment. It misconstrues "thoughts", "ideas", "notions", "concepts" and "viewpoints" as the enduring building blocks of "self-identity" or "personality". Hence, it insidiously transforms our consciousness to an anxiety-ridden fear-dominated scarcity mindset, solidifying a concept of self-identity based on self-seeking thoughts and thinking patterns. It fortifies this crippling concept by recycling the internal message that only the achievement of self-advancing goals would consolidate our real identity as a person. It produces notions, concepts, judgments, rationalizations, categorizations and mental divisions that build an invisible fortress separating us from others.

Identification with your mind, which causes thought to become compulsive. Not to be able to stop thinking is a dreadful affliction, but we don't realize this because almost everybody is suffering from it, so it is considered normal..........

Identification with your mind creates an opaque screen of concepts, labels, images, words, judgments, and definitions that block all true relationship. It comes between you and yourself, between you and your fellow man and woman, between you and nature, between you and God. It is this screen of thought that creates the illusion of separateness............

Eckhart Tolle
The Power Of Now

The feverish galloping mind frequently compares with others, particularly in terms of external achievements and material possessions. Oblivious to present-moment joys and delights, it views life as an emergency, an inevitable tragedy, a relentless battle, a continuous crisis. When it encounters failures in achieving external success, it fuels and feeds upon inner negativities, self-criticism and self-dislike. It misconceives that it could derive prowess from inner negativities. Even in human relationships, it is seeking for external security and comfort. It is oblivious to the true meaning of human bonding, of true love and affection.

Instead, subtle urges for possessiveness, manipulation and control over others spur the galloping mind.

By undertaking meditation and silent contemplation on a daily basis, we can calm the galloping mind. It will dawn on us that the endless streams of erratic thoughts are mere thoughts. They do not constitute our true essence. We do not need to seize and transmute them into tangible entities. Similarly, the attendant surges of egoistic urges and energies are transitory. There is no independent, self-existent or permanent "I", "me" or "person" orchestrating these thoughts, emotions and energies. By mindfully extending kind attention on them, they will arise and pass away. The many gaps of sacred silence and stillness which punctuate the streams of erratic thoughts unveil themselves. Gradually, we learn not to ossify our thoughts and thinking patterns into a rigid concept of self-identity. Instead, by reposing into the many gaps of sacred silence and stillness, windows of inner peace unveil.

My friend Larry Rosenberg of the Cambridge Insight Meditation Center calls it "selfing", that inevitable and incorrigible tendency to construct out of almost everything and every situation an "I", a "me", and a "mine"................Out of virtually any and every moment and experience, our thinking mind constructs "my" moment, "my" experience, "my" child, "my" hunger, "my" desire, "my" opinion, "my" way, "my" authority, "my" future, "my" knowledge, "my" body, "my" mind, "my" house, "my" land............

If you observe this process of selfing with sustained attention and inquiry, you will see that what we call "the self" is really a construct of our own mind, and hardly a permanent one, either. If you look deeply for a stable, indivisible self, you are not likely to find it other than in more thinking.

Dr Jon Kabat- Zinn
Wherever You Go, There You Are

Wealth-Creation Secret #30
The vast reservoir of inner wealth lies within the sacred gaps and spaciousness between our intentions, thoughts and sensations.

---

(3) *The Untrained Galloping Mind Is Producing And Imposing Layers Of Suffering*

Everybody's middle way is a different middle way; everyone practices in order to find out for him- or herself personally how to be balanced, how to be not too tight and not too loose.

Pema Chodron

The abyss of suffering created by an untrained mind is a key insight of the wisdom traditions. Let us trace back to the famous first discourse of the Enlightened One which he delivered to his five previous ascetic companions in the Deer Park after his Great Awakening. The Buddha's radiance amazed the five ascetics who still did not succeed in releasing themselves from existential confusion.

The Buddha spoke serenely, "There are two extremes to avoid, namely the indulgence in sense pleasures and the practice of self-mortification that deprives the body of its basic requirements. These two extremes cannot lead to enlightenment. Instead, they lead us further away from the ultimate truth.

"The path that I have discovered is called the Middle Path and there are Four Noble Truths:

"The First Noble Truth: Dukkha (*suffering*). Birth, old age, sickness and death are suffering. Sadness, anger, anxiety, fear and dejection are suffering. Contact with unpleasant things is suffering. Separation from loved ones is suffering. Not obtaining our wishes and desires is suffering. The five skandhas (*the five aggregates which make up the individual*) are suffering.

"The Second Noble Truth: Samudaya (*the arising or cause of Dukkha*). Our suffering arises from our thirst, craving and attachment. The craving for pleasure, passion, existence and non-existence causes suffering.

"The Third Noble Truth: Nirodha (*the cessation of Dukkha*). Non-craving and non-attachment lead to the cessation of suffering.

"The Fourth Noble Truth: Magga or the Noble Eightfold Path of "wise views, wise intention, wise speech, wise action, wise livelihood, wise effort, wise mindfulness and wise concentration" leads to the cessation of Dukkha.

"These Noble Truths give rise to insight, knowledge, wisdom and light, leading to Liberation, Understanding, Joy and Peace."

How do we partake of the Buddha's wisdom and share his profound insights into the human condition?

To avoid misinterpreting the Four Noble Truths, it is salutary to remind ourselves that the Buddha experiences the Great Awakening by treading the Middle Path, by avoiding extremes. Thus, to gain insight into the Four Noble Truths, it is useful to adopt the Middle Path perspective. This can be identified as the realistic perspective of a healthy person. It is a practical form of higher wisdom and higher realism that enables us to tap our inner wisdom, touch our innate sanctity and fulfill our deep potential.

By adopting this healthy and realistic perspective, we realize that the Four Noble Truths are not encouraging us to deny, repress or suppress our healthy feelings, enthusiasm and dedication to worthwhile goals. Rather, they seek to gradually train the galloping mind, healing its feverish energies, attachments, compulsiveness and emotional negativities. As explained in Chapter 3, inner cultivation does not entail that we deny, suppress or forgo healthy feelings of inner peace, joy and satisfaction. Rather, inner cultivation enables us to more effectively manage our expectations. It moderates the frequently "harsh" criteria that we impose on ourselves in order to feel at ease and contented. It enables us to gradually learn to derive intrinsic fulfillment from helping others.

By adopting this healthy and realistic perspective, we awaken to three basic aspects of "suffering":-

(a) Sensation Of Physical Pain

The first aspect is the sensation of pain that arises when our physical body is hurt or injured. Experiencing such sensations of pain is natural because they arise from a healthy nervous system and related neuro-physiological processes. We should not misunderstand that the Four

Noble Truths are encouraging us to deny or repress such sensations of pain.

For example, when our hand touched a hot kettle, we experienced a sensation of pain. When the nurse inserted a needle into our arm, we experienced a sensation of pain. When someone accidentally stepped on our toes, we experienced a sensation of pain. These experiences are normal and healthy. They naturally arise and pass away.

On the other hand, when we are afflicted with more serious disease and experienced continuous physical pain, it is healthy to consult medical doctors and seek to alleviate it. Meditation and mindfulness practice are also useful for lessening such "continuous" pain. They awaken us to the gaps of stillness and peace which punctuate such "continuous" pain. They lessen our preoccupation with and fixation on such pain by awakening us to our inner wholesomeness which no physical pain can corrode. Our sense of integrity and inner well-being is strengthened, endowing us with greater resilience to effectively manage such pain.

(b) Natural Feelings Of Sadness And Unhappiness

The second aspect refers to the natural feelings of sadness when we encounter unpleasant events. For example, when our loved ones passed away, we experienced feelings of sadness and sorrow. By undertaking meditation and mindfully extending kind attention on these feelings, we can experience them more courageously and allow them to arise and pass away. We do not cling to them or wallow in them. We do not seek to deny, suppress or flee from them. Guided by insightful awareness, by mindfully experiencing them and allowing them to arise and pass away, we nurture compassion and spiritual resilience. We can thereby continue to fulfill our responsibilities and obligations as constructive members of our families, organizations and society. Similarly, when we attain external success and affluence, we mindfully experience the spontaneous delight and joy, and let them arise and pass away. We are mindful of any subtle egoistic urges and attachment that may arise, so as not to be entangled by them.

(c) Unhealthy Ego-Based Anguish

The third aspect of suffering refers to the layers of unhealthy ego-based anguish that arises from our resistance to physical pain, from subtle non-acceptance of the impermanence of phenomenal things, from subtle attachment to external achievements and possessions, from craving for external security.

For example, when a stranger accidentally stepped on our toes, instead of allowing the sensation of pain to arise and pass away, we mentally and emotionally resist the pain. Such resistance imposes an additional layer of suffering onto the sensation of physical pain. Even when the sensation of pain has passed away, we mentally recycle it and refuse to let it go. Such mental recycling and resistance give rise to prolonged anguish. The untrained mind reasons that the stranger should have been more careful. It can also suspect that the stranger did it deliberately, thereby leading to a string of emotional negativities against the stranger.

Similarly, when our colleague was promoted while we were passed over, we naturally experienced feelings of disappointment and sadness. However, instead of allowing these feelings of disappointment and sadness to naturally arise and pass away, the untrained mind recycled them, mentally repeating stories on how we have been unfairly treated by our company, etc. These inner stories reinforce mental resistance, adding layers of anguish onto the initial feelings of disappointment and sadness, corroding our resilience and creativity.

Another example is that, owing to economic recession, numerous organizations performed poorly and many of us were retrenched. Knowing that we could not regain similar high-paying jobs in the foreseeable future, many of us need to downgrade our cars to lower-cost models or sell our houses for smaller flats. At this juncture, the untrained mind unleashes its feverish energies. It would subtly resist the change in our life circumstances, inventing and repeating mental stories about how unfortunate we are to lose our high-paying jobs and the necessity to give up many of our material possessions. Without letting go of our attachments to external possessions, without accepting the vicissitudes of life, our initial feelings of sadness would be aggravated. Mired in dejection and frustration, our ability to cope with ever-changing life circumstances is impaired.

Similarly, when our loved ones passed away, it is natural to experience feelings of sorrow and grief. However, the untrained mind subtly resists the event, adding layers of anguish onto our feelings of sorrow. Without surrendering mental resistance, without accepting the impermanence of all phenomena, we become mired in emotional negativities and inertia.

Thus, without training the galloping mind and adopting the realistic perspective of the Middle Path, natural feelings of sadness and disappointment engendered by unpleasant events are prolonged and exacerbated. We are impeded from touching our innate wholesomeness. Our roaming mind subtly recycles and dramatizes mental stories of our physical vulnerabilities, trapping us in anxieties and distracting us from the vitality of present-moment experiences.

By nurturing a healthy insightful awareness, we recognize these three basic aspects of suffering and can better appreciate (i) the origin of our natural feelings, (ii) the degree of healthiness of these natural feelings; and (iii) the extent that they may be contaminated by subtle negative urges, egoistic attachments and negative environmental conditioning.

Broadly speaking, positive and healthy feelings arise from the kind intentions of our compassionate heart, from a clear vision of our authentic life purpose, from healthy life goals that are grounded on positive personal growth. Nevertheless, owing to negative environmental conditioning, not all of our spontaneous feelings are positive and healthy. Some of our natural feelings may be contaminated by subtle negative urges. Emotional maturity hinges on the sharpness of our insight into and mindfulness of the degree of healthiness of our spontaneous feelings. We can undertake daily spiritual exercises to heal subtle negative urges and egoistic attachment that undermine our emotional health.

With ripening wisdom, we realize that the Four Noble Truths are not asserting that when we let go of our resistance to the impermanence of phenomenal things and our grasping for external security, we would be immune to sensations of physical pain or natural feelings of sadness engendered by unpleasant events. The Four Noble Truths are not seeking to transform us into pain-immune emotionless zombies. This is not congruent with the healthy perspective of the Middle Path. As long as our nervous system and neuro-physiological processes are normal and vibrant, we would continue to experience sensations of physical pain or pleasure in response to external stimuli and we would continue to experience natural feelings of sadness or joy in response to changing life circumstances.

However, the third aspect of prolonged suffering is unnecessary and destructive. It arises from the untrained mind orchestrating numerous repeating stories, concocted dramas and fantasies, depressing soliloquies and internal dialogues. We need not be held hostage by them. By quieting the galloping mind, avenues of healing its feverish, aggressive and hostile energies unveil.

May we share a lighthearted story. There was once a Zen master who had a naïve student. One day, the Zen master accidentally stepped upon a needle. He exclaimed: "Ouch!" and jumped up and down several times.

The student observed this incident and became disappointed, thinking that his master was a fake and has not even learnt to conquer physical pain. Soon, the student departed to find another teacher.

The Zen master was sad and mumbled to himself, "Hapless student, if only he had known that in reality, neither I nor the needle nor the "ouch" exclamation existed…………"

> *Wealth-Creation Secret #31*
> *Most of our everyday suffering and anguish arise from*
> *the pernicious habit of seeking to maintain an ego*
> *or a personal identity that grasps after external achievement*
> *and self-centered victory.*

(4) *The Untrained Galloping Mind Prevents Us From Attaining The Higher Perspective*

Let us share Plato's famous allegory of The Cave.

Imagine that a group of men was imprisoned since their birth in the depths of a dark cave. Their necks, hands and legs were chained, with virtually no movement. They were separated from each other and could not see or hear each other. They faced a huge wall, with a flaming torch behind them. Since they could not turn their back or neck, they had never seen the burning torch. Occasionally, their captors were come, extinguished the torch, fed and bathed them in darkness. Before the captors left, they would re-ignite the torch. The prisoners could thereby see the shadows of their captors on the wall which grew smaller and dimmer as they climbed the tortuous path that led to the narrow mouth of the cave. As time elapsed, the prisoners mistook the shadows on the wall as real entities.

Years later, the captors were ordered to liberate one of the prisoners. Released from the chains, the prisoner could finally see the faces of his captors and the flaming torch. Gradually, he realized that what he had all along mistaken as real entities were mere shadows on the wall.

The captors led the prisoner up the tortuous path toward the outside world. As he approached the narrow mouth of the cave which was guarded by soldiers, he was dazed by rays of sunlight. Slowly adjusting to the brightness of sunlight, he stepped outside the cave. His vision was overwhelmed by the splendid scenery: the resplendent flowers, shady trees, multi-colored butterflies, insects, chirping birds, scurrying animals, trickling streams, lush green hills, blue mountains and an enchanting waterfall.

Without training the galloping mind, it would chain us. Mistaking the shadows, forms and appearances of the phenomenal world as immutably real entities, we would be impeded from ascending to the higher truths.

In our journey toward the ontological Higher Reality, it is useful to distinguish between "conditional truths" and the "Higher Truth". In Chapter 3, we defined conditional truths as relative truths whereby their validity and meaningfulness depend on preconditions, countless prior causative events and the natural physical laws and processes that underpin this cosmos. Our everyday conceptualizations and logical-analytical thinking are mainly concerned with conditional truths. As we progress in our inner cultivation, we awaken to the trans-conceptual "Higher Truth" that the Phenomenal World emanates from the divine Nonmanifest Realm, and that the phenomenal realm and the nonmanifest realm are two aspects of the same Ultimate Reality. We begin to appreciate the parameters and limitations of dualistic concepts and thinking patterns.

Although dualistic "subject-object" concepts and cause-and-effect logical thinking are useful for analyzing, diagnosing and solving practical problems, they have limitations. Without the guidance of wisdom, such analytical-logical thinking can trap us in vicious cycles of misery, inner strife and emotional negativities. To fulfill our potential as co-creative partners of Divinity, we need to attain a higher perspective. However, attaining this higher perspective does not entail abandoning ordinary dualistic concepts and logical thinking. Rather, we become alert to their natural boundary and instrumental value.

For example, when crossing a busy road, we remind ourselves that, "I need to cross carefully. If I am reckless, I would be hit by a car and can become seriously injured."

From the standpoint of conditional truth, this is a sound and useful reminder. It enables us to preserve our physical existence and carry on with our lives normally. Nonetheless, from the perspective of the Higher Truth, there is no static, substantial, independent and isolated entity known as "I", "me" or "mine". Instead, our divine essence is spiritual, beyond earthly birth and death.

This higher perspective enables us to gain a clearer vision of our life purpose. It enables us to positively redefine our values and life goals that are grounded on kind intentions and healthy motivations. For example, guided by the higher perspective, the reminder to cross the road carefully is based on healthy motivations: "I need to cross carefully. If I am reckless, I would be hit by a car and can become seriously injured. I should therefore be careful and prudent, so that I can continue to be the breadwinner for my family, to fulfill my parental and filial duties, to contribute to the betterment of society."

Without the guidance of the higher perspective, the reminder may arise from subtle negative motivations: "I need to cross this road carefully. If I am reckless, I would be hit by a car and can become seriously injured. I do not wish to be seriously injured. Otherwise, I would not be able to become the star salesman of my company, unable to earn that special bonus for buying a luxurious car, unable to win over a string of attractive women, unable to gain social recognition. I also fear physical pain and death. Self-preservation and indulgence in sense pleasure are my life priorities."

Thus, the cultivation of wisdom and a healthy insightful awareness does not entail resistance against normal waking consciousness and its attendant dualistic thinking, conceptualizations and rationalizations. Rather, it seeks to gradually loosen, dislodge and deconstruct erroneous beliefs in a substantial isolated self, replacing these false beliefs with life-affirming present-moment awareness of our divine essence. More importantly, it enables us to become aware of the range of intentions, motivations and urges that underlie cognitive-dualistic thinking and rationalizations during normal waking hours. We become alert to positive and negative intentions, motivations and urges. Guided by inner wisdom, we cherish the positive intentions and motivations, while halting the unhealthy growth of negative urges and motivations.

For example, before we undertake mindfulness practice, during normal waking hours, many of us are not alert to the destructiveness of negative urges and motivations. We usually permit self-seeking thoughts, feelings and desires to drive our behavior and decision-making, so long as they do not infringe upon the law and moral norms. We continue to adhere to erroneous beliefs in an independent self. We continue to believe that satisfying the urges and yearning of this substantial "self" would yield fulfillment.

However, upon undertaking mindfulness practice, we realize that our authentic life purpose is to align our thoughts, words and deeds with the deep harmony of our true essence, so as to become co-creative partners of Divinity. We become mindful of the destructiveness of negative urges and motivations. We become mindful of the range of unhealthy self-seeking thoughts, emotional energies, desires and yearning spawned by erroneous beliefs in an inherently substantial self.

By tapping our inner wisdom, we seek to ensure that the basic motivations that give rise to everyday dualistic-logical thinking and rationalizations are positive. Cognitive-dualistic thinking and rationalizations are thereby utilized to fulfill worthwhile life goals. By tapping upon our inner wisdom, we seek to honorably fulfill daily activities, tasks and responsibilities with the overarching awareness of our divine essence, with life-affirming enthusiasm, vibrancy, flexibility and emotional maturity. We are no longer controlled and manipulated by a false self-identity. Our cognitive-logical thinking and conceptualizations rise to the higher plane of multi-dimensional perceptions and understanding. We become receptive to our innate autonomy and deep constructive potential. We avail ourselves to the higher dimension of Life. The Mystery of mysteries unveils. By extending insightful awareness and kind intentions to our thoughts, words and deeds, by letting the overarching awareness of our divine essence to permeate normal waking consciousness, we discover Divinity and enlightened living in ordinary waking hours.

Availing Ourselves To The Higher Perspective

Before we understand the idea of emptiness, everything seems to exist substantially. But after we realize the emptiness of things, everything becomes real − − − not substantial.

Shunryu Suzuki
Zen Mind, Beginner's Mind

Most humans are still in the grip of the egoic mode of consciousness: identified with their mind and run by their mind. If they do not free themselves from their mind in time, they will be destroyed by it...........

Eckhart Tolle
The Power of Now

From the standpoint of conditional truths, the First Noble Truth sounds pessimistic and gloomy, focusing on the stark facts of life: sickness, disease, death, decay, impermanence, physical vulnerabilities, humiliation and frustrations.

Nevertheless, as we continue our inner cultivation, we realize that the primary purpose of the Four Noble Truths is to introduce us to the spiritual path, to self-discovery, self-healing and self-mastery. Many Buddhist scholars have explained that the Four Noble Truths are not the deepest teachings of the Buddha. Rather, they are signposts pointing to the Higher Truth. They are the rafts that carry us over the sea of samsaric suffering.

The Buddha formulated the Four Noble Truths based on his insight into the ultimate reality. He was not being pessimistic. He was being present-moment-oriented, spontaneously receptive to the vast potentiality of life. He realized that it is the pure potentiality of life, its deep flux, change and impermanence, that makes phenomenal life possible in the first place. Such deep flux, unending change and impermanence are the intrinsic features of the Phenomenal Realm. By accepting them and foregoing resistance, we halt the multiplication of ego-driven suffering.

The Buddha's wisdom unveils that only a portion of suffering arises from physical pain. A large portion of suffering is unnecessary, self-induced and self-perpetuated. It arises from mental resistance and subtle attachments, from refusal to allow pleasant or unpleasant experiences to arise and pass away, from investing emotional and physical energies on our egoistic urges. Prolonged anguish cannot occur without our active mental consent and involvement. In addition, instead of deriving joy from performing meaningful activities, we become preoccupied with outcomes and end-results. Anxious that we cannot achieve the end-results, we succumb to non-mindfulness, restlessness and unease.

In contrast, by becoming present-moment-oriented, the Buddha discovers the root of prolonged suffering: losing touch with our divine essence and inner spaciousness. Retouching our inner sacredness restores our self-healing capacity.

These roses under my window make no reference to former roses or better roses; they are for what they are; they exist with God today. There is no time for them. There is simply the rose; it is perfect in every moment of its existence...............but man postpones or remembers; he does not live in the present, but with reverted eye laments the past, or heedless of the riches that surround him, stands on tiptoe to foresee the future. He cannot be happy and strong until he too lives with nature in the present, above time.

Ralph Waldo Emerson

On various occasions, the Buddha explained the need to nurture a skilful mindset that is receptive to our innate wholesomeness, that enables us to become mindful that there are healthy feelings, kind intentions and positive urges as well as unhealthy feelings, self-seeking intentions and negative urges. A skilful mindset is also mindful that healthy feelings and urges can be contaminated by subtle negative urges and egoistic attachment. As we continue our inner cultivation, we gain deeper insight into the origin and nuances of our feelings, intentions and urges, and extend insightful awareness and kind intentions to heal inner negativities.

Nevertheless, adopting the Higher Truth and longer-term perspective does not tantamount to trivializing the current suffering and hardships endured by the poor and the oppressed in many developing countries. Awakening to the Higher Truth perspective serves to deepen our wisdom and mindfulness practice, the ingredients for nurturing resilience and a compassionate heart to contribute to the betterment of society. As explained by Thich Nhat Hanh in *The Heart of the Buddha's Teaching*, we are not denying or fleeing from suffering:

Many people think that in order to avoid suffering, they have to give up joy, and they call this "transcending joy and suffering". This is not correct. If you recognize and accept your pain without running away from it, you will discover that although pain exists, joy also exists............. Don't get caught in theories or ideas, such as saying that suffering is an illusion or that we have to "transcend" both suffering and joy. Just stay in touch with what is actually going on, and you will touch the true nature of suffering and the true nature of joy.

If we restrict our thoughts and thinking patterns to conditional truths and the small-story perspective, we will continue to be fettered by negative self-seeking urges and energies. We will continue to misconceive our thinking and emotional patterns as constituents of our true essence. Our daily living and worldview will be warped.

By embarking on inner cultivation, we become vigilant of the limitations of adhering to a small-story perspective. We avail ourselves to the vitality and freshness of the higher perspective, allowing our worldview and motivations to undergo a positive transformation. Upon touching our true essence and catching glimpses of the Higher Reality, our level of consciousness and understanding will attain a quantum leap. Our rejuvenated awareness of Divine Reality will fruitfully guide our life direction. By aligning our daily activities with our authentic life purpose, we realize that we need not be attached to outcomes. When we have constructively defined our life goals and engage in worthwhile activities to fulfill them, we need not be attached to the end-results. Obstacles may prevent us from achieving the outcomes and end-results. Nonetheless, inspired by the higher perspective, our engagement in constructive activities is inherently fulfilling.

How do we access the higher perspective?

When his disciples enquired on the nature of the ultimate reality, the Buddha remained silent as it is not possible to describe it in ordinary dualistic language. It transcends everyday dualistic notions, concepts and analytical thinking. To a large extent, the symbolic power of human language is unable to touch it. If a person has not tasted strawberry, no matter how we attempt to describe it, that person cannot comprehend. Only direct experience can bring him the taste of strawberry.

Similarly, by undertaking meditation, silent contemplation and creative visualizations, we can catch glimpses of the Higher Reality. Such trans-conceptual trans-dualistic awakening and the subsequent daily cultivation of wisdom and spiritual qualities cannot be equated to reversion to a childhood state of blissful ignorance and dreamy immature mindset. Although a child is unreservedly happy and vibrant on many pleasant occasions, that same child can become rowdy, unruly and intractable when he is driven by the feverish energies of the galloping mind.

Thus, in the language of psychology, undertaking inner cultivation cannot be equated to reversion to a child-like pre-conceptual non-differentiated state of consciousness. It cannot be equated to reversion to a pre-egoic, pre-dualistic and pre-rational mental-emotional state that cannot effectively manage and heal negative emotions and unhealthy urges. Rather, inner cultivation deepens our emotional maturity and insight into the subtle intentions and motivations of our thoughts, words and deeds. A skilful mindset is emotionally mature and not puerile. Aware of the limitations of everyday analytical-dualistic thinking and rationalizations, a skilful mindset is trans-egoic, trans-dualistic and trans-rational, guided by inner wisdom, kind intentions and the natural laws of abundance.

Reality is free from all notions............It is our duty to transcend words and concepts to be able to encounter reality.
Thich Nhat Hanh
Living Buddha, Living Christ

Wealth-Creation Secret #32
We touch our inner affluence by realizing that
refocusing and retuning our everyday attention
will reveal the higher epiphanic perspective of life.

Spiritual Exercises: Training The Galloping Mind

The disciple Hui-K'e asked Bodhidharma, "Please help me to quiet my mind."

Bodhidharma said, "Bring me your mind so that I can quiet it."

After a moment Hui-K'e said, "But I can't find my mind."

"There," said Bodhidharma, "I have now quieted your mind."

Charles Luk
Chan And Zen Teachings

............meditation in a larger sense is really a way of being, an ability to generalize the quality of mindfulness...............you develop a continuity of awareness that allows all of your life to become an expression of your meditation practice.
Daniel Goleman

The attitude of meditative mindfulness seems so obvious to me now, and the practice seems so necessary to a clear understanding of my life. Shouldn't we all just discover these things as a natural part of our human development?
Wes Nisker

To nurture a healthy commitment to undertake meditation on a daily basis, it is useful to clarify its nature and purposes.

(1)   *Meditation Is A Time-Honored Method For Inner Exploration And For Nurturing Mindfulness*

Meditation is not negative self-withdrawal, self-absorption or self-preoccupation. It does not involve pessimistic or disaffected withdrawal from the world, evading life or cloistering ourselves in a remote place to shun the realities and difficulties of life. It is also not a technique confined to certain spiritual cults or religious sects.

On the contrary, meditation is an ancient art practiced by sages, philosophers, spiritual leaders as well as ordinary people of diverse religious and cultural backgrounds in the past ages. As long as we are individuated subjective consciousness with a phenomenal body, meditation is a valuable time-honored method for cultivating mindfulness and nurturing deep awareness of our inner wealth and resources, for attuning to deep inner peace and for fostering broadmindedness. It is a time-honored method for constructive inner exploration, for expediting our maturation and positive growth. By steadying and calming our galloping mind, it rejuvenates a healthy perspective of life priorities and enables us to touch our authentic life purpose. It connects us with our inner Light, so that we become aware of the subtle motivations and urges which underlie our daily thoughts, words and deeds.

When we speak of meditation, it is important for you to know that this is not some weird cryptic activity, as our popular culture might have it. It does not involve becoming some kind of zombie, vegetable, self-absorbed narcissist, navel gazer, "space cadet", cultist, devotee, mystic, or Eastern philosopher. Meditation is simply about being yourself and knowing something about who that is. It is about coming to realize that you are on a path whether you like it or not, namely the path that is your life.

Dr Jon Kabat-Zinn
Wherever You Go, There You Are

By touching our heart wisdom and innate sanctity, we become aware that our ego and egoistic thoughts and energies are not solid or substantial entities. Rather, they are evanescent, ephemeral and porous in nature. Thus, meditation is an effective route for loosening negative self-fixation, self-preoccupation and self-centeredness.

(2)　*Meditation Is Nourished By Deep Insight Into Our True Essence*

Meditation is............the act of being quiet with yourself and shutting down the constant monologue that fills the inner space of your being. It is stopping the constant bombardment of thoughts and the seemingly endless chatter filling your inner world.

Dr Wayne D. Dyer
Manifest Your Destiny

A method is only a means, not the meditation itself. It is through practicing the method skillfully that you reach the perfection of that pure state of total presence, which is the real meditation.

Sogyal Rinpoche
The Tibetan Book of Living And Dying

In itself, meditation is only a method. To penetrate the essence and deep significance of meditation, we need to see beyond its surface tactic or technique, and touch its marrow. Meditation will genuinely bloom and come to fruition when we touch our inner sanctity and divine essence, when we realize that we are Pure Awareness and Pure Consciousness. Guided by this overarching insight and understanding of our deep essence, we can thereby undertake meditation patiently, in tune with a peaceful heart, in tune with positive life values and belief systems. Every meditative moment becomes a miracle, manifesting inner wisdom and inner peace. Every meditative moment bears its own fruits.

It is virtually impossible, and senseless anyway, to commit yourself to a daily meditation practice without some view of why you are doing it, what its value might be in your life, a sense of why this might be your way and not just another imaginary windmills.

Dr Jon Kabat-Zinn
Wherever You Go, There You Are

(3)   *Concentration And Insight Meditations*

It's in the nature of mind to be stirred by confusing energies, like winds that blow back and forth across the surface of a clear pool, disturbing the visibility. Becoming a meditator doesn't mean stopping the ripples of the waves. Probably totally realized masters can see through all the ripples all the time. Regular seekers like myself are really happy if they can remember that they're just ripples...............

Sylvia Boorstein

In the Buddhist tradition, with which I am more familiar, the two major modes of meditation are concentration meditation and insight meditation. Concentration meditation aims to steady and calm the mind by focusing its attention on a mental or visual object, such as the inflow and outflow of our breath or a candle light. Focusing our attention on the breath is a time-honored practice. Numerous traditions and cultures have linked the breath with our life force and energy. The most natural and earthy object of meditation, it centers our mind and body on our ordinariness, nurturing a sense of humility, broadmindedness and receptiveness to the interconnected nature of life.

The focusing of attention on the breath is perhaps the most universal of the many hundreds of meditation subjects used worldwide. Steadying attention on the movement of the life-breath is central to yoga, to Buddhist and Hindu practices, to Sufi, Christian and Jewish traditions.

Dr Jack Kornfield
A Path With Heart

Apart from steadying the mind and cultivating mental "one-pointedness" via concentration meditation, it is also useful to practice mindfulness or insight meditation, which is often called Vipassana by followers of Buddhism. Insight meditation means that we learn to touch the profound "choiceless" awareness within us, to touch the Eternal Witness or Seer within us. We learn to develop keen awareness and insight into the ultimate nature of reality and the preciousness of the present moment. As explained by Dr Roger Walsh in *Essential Spirituality*, "Insight meditation is a rhythmic dance of awareness. You start by exploring the breath, then investigate whatever draws attention, and then return to the breath............You start with the breath but then go on to other experiences...........Thoughts, emotions, images and fantasies all appear in the mind, linger for a moment, and then disappear. Contrary to many people's beliefs, the task in meditation is not to squelch them, nor even to struggle with them. Rather, simply observe and

study them and they will change and pass away………"
Thus, insight meditation nurtures a healthy awareness that
our thoughts and emotional experiences do not comprise the
sanctified source of our being. They are not the building
blocks of our deep essence. We should not be gripped by
them. We should not be fixated on our *subjectivity* or self-
opinionated views. Rather, we can extend our pure, non-
judgmental and broadminded awareness to explore the
subtle origin of our thoughts and emotions. Unwholesome
self-seeking energies can thereby be weakened and healed.

In addition, undertaking insight meditation enables us to
catch glimpses of the profundity and versatility of our
consciousness whereby we can creatively shift our everyday
consciousness and transform it into epiphanic apperception
and appreciation of the non-dual nature of the Higher
Reality. We learn to access the higher truth that the
Phenomenal Realm emanates from the Nonmanifest Divine
Realm, that everyday moment is suffused with sacredness,
that every chirping bird, every leisurely goldfish, every
graceful dolphin, every dancing daffodil and flitting
butterfly, every vivacious squirrel and deer, every mulberry
tree, every tender blade of grass, every sentient being in this
cosmos, subsist in a Phenomenal Realm which is permeated
by the unseen Divine Realm.

*Do not pursue the past. Do not lose yourself in the future.
Looking deeply at life as it is in this very moment, the meditator
dwells in stability and freedom.*

The Buddha

By practicing insight meditation on a daily basis, we
nurture a capacity to watch and witness the arising and
passing away of our thoughts and emotions in a state of

composed alertness, without imposing any judgment or evaluation, without resisting unpleasant sensations and thoughts, without clinging to the pleasant ones, without investing emotional energy in them, without being carried away by complex rationalizations. Our composed attentiveness also pierces through the evanescent nature of inner forces and self-seeking urges that give rise to afflictive thoughts and emotions. We learn to watch the arising and passing away of these inner forces and energies, realizing that we can be released from their clutches and domination. We do not need to invest emotional energies in them or recycle them. Gradually, our insight into the Eternal Witness within us deepens and matures. Vast inner spaciousness unveils. We rediscover and strengthen the intuitive mode of knowing as well as our innate capacity to creatively interpret sensory and perceptual experiences. Inner freedom and autonomy are thereby restored. Clarity of our authentic life purpose gradually shines forth. The shoots of inner wisdom and broadmindedness begin to emerge.

In front of you the clouds parade by, your thoughts parade by, bodily sensations parade by, and you are none of them. You are the vast expanse of freedom through which all these objects come and go. You are an opening, a clearing, an Emptiness, a vast spaciousness, in which all these objects come and go...............

Ken Wilber
A Brief History Of Everything

(4) Meditation Enables Us To Nurture A "Wise Relationship" With Our Thinking Mind

Besides nurturing and sustaining a composed attentiveness to witness the arising and passing away of our thoughts and emotions against the background of inner spaciousness, another important purpose of meditation is to nurture a "wise relationship" with the mind and its natural processes. We learn to gain insight into the common characteristics of our thinking mind, its habitual thinking patterns, its tendency to judge, evaluate and compare, to plan and rationalize, to reflect upon the past, to display lack of attentiveness in the present moment and to be anxious about the future.

Most importantly, we become insightfully aware that our thinking mind, its range of thoughts and experiences, do not comprise our deep essence. They are not the building blocks of our inner sanctity. We become keenly aware of the instrumental nature of our thinking mind. We begin to comprehend how biological evolution has endowed us with a thinking mind with huge capacity to reflect, ponder, deliberate, rationalize and plan for the future and safeguard our survival. We also begin to comprehend that we need not be trapped by the egocentric habits of our thinking mind, its craving for self-protection and self-enhancement. By disentangling ourselves from the negative control, domination and manipulation of an egocentric thinking mind, by realizing that our thoughts and mental experiences do not comprise our deep essence, our inner wisdom will strengthen and ripen.

When we first undertake the art of meditation, it is indeed frustrating. Inevitably, as our mind wanders and our body feels the tension it has accumulated and the speed to which it is addicted, we often see how little inner discipline, patience or compassion we actually have......While we usually think of it as "our mind", if we look honestly, we see that the mind follows its own nature, conditions, and laws. Seeing this, we also see that we must gradually discover a wise relationship to the mind that connects it to the body and heart............

Dr Jack Kornfield
A Path With Heart

(5)   *Meditation Is "Anti-Competition"*

I cannot say it strongly enough: to integrate meditation in action is the whole ground and point and purpose of meditation. The violence and stress, the challenges and distractions of modern life make this integration even more urgently necessary.

Sogyal Rinpoche

In undertaking meditation, we are not competing with anybody. Importantly, we are not setting any target or seeking to achieve any specific goal. Meditation is a method for deep relaxation, for accessing deep inner peace and tranquility. It is not an inner struggle. It becomes an inner struggle only when we have yet to touch our deep essence. When we have caught a glimpse of our deep essence, we will understand that meditation is creating the optimal inner condition for us to be connected with the sanctified source of our being.

By nurturing an insightful awareness of the deep significance of undertaking meditation, any sense of desperation, urgency, inner strife and competition will slowly dissipate. In undertaking meditation, we are not challenging anybody. Rather, we are availing ourselves to the higher truth that there is no inherently substantial "I", "me" and "mine", that the everyday idea of an independent "self" is not accurate. We are nurturing a simple healthy mind-body state of being "thusness". We are nurturing a composed attentiveness and alertness to witness the "thusness" evanescence of our thoughts, sensations, feelings, emotions and inner energies.

...........after years of intense training, you can, so to speak, take out your mind and open it from the back. You will find it a very interesting spectacle. You will see, to your intense amazement, that the anger or fear or greed that had been driving you faster and faster are only forces, which you can harness and transform.

Eknath Eswaran

There is no genuine failure and debacle when we undertake meditation. We all undergo the natural cycles of meditative experiences. Sometimes we find it easier to sustain a composed attentiveness. Sometimes our mind is hyperactive, jumping around like a monkey or mustang, or galloping furiously like a wild horse in various directions. The wise approach would be to adhere to our daily fifteen-minute meditation schedule, regardless of our moods or emotions. As time passes, by adhering to our daily meditation schedule and patiently watching the arising and passing away of our thoughts, emotions and inner experiences, the galloping mind will calm down. The futility and destructiveness of being trapped and manipulated by egocentric thinking patterns will dawn on us. Thus, whenever our goal-oriented result-focused mind subtly assigns a specific objective (eg. to experience an exalted spiritual state) to our meditation practice, we should distance ourselves from these thoughts and let them pass away. We should gently remind ourselves that meditation is intrinsically fruitful, that it should be guided by an overarching awareness that our deep essence cannot be impaired by life circumstances, external events, inner experiences, thoughts or emotions, that our deep essence reflects "divine thusness", pure, timeless and inviolate.

The heart of skilful meditation is the ability to let go and begin again, over and over again. Even if you have to do that thousands of times during a session, it does not matter................as soon as we realize we have been lost in discursive thought, or have lost touch with our chosen contemplation, right in that very moment we can begin again. Nothing has been ruined, and there is no such thing as failing.

Sharon Salzberg
Lovingkindness

(6)   Patience And Consistency Are The Chief Virtues

In undertaking meditation, patience and consistency are the chief virtues. We need to patiently adhere to our daily meditation schedule, regardless of our moods or external circumstances. Paradoxically, during the trying or turbulent times in our life, we need to set aside adequate time to meditate silently and to contemplate on our life priorities and values. We can thereby sustain inner resilience, ethical vision and the strength to act as co-creators of Divinity. We can also see more clearly the evanescent nature of all phenomenal events and sustain a healthy perspective of life priorities.

Keep mindfulness even in the darkest moments, reminding yourself that the awareness is not part of the darkness or the pain; it holds the pain, and knows it, so it has to be more fundamental, and closer to what is healthy and strong and golden within you.

Dr Jon Kabat-Zinn
Wherever You Go, There You Are

Do you have the patience to wait
till your mind settles and the water is clear?
Can you remain unmoving
till the right action arises by itself?

Lao-Tzu

(7)   *Nurturing An Insightful Awareness*

You choose your future moment by moment, decision by
decision. You do this whether you are aware of it or not. If you are
not aware of it, you create your future unconsciously.

Gary Zukav
Soul Stories

By undertaking meditation on a daily basis, we are
nurturing an insightful awareness of our deep essence and
inner wholesomeness. We learn to release ourselves from the
control and manipulation of unwholesome thoughts or
afflictive emotions. We learn to more effectively manage our
inner life, its mental and emotional dynamics. As explored in
chapters 5 and 6, by nurturing and sustaining an insightful
awareness during both meditative and non-meditative
waking hours, we can more effectively attune our thoughts,
words and deeds to the harmony and potential of our deep
essence. We learn to perform each activity and task with
healthy attentiveness and concentration, which enhances our
creative thinking and decision-making ability. We also
nurture a kind of transcendental common sense whereby we
learn to see things as they are, to relish the "divine thusness"
of phenomena, without imposing and superimposing layers
of thoughts and rationalizations onto our perceptual
experiences. Furthermore, we realize that we are endowed
with immense inner freedom to unravel our neuroses and
negative attachments, to break away from unwholesome

conditioned behavior and to decide on healthy creative responses to external circumstances and events.

The spirit of mindfulness is to practice for its own sake, and just to take each moment as it comes − − −pleasant or unpleasant, good, bad, or ugly...............With this attitude, life itself becomes practice...........life itself becomes your meditation teacher and your guide.

Dr Jon Kabat-Zinn
Wherever You Go, There You Are

Practicing Concentration and Insight Meditations At Home

We sit together, the mountain and me,
Until only the mountain remains.

Li Po

- Find a quiet spot at home.

- Sit down comfortably on a cushion with legs crossed. Alternatively, we can sit on a chair.

- Place our hands comfortably on our knees.

- Breathe deeply and relax. Determine the period of our meditation session. For beginners, 10 or 15 minutes would suffice. As we become more comfortable with meditation, we can lengthen it to 20 or 30 minutes. Keep a watch nearby, so that we can check the timing as appropriate.

- Sit upright with our eyes, nose and chest in a straight line.

- We can close our eyes or let them be half-opened. Experiment with both approaches and determine which is more comfortable for us.

- Inhale gently through the nostrils and silently count as "one". Exhale gently through the nostrils and silently count as "two". Repeat this breathing-counting process for 10 minutes, so as to steady and calm the mind. Be aware of the different sensations in our nostrils, throats, chest and lungs as we inhale and exhale.

- While we are silently counting our breaths, a whole range of thoughts, memories, plans and fantasies will assail us. This is natural, given the frantic pace of modern living where the untrained mind is darting from one mental object to another. Gently smile and relax. Silently label them as "thinking" at the back of our mind and divert our attention back to breath-counting until the 10 minutes are up.

- Thereafter, we can undertake insight meditation for 5 minutes by watching in a non-judgmental, non-evaluating and non-intervening way the arising and passing away of our thoughts, sensations, feelings, emotions and inner energies. The purpose is to nurture present-moment awareness as well as awareness of the "thusness" evanescence of these inner experiences. It will gradually dawn on us that they cannot transgress upon the vast spaciousness and freedom of the Eternal Witness within us.

- Next, visualize Golden Light emanating from the depths of our being, permeating all the cells of our body. Focus our attentiveness on the warmth and affection of the Golden Light. Relax and imagine that our body is merging with the Golden Light, surrounded by its love and affection.

- Another effective way to nurture concentration and restore healthy inner silence is by repeating the name of God. We can experiment with various names, like *Heavenly Father, Divine Mother, God, Allah, Buddha, Jesus, Shiva, Divine Peace, One*, etc. before we settle for the holy name that can most effectively calm, heal and dissolve our emotional negativities and egoistic energies. We can undertake this exercise after our breath-counting meditation. Gently and slowly, we repeat the name of God for ten to fifteen minutes. In fact, whenever we experienced stress, frustration or negative emotions at home or at the workplace, we can undertake this exercise. As we wholeheartedly repeat the name of God on a daily basis, the galloping mind will lose its desperation and feverish energy. The tranquilizing and soothing effect of this exercise is profound and liberating, seeping into every cell of our body. As proclaimed by the famous spiritual teacher Ramakrishna, "Every revealed Name of the One Reality possesses irresistibly sanctifying power."

Practice your mantra two or three times a day, for five minutes each time. Practice when you wake up, at noon, and before you go to sleep............. You'll feel calmer, less hurried, less worried, and better centered. After practicing for one year, your personality will solidify at a new level of wholeness. And after you've practiced for ten years, you'll hardly recognize the person you once were.

Dr Dennis Gersten

- We can complete our meditation session by repeating slowly the following phrases, so as to connect with our inner sanctity.

May our loved ones be filled with peace and love, contentment and happiness.

May our friends and neighbors be filled with peace and love, contentment and happiness.

May I be filled with peace and love, contentment and happiness.

May all beings be filled with peace and love, contentment and happiness.

We are grateful for the peace and harmony of Divinity which envelop us.

We are grateful for the love and affection of God which permeate our being.

When you do reenter everyday life, let the wisdom, insight, compassion, humor, fluidity, spaciousness, and detachment that meditation brought you pervade your day-to-day experience. Meditation awakens in you the realization of how the nature of everything is illusory and dream-like…………

Sogyal Rinpoche
The Tibetan Book Of Living And Dying

* * * * * *

Wealth-Creation Wisdom 5
Connecting With Our Authentic Life Purpose

There are two great moments in a person's life: the first is when you were born; the second is when you discover why you were born.

Anonymous

Many persons have the wrong idea about what constitutes true happiness. It is not attained through self-gratification but through fidelity to a worthy purpose.

Helen Keller

We are here to be excited from youth to old age, to have an insatiable curiosity about the world.... we are also here to help others by practicing a friendly attitude. And, every person is born for a purpose. Everyone has a God-given potential, in essence, built into them. And if we are to live life to the fullest, we must realize that potential.

Norman Vincent Peale

Russian novelist Leo Tolstoy once told a story about a farmer who was discontented with the limited plot of land that he owned. He yearned to expand his assets.

One day, his friends informed him that large areas of fertile land were being sold at a low price at a distant village. On hearing this, the farmer rejoiced greatly. The next day, he began to travel to that village.

After traveling continuously for a week, he reached his destination. The village mayor greeted him and clarified: "By paying only ten thousand rubles, you can own as much land as you can set your feet on. Our rule is that at sunrise, you can walk as far away as you like. But you must return to the original starting point by sunset. Our village will honor that all the land which you have treaded on will belong to you."

Convinced that he could walk briskly and thereby acquire huge tracts of land for only ten thousand rubles, the farmer was exuberant. Early next morning, he paid the money to the mayor and began to walk briskly across several lush green hills. He was delighted by the fertile soil that his feet were treading on. The further he walked, the more he was captivated by the vast tracts of fertile land surrounding him. His greed deepened and he kept running well past noontime.

Only when the pinkish ray of evening light which splashed across the skyline caught his attention that the farmer realized that he need to rush back to the starting point, so as to comply with the mayor's rule. However, it was already late in the afternoon. The farmer therefore reluctantly and desperately commenced his backward journey. He ran faster and faster, breathless and exhausted. By nightfall, he finally saw the mayor waving at him. However, before he could reach the starting point, he suffered a massive heart attack. He collapsed and died on the spot, without realizing that his burial required only six feet of land.

Let us share another story about Alexander the Great. After scoring unparalleled military victories and seizing vast tracts of territories, Alexander led his victorious troops to the border of India. His adviser informed him that there lived a spiritual teacher nearby who was renowned for his wisdom and ability to predict the future. Thereupon, Alexander decided to visit him.

When Alexander reached the cave of the spiritual teacher, he and his troops marched inside. The radiance and serenity of the spiritual teacher greeted them. Alexander interrupted his meditation and enquired whether he could see the future. Filled with kind understanding, the spiritual master nodded his head. Alexander thereby enquired impatiently, "Are you able to predict whether my mighty troops can conquer the entire India within a year?"

The spiritual teacher looked gently at Alexander and replied, "Is that really important? Is conquering more lands and nations our ultimate life purpose? It appears that each of us will finally require only six feet of burial ground. If our bodies were cremated, we would require much less."

What is our ultimate life purpose? Are we destined to wander aimlessly and haphazardly in life, driven by self-seeking energies and subtle desires for self-aggrandizement? Or can we choose to touch our inner sanctity and connect with our authentic life purpose?

Wealth-Creation Secret #33
Inner success and positive wealth creation arise from
a healthy commitment to actualize worthwhile life goals.
Such commitment in turn depends on how deeply
we are connected with our authentic life purpose.

Touching Our Authentic Life Purpose

She had been jogging for only about half an hour when it happened. Suddenly a dozen young boys began to sprint in her direction. Before she had time to realize what was happening, they pounced upon her, pulled her into the bushes and began to beat her with a lead pipe. One boy continually kicked her in the face until she was bleeding profusely. Then they raped and sodomized her, and left her for dead.

Anthony Robbins
AWaken The Giant Within

This poignant account of an actual incident known as "wilding" which occurred in New York more than ten years ago is extracted from Anthony Robbins' bestseller. Nevertheless, a casual browsing through the daily newspapers revealed that incidents involving adolescents and young people willfully attacking, maiming and killing each other in modern cities continue to be frequent. In addition, criminal offences involving bands of thugs or highly-educated professionals who are motivated by personal greed and rapacity for quick gains are also common in modern societies. These harmful law-violating behavior essentially arose from inner dislocation and disconnection with our authentic life purpose.

In contrast, there are occasional incidents whereby men and women sacrificed themselves to save others. For example, during an air crash in Taiwan in year 2000, several crew members of the Singapore Airlines suffered severe burns while evacuating passengers from the wreckage of the crashed plane. It was reported that two of them eventually succumbed to the burns. During the heart-rending September 11 terrorist attacks on the twin towers in New York, many courageous rescuers lost their lives while in the midst of saving others from the blazing and collapsing buildings. Their sacrifices once again testified to the fortitude and nobility of the human spirit.

Inside you is untapped strength of will, of spirit, of heart. The kind of strength that will not flinch in the face of adversity. You have only to remember your purpose, the vision that brought you to Earth – – – the vision that will take you to the stars – – – to the depths of the oceans and up the stairway to the soul.

Dan Millman
Everyday Enlightenment

To live up to the full measure of our humanity, to avoid harming and ruining our own lives and those of others, we need to connect with our authentic life purpose.

How do we touch and connect with the deep significance of our lives?

The perennial wisdoms reveal that we can do so by probing within, by mining our inner wealth. By undertaking meditation, silent contemplation and creative visualizations on a daily basis, we lay the groundwork for connecting with the deep significance of our existence. We learn to tame the galloping mind and dislodge false beliefs in an independent isolated self. Holistic insights into our authentic life purpose will gradually dawn on us, leading us toward effective self-mastery, toward positively recreating our phenomenal self and re-appraising our values and life priorities.

Touching our deep essence is analogous to touching and eating a precious plum. Connecting with our authentic life purpose occurs when we become aware of the fragrance and sweetness of the fruit. We experience genuine fulfillment and inner peace by aligning our values and life goals with the deep harmony, freewill and constructive potential of our higher dimension.

With ripened wisdom, the following overarching insight, principle and value will dawn on us:

Overarching Spiritual Insight: Our phenomenal self emanates from the divine Nonmanifest Realm. It is innately wholesome. Our true essence partakes of Divinity. It is eternal, beyond earthly life and death, beyond time and space. This is an aspect of Divine Thusness. On the other hand, all phenomenal things, including our physical body, are impermanent and subject to constant change. Such incessant change and impermanence are also an aspect of Divine Thusness. We connect with the higher perspective when we awaken to the ultimate truth that both the Manifest Realm, which is characterized by incessant change and impermanence, and the pure potentiality of the sublime Nonmanifest Realm are two aspects of Divine Thusness.

Overarching Spiritual Principle: Our authentic life purpose is to attune our values, beliefs, life goals, intentions, daily thoughts, words and deeds to the higher wisdom, harmony, freewill and constructive potential of our divine essence.

The famous Golden Rule and Silver Rule are derived from this overarching spiritual principle:-

- Golden Rule: "Do unto others what you wish others to do unto you."

- Silver Rule: "Do not do unto others what you do not wish others to do unto you."

Overarching Spiritual Value: To fulfill our authentic life purpose, we uphold and commit ourselves to the cultivation of wisdom and positive spiritual qualities which include compassion, inner peace, contentment, broadmindedness, empathy, insightful acceptance and non-resistance, self-forgiveness and forgiveness of others, patience, generosity, non-attachment to outcome, humility, simplicity, present-moment awareness and reverence for life.

Guided by these overarching spiritual insight, principle and value, we cross over the invisible boundary, stepping into the sanctified territory which underpins authentic living. We rise to a higher echelon of inner freedom, vitality and flexibility. We rise to a higher galvanizing plane of ethical vision and discernment. We rise to a higher level of inspired acumen which attunes our words and deeds to the deep consonance of authentic living. By allowing our phenomenal self to enter the gateways of fruitful living, by awakening to the intrinsic fulfillment of contributing to the well-being of others, we begin to embody the sincerity of inner freedom and grace. An epiphanic vision of our higher dimension will dawn on us. It reveals that we are destined to emerge from the chrysalis of five-sensory three-dimensional existence. It unveils our innate potential to cross over the invisible boundary and rejoin the higher arena of authentic living.

English writer Lewis Thompson once wrote, "Christ, supreme poet, lived truth so passionately that every gesture of his, at once pure Act and perfect Symbol, embodies the transcendent." The purpose of our life is to embody the transcendent, to manifest and bring forth through pure-hearted intentions, empathic words and altruistic deeds the divine qualities inherent in our being.

If one advances confidently in the direction of his dreams and endeavors to live the life which he has imagined, he will meet with success unexpected in common hours. He will pass an invisible boundary; new universal and more liberal laws will begin to establish themselves around and within him; and he will live with the licenses of a higher order of being.

Henry David Thoreau

I still believe that standing up for the truth is the greatest thing in the world. This is the end of life. The end of life is not to be happy. The end of life is not to achieve pleasure and avoid pain. The end of life is to do the will of God, come what may.

Martin Luther King

Wealth-Creation Secret #34
Aligning our intentions, words and deeds with the divine essence
and spiritual foundation of our life
is to tap the natural laws of abundance.

Reappraising Our Values

Every time a value is born, existence takes on a new meaning; every time one dies, some part of that meaning passes away.

Joseph Wood Krutch

There is an unbelievable power in living your values: a sense of certainty, an inner peace, a total congruency that few people ever experience.

Anthony Robbins

Visit a beautiful and serene seaside. Relax and undertake breath-counting meditation and creative visualizations as outlined in chapter 1.

Thereafter, close our eyes and breathe gently. Reflect on our current values, dominant beliefs and life goals for 5 minutes. Are they conducive to the cultivation of wisdom and positive spiritual qualities?

Gently open our eyes. Obtain a pen and a blank sheet of paper. List down our guiding values and main life goals. Broadly speaking, values refer to those principles and things that we consider to be important to our well-being and happiness, and life goals refer to those longer-term goals and objectives that we seek to attain.

Reflect on our current values and life goals. Gently ask ourselves whether they are driven by egoism and narrow self-love, by unhealthy attachment to material comfort, financial success, self-aggrandizement, sense pleasure and social recognition? Does our value hierarchy ignore the spiritual dimension of our being? Can our current values and life goals lead to inner peace and genuine fulfillment? It may be useful to refer to the research findings of Dr Shalom Schwartz, who conducted comprehensive studies on "values" in the 1990s. Dr Schwartz identified ten motivational domains which represent universal human goals that guide our behavior:-

Motivational Domain	*"Schwartz's values" list*
Power	Social power, authority, wealth, public image, social recognition
Achievement	Capability, ambition, influence, intelligence
Hedonism	Pleasure, enjoyment, self-indulgence
Stimulation	Daring, variety, excitement
Self-direction	Curiosity, creativity, freedom, independence, self-respect
Universalism	Environment, nature, beauty, social justice, wisdom, equity, peace, inner harmony
Benevolence	Helpfulness, honesty, forgiveness, loyalty, responsibility, spirituality, friendship, love, meaning in life.
Tradition	Acceptance, devotion, humility, respect for tradition, moderation
Conformity	Obedience, honor, politeness, self-discipline
Security	Cleanliness, reciprocation of favors, social order, sense of belonging, health.

Outlined below is the gradual transformation in my values and life goals before and after touching my deep essence. Inner peace, contentment and genuine fulfillment are the natural fruits when we connect with our authentic life purpose and align our daily activities toward fulfilling it:-

Before *(Personal Values based on* *by lack of spiritual* *Insight, consciousness)*	*After* *(Personal Sub-Values in alignment* *with the overarching Spiritual* *Principle & Value)*
1. Intellectual Achievement	*1. Self-acceptance based on* *cultivating wisdom* *and a compassionate heart*
2. Financial success	*2. Financial independence* *based on a healthy simple lifestyle* *and "spending within our means"*
3. Material Enjoyment	*3. A healthy non-attachment to* *material comfort*
4. Social recognition	*4. Commitment to worthwhile life* *goals and activities, without* *attachment to recognition* *from others*
5. Physical Health	*5. Spiritual, mental, emotional* *and physical well-being based on* *cultivating wisdom and* *positive spiritual qualities*
6. Love and Acceptance *by others* *members*	*6. Nurturing kind intentions* *and affection toward family* *and friends, and forgiving* *their shortcomings*
7. Freedom	*7. Inner freedom and peace*

Emerson Lee

8. Fairness of treatment
by others
spiritually

8. Nurturing and extending kind
understanding toward the
unconscious thoughts, words
and deeds of others.

9. Cultivating wisdom and
touching our innate
wholesomeness.

10. Accessing inner affluence
to create external wealth for
worthwhile purposes.

Life Goal:
To become a highly
successful manager
and retire at age 50
to enjoy material
wealth.

Life Goal:
To undertake inner
cultivation as part and parcel
of healthy everyday living;
to engage in worthwhile activities
that contribute to the well-being
and positive growth of others;
to disseminate the perennial
wisdoms to the younger generation.

Wealth-Creation Secret #35
When divorced from the guidance of compassion,
broadmindedness and moral values, wealth creation would
corrupt our phenomenal being. Only by aligning our wealth
creation efforts with positive moral values that seek to enhance
the well-being of others can we reap the
fruits of inner and outer affluence.

Redefining Our Life Goals

I think the years I have spent in prison have been the most formative and important in my life because of the discipline, the sensations, but chiefly the opportunity to think clearly, to try to understand things.

Jawaharlal Nehru

Redefining our values and life goals enable us to reclaim our freewill. We become aware of the pernicious effects of negative environmental conditioning in modern societies. It dawns on us that when our values, beliefs and life goals are oriented toward contorted beliefs in an inherently substantial self, toward self-protection, self-aggrandizement and narrow self-love, they will lead us further and further away from our authentic life purpose. We will sink deeper into deleterious thinking and emotional patterns. Our waking hours are marked by inner strife and unease. We are forfeiting genuine freedom of choice that is not distorted by self-seeking urges. In due course, we end up undermining and sabotaging our lives.

Popular books and courses on self-improvement stress the need for us to prioritize our value, beliefs and life goals. This is conducive to gaining deeper self-understanding. Nonetheless, genuine self-mastery requires us to quantum-leap to a higher plane, to touch our deep essence and authentic life purpose. Without doing so, it is difficult to develop a healthy insightful awareness to differentiate between positive and negative intentions, between healthy and unhealthy motivations that underpin our values and life goals.

If our values and life priorities are unclear and not attuned to our authentic life purpose, if they are distorted by unhealthy egoistic motivations, they will reinforce self-seeking energies and urges. Instead of illuminating a healthy path, they lead us further away from genuine fulfillment.

On the contrary, by connecting with our authentic life purpose, we can effectively reappraise and redefine our current values and life goals. We can modify or discard those that reinforce unhealthy intentions and narrow self-love. We regain genuine freewill and autonomy by extricating ourselves from the control of subtle unhealthy intentions and urges. We can thereby embark on the path of creatively reinventing ourselves and manifesting our constructive potential.

To me, ultimate power is the ability to produce the results you desire most and create value for others in the process. Power is the ability to change your life, to shape your perceptions, to make things work for you and not against you. Real power is shared, not imposed. It's the ability to define human needs and to fulfill them — — both your needs and the needs of the people you care about.

Anthony Robbins
Unlimited Power

Six Valuable Approaches Toward Attaining Healthy Life Goals

The great at anything do not set to work because they are inspired, but rather become inspired because they are working. They don't waste time waiting for inspiration.

Ernest Newman

Below are six valuable approaches that sustain our connection with and commitment to the deep significance of our lives, enabling us to work toward healthy life goals.

- Approach 1: Nurturing a healthy insightful awareness and kind intentions
- Approach 2: Nurturing positive beliefs and attitude
- Approach 3: Nurturing a healthy self-esteem and deep faith in our innate worth
- Approach 4: Nurturing intrinsic motivation and enthusiasm in working toward worthwhile life goals
- Approach 5: Identifying our natural aptitude and talent
- Approach 6: Applying the Vision-Fulfillment Technique in working toward positive long-term goals

Approach 1: Nurturing a healthy insightful awareness and kind intentions

Kindness in words creates confidence.
Kindness in thinking creates profoundness.
Kindness in giving creates love.

Lao Tzu

Start by doing what is necessary, then what is possible, and suddenly you are doing the impossible.

St Francis of Assisi

Nurturing a healthy insightful awareness that is clear, transparent and uncluttered by the non-essentials and superficialities of our life is foundational to authentic living. It sustains our connection with the deep significance of our lives. It is cultivated by undertaking silent meditation, contemplation and creative visualization on a daily basis. It enables us to catch ourselves slipping into spiritually unconscious behavior and to sprinkle seeds of kind intention into our thoughts, words and deeds.

Recall a time when we experienced deep harmony and inner fulfillment from having performed a kind deed. Recall a time when we assisted a stranger based on goodwill, without expectation of return. Recall a time when we secretly extended a helping hand to a friend out of kindness, without his or her knowledge. Recall a time when we experienced deep sympathy and sadness for the innocent victims of crimes, of terrorist acts, of civil commotions and wars, of earthquakes, floods, hurricanes and other natural disasters. Recall a time when we experienced a profound ineffable sense of deep kinship with humanity, of sharing the anguish of the deprived, the diseased, the needy, the homeless, the unwanted elderly folks, the social outcasts.

Recall a time when we experienced heartfelt admiration for courageous men and women who sacrificed their lives to save others. Recall a time when we were deeply touched and inspired by the lives of past sages and great men like Gautama Buddha, Jesus, Prophet Mohamed, Confucius, Socrates, Abraham Lincoln, Mahatma Gandhi, and Mother Teresa who became enduring torches of wisdom, compassion, broadmindedness and fortitude, illuminating a brighter path for humanity.

Recall a time when the depth of our soul was ignited by the deep affection of our beloved one. Recall the first time when we looked into the sparkling eyes of our newborn child and witnessed hope and divinity in its pristine beauty. Recall a time when we were totally absorbed and awed by the wonders of Mother Nature, her majestic canyons, immense waterfalls, panoramic snow-peaked mountains, boundless oceans.

During these life-affirming life-invigorating moments, our narrow vision of life and parochial sense of self-sufficiency evaporated. We were pervaded by a pulsating sense of immediacy. We touched the marrow of our being. We touched the deep mystery, profundity and harmony of our being. Ineffably, subconsciously, mysteriously, we could sense and intuit that behind the observable vastness, immensity and multifarious nature of the world of constantly changing phenomena and appearances, the web of life is inextricably weaved together, that a higher invisible realm is subsisting as the miraculous foundation of life.

This keen sense of awareness and immediacy is replicated during meditation, silent contemplation and creative visualization. By calming the roaming mind, we center our awareness on the sacred aspect of our being, from which arose our profound and inexplicable kinship and connectedness with the web of life. As we deepen our mindfulness practice, it dawns on us that this keen sense of awareness and immediacy pervades our normal waking and thinking consciousness. In fact, it is the sublime overarching foundation and background of our everyday sensations, thoughts and feelings during normal waking hours. By dissipating the cluttered false beliefs in an isolated self, we retouch this keen sense of awareness and immediacy during normal waking hours, the pulsating core of our being.

When we allow our natural and healthy insightful awareness to shine forth during meditative moments and during our waking hours, we perceive more clearly the non-substantial nature of our physical self. We perceive more clearly the non-substantial, transparent and evanescent nature of our sensations, thoughts, feelings, inner negativities, fear, anxiety and uncertainty.

During meditative moments, we allow our healthy insightful awareness to dilute and dissipate these inner negativities, to catch ourselves slipping into spiritually unconscious behavior, to nurture our capacity to sprinkle kind intentions into our thoughts, words and deeds.

During non-meditative waking hours, we commit ourselves to gently "watch over" the subtle arising of our thoughts, words and deeds and create sufficient inner space to attune them to our heart wisdom. We gradually learn to let our everyday sensations, thoughts and feelings to become aligned with the deep wisdom, spaciousness, broadmindedness and harmony of our insightful awareness. By doing so, we learn to replicate the meditative sense of inner peace, ease and freedom during non-meditative waking hours. The negative patterns of self-seeking urges and compulsiveness will shrivel and diminish against the overarching background of our healthy insightful awareness. The sense of neurotic urgency, emergency and competition that plagues our waking hours gradually lessens. Authentic living coupled with moments of grace and peace unfolds before our eyes.

By replicating our meditative sense of keen awareness and broadmindedness, we can more effectively cultivate kind intentions during our non-meditative waking hours. Kind intentions refer to our sincere intentions to contribute to the well-being and positive growth of others when we are attuned to our heart wisdom. We are thereby induced to engage in worthwhile activities that create value for others. Material wealth emerges a natural by-product of engaging in worthwhile activities and a conduit for contributing to the well-being of others.

With ripening wisdom, we become gently mindful over our thoughts, words and deeds. We become gently mindful over our subtle intentions, motivations and urges. When we engage in a certain act, we create sufficient inner space and gently ask ourselves whether they arise from kind intention. If positive, we can confidently proceed to gather the requisite practical and technical knowledge and skills to perform the act. Regardless of the outcome or end-result, we learn to derive intrinsic fulfillment from performing a worthwhile act that is guided by heart wisdom.

It dawns on us that authentic living and effective self-mastery do not entail forgoing everyday logical-dualistic thinking and reasoning. By replicating the meditative insightful awareness in our non-meditative waking hours, we perceive more clearly the instrumental nature of logical-dualistic thinking and conceptual-symbolic knowledge. Whether our daily thinking and reasoning is healthy or unhealthy depends on our subtle intentions and motivations. By ensuring that our basic intentions and motivations are kind and attuned to the deep harmony of our being, our thinking and reasoning capacity can assist us to work toward worthwhile goals that contribute to the well-being of others.

We engage in inner cultivation, in meditation, contemplation, creative visualizations and repeating the name of God not to cast away our common sense-thinking and natural emotions. Rather, we are seeking to gain insight into the subtle intentions, motivations and urges that drive our everyday thoughts and feelings. We seek to nurture a healthy discernment and capacity to distinguish between kind intentions and negative self-centered intentions, motivations and urges.

A spiritually mature person is not devoid of intentions, motivations or emotions. He does not forgo his natural reasoning and emotional capacity. Rather, he is mindful of the subtle intentions that underpin his values and life goals, that drive his daily thinking, emotional and behavioral patterns. He has developed a skilful mindset which enables him to create sufficient inner space not only to "watch over" the arising of subtle intentions and urges, but also to transform negative intentions into positive empowering ones as well as to nurture constructive thinking and emotional habits. He has developed a skilful mindset which appreciates the instrumental value of functional knowledge and technical skills, making him wary that he should not misuse them for selfish purposes. He has developed a skilful mindset which enables him to effectively quiet down his judgmental galloping mind, attuning him to the sanctified source of his being and the divine spark in others.

Wealth-Creation Secret #36
The marrow of the perennial wisdom consists of
the art and science of sustaining an insightful awareness.
As we progress in our spiritual path, we will realize that
such insightful awareness will gradually broaden and deepen
into insightful compassion, insightful wisdom, insightful self-
forgiveness and forgiveness of others, insightful acceptance of the
adversities of life as catalysts for growth,
and insightful reverence for life.

Approach 2: Nurturing Positive Beliefs And Attitude

"As he thinketh in his heart, so is he."

Proverbs 23:7

The deepest ocean, the tallest mountain, the most powerful animal cannot believe. Only man can believe. The height of man's success is determined by the depth of his belief.

Zig Ziglar

Most of us seriously want to get rid of the pain, the illness, and frustrations, but we still want to maintain our old self-concept. Perhaps that is why we are going in circles, because we rigidly hold on to our old belief system.

Dr Gerald Jampolsky

In 1967, Martin Seligman, a graduate student at the University of Pennsylvania, conducted an experiment that resulted in a major breakthrough in the field of human psychology. After conducting a number of experiments in which dogs received an electric shock, Martin Seligman noticed that some of them did not respond. They simply laid down and endured the pain. At that time, there was no theory in the field of psychology that could explain such behavior.

Seligman creatively designed a two-stage experiment to test his ideas on why some dogs passively received the electric shocks and did not actively find an escape route. In Stage One of his experiement, dogs in Group A were harnessed and administered a mild shock. They could stop the shock by pressing a bar with their nose and they soon learned to do it. Group B dogs were placed in the same harness and administered the same shock but had no method of stopping it. These dogs soon learned to accept the pain passively. Group C was called the control group. They were put in a harness and given no shock.

The next day, Seligman conducted Stage Two of his experiment. One at a time, he put all of the same dogs in a device called a "shuttlebox" — a large cage with a low fence dividing it into two compartments. Each dog was placed on one side where it received a mild electric shock. Each could escape from the electric shock by leaping over the low fence to the next compartment in the cage.

Group A and Group C dogs promptly figured out how to cross over the low fence to escape from the electric shocks. However, Group B dogs displayed a different response. They laid down and whimpered. They did not seek a way to escape from the electric shocks.

What Martin Seligman and others discovered was that these dogs had learned to be "helpless", a behavior that virtually destroyed their motivation to act. Scientists had since discovered that many other types of animals as well as human beings can acquire this destructive behavior and mindset. Thus, "learned helplessness" refers to a self-sabotaging mindset and behavior that has internalized the belief and attitude that when we encounter an obstacle, whatever we do, our actions are not meaningful and are not conducive to overcoming the obstacle. We relinquish hope and our motivation to act.

This theory of "learned helplessness" could also solve a traditional riddle about an Indian boy who could tie a large elephant to a thin pole with a rope. The large elephant could easily break away from the thin pole but it did not. When the passer-by enquired, the boy said, "It would not try to escape, even though its giant strength can easily enable it to do so. When it was a young animal, my father had sought to tame it by chaining it to a huge tree. After struggling for several days to break the chain, it learnt that it was futile to do so. Thereafter, even though it is now a large grown-up animal, it no longer attempted to escape."

Do we sometimes act passively like the large elephant? Although we have tremendous constructive potential, did we awaken to it and learn to use it? Did past setbacks deter us from putting in our best in working toward worthwhile goals?

The birth of excellence begins with our awareness that our beliefs are a choice. Belief can be a conscious choice. We can choose beliefs that limit us or choose beliefs that support us.
Anthony Robbins

Our beliefs are founded on our worldview, from our experiences of external events, from the way we interpret and perceive our experiences, from environmental conditioning, from family upbringing and educational background. Our beliefs deeply influence our mindset, inner reality, thinking and emotional patterns, attitude toward external events, life goals and daily behavior. For example, with positive beliefs, we energize ourselves to accomplish many constructive goals. With negative beliefs, we deter ourselves from attempting to work toward worthwhile goals and can acquire a mindset that constantly pictures us as helpless victims. Erroneous beliefs that we cannot positively transform our worldview and self-perception, that we cannot become a constructive force in the world, will severely constrain and limit us.

To fulfill our deep potential, we need to nurture a healthy insightful awareness and awaken to the higher truth that we have the innate potential and freedom to choose, craft and formulate positive empowering beliefs that galvanize us to become a constructive force in the world. This important topic on our innate ability to redefine our beliefs and positively reinterpret our sensory experiences is further discussed in chapter 6.

Wealth-Creation Secret #37
Genuine positive beliefs and positive thinking are
devoid of fixation on self-centered victory.
Rather, they arise from the conviction that
our efforts and commitment to actualize worthwhile goals
are inherently fulfilling and valuable.

Approach 3: Nurturing A Healthy Self-Esteem

Everyone has his own specific vocation or mission in life to carry out a concrete assignment............Therein he cannot be replaced, nor can his life be repeated. Thus, everyone's task is as unique as is his specific opportunity to implement it.

Viktor Frankl
Man's Search For Meaning

No matter how intelligent, attractive, or talented you may be —
— to the degree you doubt your worthiness, you tend to sabotage your efforts and undermine your relationships. Life is full of gifts and opportunities; you will open to receive and enjoy them to the

degree that you begin to appreciate your innate worth, and to offer to yourself the same compassion and respect that you would give to others.

Dan Millman
Everyday Enlightenment

Healthy self-esteem arises from touching our heart wisdom. It is founded on the insight that external success and failures cannot diminish our innate wholesomeness. It is founded on the insight that our deep essence partakes of Divinity, that we are surrounded and engulfed by Divinity. We physically live and die, become spiritually reborn, resurrected and transformed in the arms of Divinity. Without guidance from our heart wisdom, self-esteem becomes narrow self-love, narcissism and self-centeredness in various guises.

Nurturing conviction in our innate goodness is pivotal in fostering healthy self-esteem. Let us undertake a simple exercise to touch and rediscover our innate goodness.

For the next 15 minutes, undertake breath-counting meditation and creative visualizations as outlined in chapter 1. Let our higher consciousness and awareness merge with our inner Light and sanctity.

Thereafter, gently open our eyes. Recall three good deeds that we have done in the past which are motivated by kind intentions and write them down on a sheet of paper. They need not be grand things. Let me share my examples.

- First deed: During schooldays when I was fifteen, together with some classmates, I volunteered to spend a day selling little stickers relating to a national fund-

241

raising campaign to assist needy cancer patients. I could still vividly remember the sense of fulfillment and satisfaction when, at the end of a tiring day, I passed a can filled with coins to the organizer.

- Second deed: I once had a sincere friend who needed a sum of money to tide over a period of financial difficulty. I was glad that I had the financial resources to assist this friend based on goodwill.

- Third deed: For the past seven years, I worked as a finance manager in a large public institution. Although the pay is lower when compared to the private sector, I decided to contribute my best years to public service, as it brings me greater fulfillment. I also encountered more opportunities to render my services to the public. In one incident, I went beyond my call of duty to assist a needy family which desperately required assistance to provide for the subsistence needs of their children.

By awakening to our basic goodness and the seed of kind intention within us, we touch the bedrock and foundation of healthy self-esteem. The seed of humaneness is embedded within us. By allowing our words and deeds to be guided by innate kindness, we rediscover our inner assets. Such rediscovery strengthens a healthy self-esteem and enables us to harmoniously connect with our authentic life purpose. To reiterate, they are:-

- The capacity to gain insight into our divine essence and awaken to our authentic life purpose.
- The capacity to touch and relax into the embrace of inner spaciousness and deep peace.

- The capacity to tap our heart wisdom to tame and train our roaming thinking mind, to dislodge erroneous concepts of self-identity, to heal emotional negativities and inner strife.
- The capacity to nurture a healthy insightful awareness and allow it to guide our words and deeds.
- The capacity to forgive ourselves and others, to emphathise with and be receptive to the suffering of others.
- The capacity to be guided by heart wisdom and to sprinkle kind intentions into our thoughts, words and deeds.
- The capacity to positively re-create ourselves and align our worldview, belief and value systems with the natural laws of abundance.
- The capacity to tap our heart wisdom to nurture positive habits, positive thinking and emotional patterns, and a resilient character.
- The capacity to tap upon our inner wisdom to creatively and effectively solve daily problems.
- The capacity to commit ourselves to worthwhile life goals and activities that contribute to the well-being of others.

Tapping these inner assets will gradually dissolve erroneous beliefs that we are only five-sensory three-dimensional beings without a higher dimension. It will unleash our constructive potential and imbue us with healthy determination and tenacity to work toward worthwhile goals.

You can't live a perfect day without doing something for someone who will never be able to repay you.

Dr Ellen McGrath, a specialist in fostering self-esteem, highlighted that *"maintaining self-esteem is a lifelong psychological workout, no matter who you are. Self-esteem is not an end goal. It's a mental muscle which must be developed and maintained through exercising it our whole lives............ When we build up the self-esteem muscle deep inside ourselves, we learn to like and respect who we are, no matter what is happening around us."*

Dr McGrath also recommended that "a passion a day keeps the doctor away". If we can pursue one of our healthy passions for just 15 minutes a day, it will foster a vibrant self-esteem. For the past few years, I have followed this advice and found that it is very effective. On my part, I am deeply interested in creative writing and sharing some of my insights on the benefits of inner cultivation. By devoting 15 minutes to half an hour a day to writing, I reconnect with my creativity, which simultaneously nurtures a healthy self-esteem.

Thus, you may wish to identify one or two of your healthy interest and follow Dr McGrath's advice to spend 15 to 30 minutes a day on it. Let our unique talent to slowly mature and blossom. This routine will bolster healthy self-esteem and self-appreciation.

Many people fail to set and achieve goals because they have lost the ability to inspire themselves.

Dr. Gerry Sexton

Nurturing healthy self-esteem also entails healing inner negativities. Broadly speaking, there are two types of inner negativities. The first type refers to the more specific negative mental-emotional states that are produced by frustrating or adverse events. Anger, resentment, hatred, enmity, sorrow, disappointment, jealousy and envy are common examples.

The second type refers to a continuous gnawing sense of unease, unhappiness, desperation, discontent, disillusionment, anxiety and fear that pervades our daily thoughts and emotional patterns.

From the higher perspective, both types of inner negativities arise from losing touch with our true essence. It gives rise to inner dislocation, a pervasive sense of insecurity and erroneous beliefs in the overriding importance of self-aggrandizement. In addition, we are subject to continuous negative environmental conditioning that champions the supremacy of sense pleasure and material acquisitions, the glamour of being rich and famous. Our self-concept, self-image and worldview are distorted by these continuous bombardments. A competition-riven scarcity mindset evolved, fuelled by the feverish energies and desperation of the galloping mind. Ceaselessly, we compare our achievements with those of others, with our friends, neighbors and siblings. Such continuous comparison generates inner strife and discontent. To out-rival others, we impose excessive demands and overtaxing goals on ourselves. We may even resort to imprudent tactics and shortcuts. When external goals, social recognition and worldly success prove to be beyond our grasp, frustrations, disillusionment, self-dislike and self-rejection would afflict us.

Alternatively, even if we succeeded in achieving outward prizes, without restoring inner peace and the natural ability to appreciate the simple joys in life, genuine fulfillment would elude us. A gnawing sense of fear and insecurity will contaminate our daily existence. Lulled by the false belief that we need to amass material possessions and external power to attain fulfillment, we sink deeper into the abyss of inner dislocation.

To halt this harmful descent and to heal self-rejection, touching the higher dimension of our being is crucial. The spiritual exercises outlined in the previous chapters are valuable in this regard. They plant, water and cultivate transformative insights that inner wisdom is always available to guide us.

To awaken to the higher truth that external success or failure cannot affect our inner wholesomeness is to quantum-leap to a higher mental horizon and a higher plane of healthy self-esteem. The good news is that undertaking spiritual cultivation nurtures and cross-fertilizes a range of positive spiritual qualities, like patience, compassion, forgiveness, empathy, broadmindedness, generosity and reverence for life. Besides being antidotes to mental-emotional negativities, these spiritual qualities enhance positive growth and deepen our insights into our inner worth.

Wealth-Creation Secret #38
A healthy self-esteem is not built from external achievements.
A healthy self-esteem is the natural fruit of our commitment
to stay connected with our divine essence.
A healthy self-esteem arises from a deep awakening
to the higher truth that external circumstances and events
cannot impair our inner worth.

Approach 4: Nurturing intrinsic motivation and enthusiasm in working toward constructive life goals

If a man is called to be a streetsweeper, he should sweep streets even as Michelangelo painted, or Beethoven composed music, or Shakespeare wrote poetry. He should sweep streets so well that all the hosts of heaven and earth will pause to say, here lived a great streetsweeper who did his job well.

Martin Luther King

When you see ordinary situations with extraordinary insight it is like discovering a jewel in rubbish. If work becomes part of your spiritual practice, then your regular, daily problems cease to be only problems and become a source of inspiration.

Chogyam Trungpa

If you develop a pure and sincere motivation, if you are motivated by a wish to help on the basis of kindness, compassion, and respect, then you can carry on any kind of work, in any field, and function more effectively with less fear or worry.......... Even if you fail to achieve your goal, you can feel good about having made the effort.

The Dalai Lama

Studies repeatedly indicated that many of us are not deriving fulfillment and satisfaction from our current jobs. The list of frequent grumbles include: "my working life is ruined by a tyrannical supervisor", "my pay is a pittance when compared to my boss", "my colleagues are so selfish and unhelpful", "promotions are reserved for the elite and favorites of our boss", "there is no promotion and career prospect for me as my boss is biased against me and disregard my good performance", "there is no job security since everything depends on results, profits and bottomline......."

247

In our intensely competitive working environment, it is difficult to nurture intrinsic motivation and fulfillment from our job. However, all the more we should learn to do so, to learn to put in our best and excel. This is the foundation of inner and outer success.

We need not be mired in a particular job if we do not like it. Nonetheless, before we look for another job, it is important to learn from the negative aspects of our current job. It is important to cultivate foundational wisdom, spiritual qualities and emotional maturity that are required of us no matter where we work. If we do not commit ourselves to continuous learning, to continuous broadening and upgrading of our technical-functional skills, to cultivating higher wisdom, emotional maturity and spiritual qualities like patience, understanding, forgiveness, empathy, broadmindedness and perseverance, no matter where we work, we will encounter similar patterns of inner strife, frustrations and discontent.

Someone remarked to the famous French philosopher Blaise Pascal, "If I had your brains, I would be a better person." Pascal thereupon replied, "Be a better person and you will have my brains."

This seemingly cryptic remark of Pascal contains an ocean of truth. By realigning our values and life goals to our authentic life purpose, to upholding integrity and honest living, we experience continuous waves of enthusiasm and moral courage to pursue constructive activities. Guided by heart wisdom, we learn to derive intrinsic motivation and fulfillment from engaging in activities that are attuned to the deep harmony and potential of our being. The achievement of outcomes and end-results become secondary. We learn to put in our best in performing every worthwhile activity. A natural law of success is that when we put in our best in performing each daily activity and task, the higher is the likelihood of attaining the positive end-result.

Further, aligning our values and life goals with our authentic life purpose would unleash our creativity and enhance the quality and acuity of our thinking. As emphasized by Dr David Shultz in his bestseller The Magic of Thinking Big, the foremost secret of success lies in the higher truth that "it is not our inborn intelligence, but the quality of our thinking that guides the use of our intelligence that makes the difference". By availing ourselves to this secret, by aligning our values and life goals with our deep potential, the quality of our consciousness and thinking will quantum-leap to a higher plane. This is the higher plane from which successful men and women derive the enthusiasm, broadmindedness, ethical vision and moral courage to accomplish worthwhile deeds.

Never underestimate your own intelligence and never overestimate the intelligence of others. Concentrate on your assets. Discover your superior talents. It is not how much many brains you have got that matters. It is how you use your brains that matters.

David Shultz
The Magic Of Thinking Big

By attaining this higher perspective, we perceive more clearly the coherence, interconnectedness and interwoven fabric of our lives. Let us recount the story of the bricklayer.

A passer-by saw four bricklayers.

He approached the first bricklayer and enquired what he was doing. "Can't you see that I am laying bricks," he grumbled.

When he approached the second bricklayer, the nonchalant reply was, "I am building a wall."

The third bricklayer was more cheerful and said, "I am building a modern school for children in this neighbornood."

The fourth bricklayer was more enthusiastic and replied, "I am contributing to building the future of this nation."

If you can't do great things, do small things in a great way. Don't wait for great opportunities. Seize common, everyday ones and make them great.

Napolean Hill

Commit your work to the Lord, then it will succeed.

Proverbs 16:3

Whatever you do, work at it with all your heart, as working for the Lord, not for men.

Colossians 3:22-23

We need to learn to inspire ourselves to put in our best to create value for others, to assist others in their positive growth, regardless of human commendation and recognition. When we avail ourselves to inner wisdom and learn to view Divinity as our true long-term employer, we begin to see things in their proper perspective. We no longer hanker after human approval and external prizes. Instead, we learn to derive intrinsic satisfaction and fulfillment from engaging in tasks and activities that are guided by worthwhile purposes.

Let us share the memorable story of little Annie.

Many years ago, in a mental institution in Boston, a young girl known as little Annie was locked in a dudgeon. Although this institution was one of the more enlightened ones for treating the mentally ill, the dudgeon was reserved for the "hopelessly" insane. In little Annie's case, the doctors had given up hope.

However, an elderly nurse refused to accept the doctors' view. She believed that there was hope in all of God's creations and was determined to nurse little Annie back to good health.

On many occasions, Little Annie was violent and aggressive against anyone who visited her dudgeon. Nevertheless, the patience and affection of the elderly nurse slowly changed her. During each visit, the elderly nurse would bring brownie biscuits to little Annie and placed them outside her dudgeon. Initially, little Annie ignored the elderly nurse. But gradually, little Annie became aware of the elderly nurse's lovingkindness and started to eat the brownie biscuits.

Many days passed. The elderly nurse continued to show her love and concern for little Annie and would bring brownie biscuits during each visit. After a period of time, the doctors were surprised to observe that little Annie had become more normal and receptive to advice. In due course, they decided that it would be safe to transfer little Annie to the normal hospital room for treatment.

Soon, little Annie recovered and the doctors finally decided that she could return home. Thereupon, little Annie decided that she would become a nurse. She was determined to emulate the example of the elderly nurse and bring love and hope to the less fortunate.

Years later, the Queen of England, while pinning her country's highest honor on a foreigner, asked Helen Keller, "How do you account for your remarkable accomplishments in life?"

Without hesitation, Helen Keller replied, "Had it not been Anne Sullivan ("little Annie"), the name Helen Keller would have remained unknown."

It was little Annie who did not give up hope on Helen Keller who was stricken by a disease at a very young age and became blind and deaf. Anne Sullivan continued to shower love and affection on her, encouraging her to lead a normal life despite her physical disabilities. In turn, Helen Keller influenced millions with her courage and dedication to help and inspire others.

Always do your best. Your best is going to change from moment to moment; it will be different when you are healthy as opposed to sick. Under any circumstances, simply do your best, and you will avoid self-judgment, self-abuse, and regret.

Don Miguel Ruiz

I once heard a story about a young minister encountering an elderly shoemaker. They began a friendly conversation and the young minister discovered that the shoemaker was a wise man. Nonetheless, he ineptly remarked, "How good and surprising it is to meet a Christ-like person in a lowly occupation."

The elderly shoemaker replied with a smile, "Nope, my occupation is not lowly in the eyes of God. I believe that making a pair of shoes is just as sacred as preaching a sermon. What is important is the quality of heart wisdom and love that we bring to our daily activities."

We believe sweat on the brow from honest labor is one of life's glorious sights and to show your fellow man the dignity and value of work.........that real satisfaction comes from total effort fully expended in quest of a worthy ideal.

Zig Ziglar

And what is it to work with love?

It is to weave the cloth with threads drawn from your heart, even as if your beloved were to wear the cloth.

It is to build a house with affection, even as if your beloved were to dwell in that house.

It is to sow seeds with tenderness and reap the harvest with joy, even as if your beloved were to eat the fruit.

Kahlil Gibran
The Prophet

Wealth-Creation Secret #39
What is the essence of the natural laws of external affluence?
It is the commitment to nurture intrinsic fulfillment and joy
in performing deeds that enhance the well-being of others.

Approach 5: Identifying Our Natural Aptitude And Talent

Men are not chained to the conditions of their births; they could better their station in life and harvest the fruits of their own talents and industry.

Abraham Lincoln

What is success? I think it is a mixture of having a flair for the thing that you are doing; knowing that it is not enough, that you have got to have hard work and a certain sense of purpose.

Margaret Thatcher

Use what talents you possess. The woods would be very silent if no birds sang there except those that sang best.

Henry Van Dyke

Let us share the following traditional story.

There was once a notorious bandit in India who, after many successful raids, realized the terrible suffering he had inflicted upon the villagers. Yearning to atone for his sinful deeds, he visited a famous Hindu master. He confessed to the master, "I am a sinner. I have robbed the rich as well as the poor, and had caused much sufferings. Am I incorrigible and hopeless? How can I make amends?"

The Hindu master looked at him compassionately and asked, "Yes, you can make amends. Do you have any talent or unique skill?"

"No, I have no talent or unique skill," replied the bandit morosely.

"I think you are good in something. God has always fairly endowed each of us with some special gift or talent. Ponder over this matter and visit me again two days later with the answer," advised the master.

The bandit returned to his hideout and pondered deeply. Two days later, he visited the master and said, "I think I do not have any talent or special gift, except for stealing."

"Aha," exclaimed the Hindu master. "That is precisely the skill that you need to liberate yourself from inner torment and anguish. Now go to a quiet place and patiently watch your breath. Use your vast imagination to steal the stars and planets in the sky and dissolve them into the immense spaciousness of your pristine mind which is filled with natural lovingkindness. Sooner or later, you will awaken."

Realize that God wants you to be successful, but it's your responsibility to learn and follow God's vision for your optimal future.

Kirbyjon Caldwell
The Gospel of Good Success

In The Seeds of Greatness, Denis Waitley wrote, "*Our careers are a blend of natural abilities, environmental modeling, acquired skills and experience. Many times our careers hinge heavily on the economic requirements at a pivotal age and family considerations. If we are to develop our lives along the path of greatest wisdom, however, we should give serious thought to discovering our inherent abilities as early as possible.*"

To tread the royal road to inner and outer success, we need to identify our "inherent abilities", our natural aptitude and talent that can create value for others. Aligning healthy life goals with our natural aptitude and talent imbues us with higher levels of enthusiasm in working toward them. This time-tested approach for arriving at genuine success is emphasized by Dr Deepak Chopra in *The Seven Spiritual Laws Of Success*:

I am going to ask myself how I am best suited to serve humanity. I am going to answer that question and then put it into practice. I am going to use my unique talents to serve the needs of my fellow human beings – – I will match those needs to my desire to help and serve others.

How do we identify our inherent abilities, natural aptitude and talent?

The basic steps are as follows:

First, reflect on the list of positive activities in which we have a passionate or keen interest.

Second, ascertain which of these positive activities can effectively serve the needs and requirements of humanity and enhance their well-being, whether it be related to their physical, emotional, intellectual, economical or spiritual needs. We should ensure that the activities that we have a passionate and keen interest are conducive to creating value for others as well as to our personal growth and maturation. We can thereby avert pursuing activities that would reinforce self-centeredness and self-seeking urges.

Third, reflect on whether we have the inherent abilities or natural aptitude to undertake these positive activities, so as to effectively serve the needs of humanity. Generally, our inherent abilities would fall within the following eight "domains" of intelligence as identified by Professor Howard

Gardner in his influential theory on "multiple intelligences". I have summarized and interpreted them as follows:-

(1)   Linguistic intelligence: an aptitude in written or oral expressions; mastery of a language or languages; sensitivity to and keen awareness of how the proficient use of words can enhance effective communication and inspire others.

(2)   Musical intelligence: sensitivity to tempo, pitch, tone and timbre; an ability to create musical arrangements that can effectively convey diverse ideas, feelings and emotions.

(3)   Logical-mathematical intelligence: an aptitude for inductive and deductive reasoning; an aptitude in computing numbers and solving abstract mathematical problems.

(4)   Spatial intelligence: an ability to visualize objects, their design, constituents and layout, and to transform these mental visualizations into concrete objects.

(5)   Kinesthetic intelligence: an ability to use body movements to effectively convey ideas, feelings and emotions.

(6)   Interpersonal intelligence: an ability to gain insight into and effectively manage the mental-emotional dynamics underlying human relationships and interactions.

(7)   Intrapersonal intelligence: an ability to understand our inner landscape, intentions, motivations, feelings and level of psychological-spiritual maturity.

(8)   Naturalist intelligence: an ability to gain a holistic insight into the intricate workings, deep harmony and interconnectedness of Nature; an ability to experience basic unity and oneness with Mother Nature.

All of us have some of these abilities in a smaller or larger measure. The important point is to nurture and develop those abilities with which we are endowed in a larger measure which can be defined as our "aptitudes" or "talents". We can do so by identifying and enrolling in appropriate functional courses or degree programs. We should also seek to match our aptitudes or talents with worthwhile activities which we have a healthy enthusiasm or passion in undertaking. By constantly enhancing our natural competency, aptitudes and talents, they will mature gradually. Wealth creation becomes a natural by-product of our refined competency, aptitudes, skills and talents that are oriented toward creating optimal value for others.

Wealth-Creation Secret #40
Discover the range of inner assets at our disposal.
They are precious gifts from Divinity.
When we utilize these gifts to enhance the well-being of others,
we will realize that each of us has immense potential
in becoming constructive partners of Divinity.

Discover your divinity, find your unique talent, serve humanity with it, and you can generate all the wealth that you want. When your creative expressions match the needs of your fellow humans, then wealth will spontaneously flow from the unmanifest into the manifest...............

Dr Deepak Chopra
The Seven Spiritual Laws of Success

The expression of our gift need not be grand. Everyone who writes poetry does not need to publish ten volumes and win the National Book Award. The farmer in rural Asia who works his family's meager land for survival can plow with a song on his lips, can bring his inspired prayers to the mosque, can add his poetic voice to the village. He too is transforming the world.

Dr Jack Kornfield
After The Ecstasy, The Laundry

Approach 6: Applying The Vision-Fulfillment Technique

If Joan of Arc could turn the tide of an entire war before her eighteenth birthday, you can get out of bed.

E. Jean Carroll

Most people spend more time planning Christmas and holidays than they spend planning their life.

Denis Waitley

Deep within humans dwell those slumbering powers; powers that would astonish them, that they never dreamed of possessing; forces that would revolutionize their lives if aroused and put into action.

Orison Marden

Besides identifying our natural aptitude and talent, we need to learn what I label as the "Vision-Fulfillment Technique". This technique entails writing down our long-term vision, long-term goal, and the detailed activities that we need to undertake to achieve the long-term goal.

I was fortunate to learn this technique during my schooldays. For example, regarding tertiary education, I wrote down my vision and longer-term goals when I was an adolescent. I targeted to attain the requisite post-graduate training so as to become a professional and a manager. By writing down my longer-term goals (eg. 3-year, 5-year and 10-year goals) and identifying the necessary activities to achieve those goals, by mid-twenties, I attained with commendable results a Bachelors' degree in Economics and Philosophy, a Masters Degree in Accountancy and another Masters Degree in Business Administration.

Nonetheless, with maturing wisdom, I realize that this technique is inadequate by itself. To fulfill our deep constructive potential and attain genuine fulfillment, its application needs to be guided by heart wisdom and a clear vision of our authentic life purpose. If we allow ourselves to be driven by self-seeking urges, our vision and longer-term life goals would become distorted and oriented toward self-aggrandizement. Even if we achieved these goals, they cannot lead to genuine fulfillment.

Thus, it is important to have a balanced vision of our authentic life purpose on which we can graft positive life goals. By nurturing enthusiasm and deriving intrinsic fulfillment in working toward worthwhile goals, we create value for others and become constructive members of our families and societies. External wealth will follow as a natural by-product of our enthusiasm and commitment to contribute to the well-being of others.

Total success is the continuing involvement in the pursuit of a worthy ideal, which is being realized for the benefit of others — — rather than at their expense.

Denis Waitley, Seeds of Greatness

To summarize, after connecting with our heart wisdom and authentic life purpose, we can apply the following 7-step vision-fulfillment technique to work toward healthy life goals. This technique is distilled from years of studying the strategies and techniques adopted by successful men and women from all walks of life. To illustrate, I would like to share my experiences of how I apply this technique to fulfill my vision of becoming an inspirational author.

(1)   Write down as clearly as possible our vision.

Example:

Vision Statement: To share useful insights on tapping the perennial wisdoms in attaining inner and outer success, so as to contribute to the well-being of others.

(2)   Write down the key long-term goal that will contribute toward fulfilling this vision. It is prudent to set a realistic timeframe of 3 to 5 years to attain this key long-term goal.

Example:

Key Long-Term Goal: To become an inspirational author in 5 years' time, based on my interest in creative writing, so as to share useful insights on tapping the perennial wisdom in attaining inner and outer success.

(3)   Privately pin up our vision statement and key long-term goal at our working table at home, so that we can read it aloud to ourselves at least two times a day.

(4)   Do detailed and comprehensive research. Read up useful books relating to the attainment of this key long-term goal. Find opportunities to converse with people who have attained worthwhile goals that are identical to ours and tap upon their valuable experiences.

Example:

(a)   To purchase and read about 150 valuable books on the perennial philosophy, religions, human development, organizational management, peak performance and leadership over a span of 2 years to broaden my knowledge base.

(b)   To undertake meditation, creative visualizations and other spiritual exercises on a daily basis to nurture a healthy insightful awareness. To practice mindful living during normal waking hours, so as to gain personal experiences and understanding of the usefulness and benefits of applying the perennial wisdoms.

(5)   Based on our research, readings, studies and conversations with our mentors and teachers, devote two weeks of our leisure time to silently contemplate, brainstorm and write down the detailed activities that we need to complete in order to attain our key long-term goal. Thereafter, we can consider to show this list of detailed activities to our trusted mentors or teachers with the requisite expertise for their advice. If their advice or comments are valuable, we can modify the list of activities.

Example:

(a)   List of activities to attain key long-term goal. To read about 150 useful books pertinent to the subject matter of the book which I intend to write.
(b)   To collate useful stories and quotations for preparing the first draft of the book.
(c)   To allocate a certain amount of time after office hours for preparing the first draft.
(d)   To place a journal book beside my bed, so as to jot down any inspiring thoughts during early hours of the morning.

(e)   To plan the overall content, format and structure of the book.

(6)   Write down a schedule on the amount of time that we plan to allocate on a daily basis to work on the detailed activities. Do not be over-ambitious. Assign a realistic timeline to complete each activity. Depending on our financial situation, we do not need to resign from our full-time job. Nurturing our aptitudes and talents takes time. Working on our worthwhile long-term goal takes time. If our current full-time job does not align with our deepest interest, and our financial circumstances forbid us to resign, we can still plan to allocate 15 to 30 minutes a day to undertake activities that will lead to the achievement of our key long-term goal.

Example

(a)   To spend an average of 45 minutes per day over a period of 2 years to read about 150 books relating to subject matter which I intend to write on.

(b)   To collate useful stories and quotations for preparing the first draft. This is a continuous activity.

(c)   To allocate 30 minutes to creative writing in the evening after office work and spend 2 hours on creative writing on Sundays. This is a continuous activity over a 2-year period. Target to complete the first draft of the book in 30 months by 200X. Target to spend another 6 months revising the first draft. Target to complete the final draft of the book for perusal by the publisher by 200Y.

(7)   On a monthly basis, assess the rate of our progress toward completing each key activity. Learn to derive fulfillment and satisfaction from completing each key activity. If there are any significant obstacles or setbacks, reflect on them as valuable learning opportunities. Reflect on

whether we need to modify our activities or overall strategy. Guided by our heart wisdom and healthy life goals, we can be creatively flexible in modifying our strategies and approaches in working toward our key long-term goal.

Wealth-Creation Secret #41
Patience, perseverance, optimism and commitment to work toward positive outcomes are the cornerstones of wealth creation.

We are visitors on this planet. We are here for ninety, a hundred years at the very most. During that period we must try to do something good, something useful with our lives. Try to be at peace with yourself and help others share that peace. If you contribute to others' happiness, you will find the true goal, the meaning of life.

The Dalai Lama

* * * * * *

Wealth-Creation Wisdom 6
Healing & Positively Transforming
Emotional Negativities

Go ahead, light your candles and burn your incense and ring your bells and call out to God, but watch out, because God will come and He will put you on His anvil and fire up His forge and beat you and beat you until He turns brass into pure gold.

Sant Keshavadas

If there be anywhere on earth a lover of God who is always kept safe, I know nothing of it, for it was not shown to me. But this was shown: that in falling and rising again we are always kept in that same precious love.

Dame Julian Of Norwich

The greatest discovery of my generation is that human beings can alter their lives by altering their attitudes of mind.

William James

There was once a rich merchant who sent his son, a young man named David, to an elderly wise man to gain wisdom. For five years, besides teaching him Greek sciences and philosophy, the wise man assigned a senior disciple to insult David at least three times a day. Whenever David was insulted, he was not permitted to rebut, but to accept the insults silently and with patience. In addition, for each insult, David would need to fork out a copper coin from a bag of coins given by his father and hand it to the disciple.

At the end of five years, David was told to visit the capital of the country to earn his livelihood. After traveling for one week, he arrived at the gateway of the wealthy capital. A disheveled beggar was sitting under a tree near the gateway. Upon seeing David, the beggar accosted him and vehemently scolded and insulted him. David listened patiently. When the beggar began to quiet down, David bowed at him sincerely and proceeded to enter the capital.

The beggar was astounded by David's patience and quickly enquired how did he manage to rein in his anger?

David smiled serenely and explained with a dose of humor, "For five years, whenever I was insulted, I need to fork out a copper coin and pay. This was the instruction from my teacher. However, when you insulted me just now, I was not obliged to pay. Can you imagine my sense of relief? Although I am now penniless, do not worry. When I found a job in the capital and earn some coins, I will share them with you."

The beggar was amazed and said, "Your teacher's wisdom is indeed profound. For the past ten years, I was directed by the sovereign of this great country to look for someone with immense patience, deep insights and learning to assist him, but to no avail. I think we have finally found the right person."

Let us share another illuminating story.

A Japanese warrior visited a Zen master to enquire on some philosophical issues.

"What do you wish to know?" asked the Zen master.

"Explain to me the existence of heaven and hell, and how do I enter heaven."

The Zen master looked deeply at the Japanese warrior, who is filled with aggressive energy.

"What makes you think that you are able to comprehend such deep issues. You are simply brutish and uncultured. You are wasting my time." The Zen master deliberately spoke in a contemptuous manner.

The warrior was astounded, deeply offended by the words of the Zen master. Nobody ever spoke derisively to a Japanese warrior without facing the prospect of instant death.

"Are you too dumb to understand my words. Do not waste my time and get out of this monastery!" shouted the Zen master.

The warrior exploded with anger. Withdrawing his lethal sword in lightning speed, he lifted it menacingly and was about to strike at the monk's skull when he heard the words, "This is the gate to hell."

The warrior was once again astounded. Gradually, he realized that his impulsive rage and hostility were accurately interpreted by the Zen master as "hellish" in their destructiveness. Breathing deeply, he replaced his sword and bowed respectfully before the Zen master.

"And this is the gate to heaven," said the Zen master.

Even if you are a millionaire, you are still subject to the destructive effects of anger and hatred. Nor can education alone give you a guarantee that you will be protected from these effects. Similarly, the law cannot give you such guarantees or

*protection.........The only factor that can give you refuge or
protection from the destructive effects of anger and hatred is your
practice of tolerance and patience.*

The Dalai Lama

Wealth-Creation Secret #42
*If we can become more attentive to the evanescence of
our emotions and feelings, and watch them dance and quiet
down, like an affectionate grandmother watching the playfulness
of her grandson and restraining him whenever appropriate,
we are on the threshold of enlightenment.*

IQ Versus EQ And Spiritual Maturity

As emphasized in chapter 2, the cultivation of wisdom
and spiritual qualities is conducive to the effective
development of problem-solving and creative thinking skills.
It is also conducive to the effective development of
communication, listening, rapport-building, conflict-
resolution and leadership skills. Guided by wisdom and
spiritual qualities, we can sincerely and more effectively
harness functional-technical knowledge and skills for
attaining worthwhile goals.

Thus, the crucial question is, *"Without attaining genuine
self-understanding, without cultivating foundational wisdom and
spiritual qualities,* can we effectively contribute to the creation
of economic value and wealth for our organization?"

During my younger days, like many professionals who
graduated from mainstream business education, I thought
that cognitive intelligence (IQ) was the key factor
underpinning optimum work performance. After working

268

for many years as financial controller and as a senior manager, I am convinced that this model of thinking is not accurate. Cognitive intelligence which underlies the development of our functional-technical skills is not sufficient for sustaining optimum work performance. Emotional intelligence (EQ) and spiritual maturity are the second and third key factors in sustaining optimum work performance.

For many years, the Conventional Paradigm on seeking personal excellence did not emphasize the importance of EQ. This is quite understandable since the conventional paradigm subscribes to the empiricist-scientific model of personal development. Emotional intelligence and maturity appear to be nebulous things, difficult to quantify, measure and verify.

Since the 1980s, which culminated in the publication of Dr Daniel Coleman's Emotional Intelligence, the world of management begins to accord formal recognition to the importance of EQ in sustaining optimum performance.

Although mainstream management experts and psychologists begin to recognize the importance of EQ, they did not dwell further into the roots of EQ. They did not further explore how wisdom and spiritual qualities are essential to the effective cultivation of EQ. They are hemmed in by the conventional paradigm of personal development.

To attain a quantum leap in cultivating EQ and leadership ability, a similar quantum leap in our conceptualization of and personal experiences in cultivating EQ is required. We need to broaden our mental horizon and tap upon the time-honored teachings of the wisdom traditions.

In his groundbreaking book *Emotional Intelligence*, Dr Danile Coleman defined "emotion" as "a feeling and its distinctive thoughts, psychological and biological states, and range of propensities to act". Although there are countless blends, variations and nuances of feelings and emotions, psychologists have proposed the following major categories:-

- Anger, which encompasses resentment, discontent, indignation, sullenness, soreness, exasperation, vexation, agitation, irascibility, acrimony, grudge, enmity, antagonism, acrimony, hostility, wrath, and at the extreme, pathological hatred and aggressiveness.

- Dislike, which encompasses distaste, nausea, loathing, antipathy, aversion, abhorrence, repulsion, scorn and disdain.

- Sadness, which encompasses dejection, gloominess, disappointment, disillusion, sorrow, anguish, despondency, melancholy, self-pity, pessimism, cynicism, despair and at the extreme, pathological depression.

- Surprise, which encompasses astonishment, amazement, shock and wonder.

- Fear, which encompasses shyness, diffidence, timidity, apprehension, anxiety, misgiving, suspicion, nervousness, consternation, agitation, trepidation, horror and at the extreme, phobia and psychopathic dread.

- Guilt, which encompasses remorse, regret, shame, embarrassment, humiliation, compunction and repentance.

- Enjoyment, which encompasses happiness, joy, hopefulness, cheerfulness, ease, relief, contentment, delight, vitality, self-confidence, satisfaction, exhilaration, bliss and at the extreme, drug-induced or pathological mania.

- Love, which encompasses acceptance, friendliness, kindness, fondness, liking, affection, emotional closeness, intimacy, trust, adoration, devotion, infatuation and agape.

Each relationship you have with another person reflects the relationship you have with yourself.

Alice Deville

What we experience is our state of mind projected outward. If our state of mind is one of well-being, love and peace, that is what we will project and therefore experience. If our state of mind is one filled with doubt, fear and concern about illness, we will project this state outward, and it will therefore be our experiential reality.

Dr Gerald Jampolsky

Based on the Wisdom Paradigm on personal growth, as outlined in Chapter 2, emotional maturity can be classified into Intrapersonal-EQ and Interpersonal-EQ.

(i) Intrapersonal-EQ refers to compassionate awareness and deep understanding of our feelings and emotions in the moment, and how such feelings and emotions can influence our thinking, decision-making and behavior. The cultivation of wisdom and spiritual qualities is foundational to cultivating intrapersonal-EQ. A person with high intrapersonal-EQ can effectively differentiate between *healthy* feelings (eg. inner peace, contentment, joyful spiritual state) and *unhealthy* feelings (eg. resentment, antagonism, frustration, hostility, aggressiveness). He is mindful that his thinking, decision-making and behavioral pattern need not be influenced and distorted by unhealthy feelings and emotions. He is able to create adequate inner space to heal and positively transform unhealthy feelings and emotions.

(ii) Interpersonal-EQ refers to compassionate and empathic awareness and understanding of the feelings and emotions of another person or group of people in the moment, and how such feelings and emotions can influence their thinking, decision-making and behavior. Interpersonal-EQ arises from Intrapersonal-EQ. Hence, it also arises from the cultivation of wisdom and spiritual qualities, like compassion, empathy, patience, forgiveness, non-judgemental attitude and altruism. These spiritual qualities enable us to adopt the other person's perspective and are essential to the development of effective communication, listening, rapport-building and conflict-resolution skills.

A person with high interpersonal-EQ can effectively differentiate between *positive* and *negative* feelings/emotions of another person or group of people. Depending on his emotional and spiritual maturity, he can assist people who are trapped by negative emotions.

Thus, based on the Wisdom Paradigm of personal growth, an emotionally mature person has high intrapersonal-EQ and interpersonal-EQ.

Although the conventional paradigm has begun to recognize the importance of EQ to achieving optimum work performance, *it did not explore the critical link between developing high EQ and the cultivation of wisdom and spiritual qualities. It did not explore the foundation of emotional intelligence.*

Without understanding the source and foundation of EQ, without exploring the critical linkage between developing EQ and the cultivation of wisdom and spiritual qualities, our efforts to cultivate emotional maturity are handicapped.

Wealth-Creation Secret #43
When we embrace the imperative of laying a spiritual foundation to our lives, our cognitive and emotional intelligence will rise to a higher plane, our worldview and mental horizon will broaden and positive growth will occur.

The Four Impediments To Optimum Performance

Without adequate emotional maturity, we will encounter what I depict as the Four Impediments to optimum work performance. These Four Impediments refer to *unconstructive interactions or relationships with our boss; with our colleagues; with our subordinates; and with ourselves.*

These unconstructive interactions or relationships arise from a vicious cycle of emotional negativities and negative mental states. Although we may have highly competent functional knowledge and technical skills, without healing these unconstructive relationships, the realization of our potential is hampered. Our motivation and enthusiasm to put in our best and excel in our jobs is impeded.

The Four Impediments are mainly driven by emotional negativities and negative mental states. Our experiences of such emotional negativities (eg. anger, hatred, resentment, frustration, discontent and anxiety) can exist at the conscious or subconscious level. Without nurturing a healthy insightful awareness, it is likely that we are not conscious of the significant extent in which our behavior, thinking and decision-making are being driven by negative emotions. When our managers and employees are unable to effectively resolve negative mental-emotional states, individual as well as team performance will be compromised.

The stark truth is: Although we can skip from one vocation to another hunting for the most rewarding job, the best boss, the ideal workplace, or we can be our own boss, sooner or later, we will realize that constructive working relationships hinge on EQ. Without cultivating emotional and spiritual maturity, no matter where we work and no matter what type of business we engage in, emotional negativities would continue to besiege us, undermine our leadership competency and hinder us from optimizing work performance.

<u>*The First Impediment.*</u> Modern workplaces are marked by demanding performance targets and increasing competition for management recognition and organizational resources. In particular, our bosses are pressurized to excel. They are inclined to benchmark our performance against the standards adopted by world-class organizations.

As we encounter more and more instances of what we *perceive* as over-demanding performance standards or unreasonable treatment from our bosses, we become defensive and experience emotional negativities (eg. anger, resentment, frustration, dejection, etc). When these negative emotions accumulate, we will engage in subtle emotional and psychological strivings with our bosses. These lead to unconstructive relationship with them.

The Second Impediment. Similarly, as modern workplaces are marked by demanding performance targets, the likelihood of rivalry among employees increases. As we encounter more instances of defensive, self-protective and self-seeking behavior from our colleagues, we will experience negative emotions. When they accumulate, we will engage in subtle psychological strivings with our colleagues.

The Third Impediment. Effective relationship with our subordinates depend on our interpersonal skills and leadership competency. If our relationships with our bosses or peers are unconstructive and lead us to experience emotional negativities, they will adversely affect our relationship with our subordinates. A common occurrence is that we tend to vent such negative emotions on our subordinates. If we are unable to effectively heal these negative emotions, our leadership competency is corroded.

The Fourth Impediment. A pivotal truth is that unconstructive interactions or relationships with our bosses, colleagues and subordinates arise from unconstructive relationship with ourselves. Unless we can cultivate a healthy relationship with ourselves based on wisdom, compassionate self-understanding and vibrant self-esteem, the soundness of our relationships with others is compromised.

Wealth-Creation Secret #44
Inner and outer success depend first and foremost on sustaining
a meaningful and constructive relationship with ourselves.

Factors That Give Rise To Emotional Negativities

Emotional negativities that drive the above Four Impediments arise from a range of factors. They include an untrained and spiritually unconscious mind; work-related stress; emotional and psychological strivings with our bosses and colleagues; and adverse events that occur within and beyond the workplaces.

An Untrained Mind And A Scarcity Mindset. As described in Chapter 4, when we are driven by an untrained galloping mind and hemmed in by a scarcity mindset, we tend to perceive life situations as zero-sum competitions. This anxiety-ridden emergency-oriented scarcity mindset arises from unhealthy self-absorption and erroneous beliefs in an inherently substantial self. It gives rise to emotional negativities, worries and frustration. Consuming much of our mental energy, it exerts a negative impact on our work performance and leadership competency.

Work-Related Stress. It is well-recognized that inability to effectively manage work-related stress will undermine work performance. Specifically, modern workplaces are usually marked by lengthy working hours, heavy workload, demanding performance targets and increasing competition for management recognition. We are facing mounting work-related stress and pressure.

Without effectively healing work-related stress and pressure, they will snowball. We will experience physiological tension, unease, frustrations and anxieties. They sap our vibrancy and corrode our enthusiasm to realize our deep potential, to put in our best and excel in our jobs. Besides undermining our work performance, they hinder us from developing constructive relationships with others.

Emotional And Psychological Strivings With Our Superiors And Colleagues.

These emotional-psychological strivings usually arise from an accumulation of instances whereby we *perceive* that we have suffered some unreasonable or unfair treatment from our bosses or colleagues, especially those that hurt our sense of self-importance. Our *perception* of being mistreated or slighted produces a negative mental state. This in turn generates emotional negativities that reinforce negative mental states. A vicious cycle occurs.

Without healing this vicious cycle, it becomes entrenched, gnawing at us psychologically, consuming much of our mental energy. It undermines our work performance and leadership competency. It corrodes our analytical, problem-solving and creative thinking ability. It saps our enthusiasm to put in our best, causing us to lose concentration and become irritable. This vicious cycle afflicts our workplaces with emotional wounds, leading to sub-optimal employee behavior.

"Uncontrolled" Emotional Outburst Or Over-reaction. Sometimes, we find ourselves in a reactive or pessimistic state. When difficult customers or our demanding bosses raised their voices at us, we experienced a surge of anger. We are highly tempted to shout back. We can, in fact, lose control and react by shouting back, although we may later regret such "over-reaction" or being "emotionally hijacked". To optimize work performance, we need to effectively manage such emotional outbursts.

Adverse Factors Or Events Within The Workplaces. Typically, our enthusiasm to excel in our jobs depend on a range of favorable factors within the workplaces. They include high salary, supportive bosses, challenging jobs, appreciation from management, inspiring leadership of senior management, good corporate performance, and so forth. However, our fast-paced, highly competitive and profit-driven corporate environment is usually not characterized by these favorable factors. Instead, we encounter all types of adverse events in our workplaces.

For example, our pay package is closely tied to individual performance or contribution to departmental profits, where "lifetime" job security has become an archaic concept; we encounter promotions that are reserved for "elite" colleagues; "uncooperative, jealous and ungrateful" colleagues; unreasonable or fastidious customers who make our jobs uninspiring; emotional and psychological strivings among colleagues, etc. Without undertaking inner cultivation to tap our inner wisdom, these adverse factors can corrode our enthusiasm to put in our best and excel in our jobs.

Non-Fulfilling Relationships Beyond The Workplaces. Work-related emotional negativities can have adverse spillover effects on our lives after working hours. For example, they induce us to worry about our unproductive relationships with our bosses and colleagues. Our family life and the quality of our relationships with our spouses, children and loved ones would be negatively affected. In turn, non-fulfilling relationships with our family induce us to experience negative emotions and negative mental states that in turn adversely affect our work motivation.

Adverse Events Beyond The Workplaces. We are assaulted by emotional negativities when we encounter adverse or unpleasant events outside the workplaces. They include quarrels with our spouses, children, neighbours or friends; unfortunate accidents involving our loved ones; unexpected financial losses in the stock market; unexpected physical illness, etc. They impose significant stress on us, undermining our analytical and problem-solving ability.

In a longer-term context, in encountering unpleasant events within and beyond our workplaces, deeper existential issues will gnaw at us. They are couched in questions like, "What is the appropriate work ethic in such highly competitive corporate environment?", "What is the true meaning of working more than 50 hours per week? Am I pursuing my own dreams or seeking to fulfill someone's expectations?", "Why does my friend die of cancer at such a young age?" "Why did my neighbour's son become a cripple due to a car accident?" "Why did the terrorists succeed in crashing their planes into the World Trade Centers at New York, killing thousands of innocent people?" "Why is life so unpredictable?" "Does my life has any ultimate meaning?"

There are no easy answers which can resolve all these factors that give rise to emotional negativities. Nevertheless, by tapping upon the perennial wisdoms, we can learn from the following time-tested approaches to heal and positively transform emotional negativities.

(1)   Gaining Insight Into And Healing The "Root Causes" Of Emotional Negativities

............*first, by understanding that afflictive thoughts and emotions are destructive and negative, and, second, by trying to strengthen our positive thoughts and emotions, which are their antidotes, we can gradually reduce the force of our anger, hatred, and so on.*

The Dalai Lama

If we face our feelings with care, affection, and non-violence, we can transform them into a kind of energy that is healthy and nourishing.

Thich Nhat Hanh
The Heart of the Buddha's Teaching

When we fought against negative emotions, were we pushing, shoving and punching these invisible energies? Did we encounter more resistance? Could we overcome negative emotions by giving vent to them, like screaming them out, banging our fists against the wall, reactively aggressively against others, ventilating our hostile emotions on others or indulging in sense enjoyment? Are we treating the symptoms? Do these approaches develop into negative habits that further corrode our inner peace and impair our relationships with others? Did our negative emotions disappear for a short while, only to return and haunt us with greater ferocity? During darker moments, negative emotions seem like unbreakable chains holding us in permanent bondage.

There is a psychological myth that venting your anger is the healthy thing to do. The problem with venting anger is that you can't take back what you said or did to the person receiving it. The act of venting anger becomes habit forming.

Denis Waitley, Seeds of Greatenss

These days, we are often told that faster is better, but when it comes to emotional reaction time, slower is often the wiser way to go. Meditation helps us extend our reaction time. In this way, we are given another second or two more before we respond.

Lama Surya Das
Awakening The Buddhist Heart

By undertaking daily meditation, it will gradually dawn on us that negative emotions like anger, resentment, hostility, vindictiveness, frustration and jealousy need not be invisible chains. They are not substantial entities or unconquerable forces. Rather, they are evanescent and non-substantial in nature. It is our erroneous self-concept and beliefs in an isolated self which solidify these inner energies. Our erroneous beliefs are implanted and strengthened by years of negative environmental conditioning which reinforce deceiving messages that peace and joy are founded on material wealth, social recognition and romantic relationships.

Most contemporary psychological research shows that when one expresses anger quite often in one's life, it leads to the easy expression of anger. Expressing anger becomes a habit. Many people assume that we have a certain amount of anger inside, and that if we do not want to keep it inside, we have to put it outside; somehow if it is outside, it is not going to be inside anymore.

Anger seems like a solid thing. But in fact, we discover, if we observe carefully, that anger has no solidity. In reality, it is merely a conditioned response that arises and passes away.

Sharon Salzberg
Lovingkindness

Thus, the first fruitful approach to healing negative emotions is to gain insights into their roots and non-substantial nature. Such insights are therapeutic and curative. They endow us with the capacity to create adequate inner space to watch the arising and passing away of negative emotions. Gradually, we loosen and dislodge false beliefs in a separate self that demands constant protection and gratification. We loosen, decondition and break away from the pernicious habit of venting anger and resentment on ourselves and others. We learn to sprinkle kind intentions into our daily thoughts, emotions and deeds, and patiently surround negative emotions and hostile energies with kind understanding. We can positively transform and channel our inner energies toward worthwhile deeds that are conducive to our positive growth and the well-being of others.

As we continue to cultivate the inner space for the arising and passing away of unhealthy thoughts and emotions, we regain our freewill to effectively manage our mental-emotional states and behavioral response to external events. We loosen ourselves from the festering grip of inner negativities. We awaken to the emotional and psychological wounds at our workplaces and in our homes. It dawns on us that cultivating wisdom and spiritual qualities is foundational to emotional maturity. It dawns on us that our supervisors, colleagues, family members, friends and neighbors also suffer from inner dislocation and negativities. Guided by heart wisdom, we gradually disentangle ourselves from the pernicious habit of reacting vindictively against the defensive and spiritually unconscious deeds of others. We awaken to the need to gradually heal the vicious cycle of inner negativities that corrodes individual and organizational performance.

If you have been disappointed by strained relations with a friend or loved one, you must realize that each relationship is unique. Don't let tension with one person convince you that you lack the ability to be a good friend or a loving family member.

Dr David Niven

Wealth-Creation Secret #45
The good news is that cultivating wisdom and spiritual resilience will enhance not only our work performance, but guide and sanctify our daily activities in all areas of our life.

---

(2)   Nurturing An Abundance Consciousness

Another effective antidote to inner negativities which in many instances arose from a competitive-riven scarcity mindset is to nurture a healthy abundance consciousness. As outlined in chapter 1, by awakening to the higher truth that we are enveloped and surrounded by immense natural beauty and affluence, and that we can enjoy deep inner peace and contentment without being entangled in the frenzied pursuit of worldly prizes, a healthy abundance consciousness will burgeon. We rediscover the bliss and tranquility of walking along the beach, watching the evening sunset, enjoying the refreshing sea breezes and spiritually merging with the boundlessness of the blue oceans. We rediscover our capacity to open ourselves to simple joys, of relishing the uniqueness and vitality of each miraculous moment. By shedding an egocentric scarcity mindset, by redefining life priorities and allocating more time to reconnect with Mother Nature, `we can alleviate much of our daily work-related stress. It is within our reach to choose a more healthy, balanced, uncluttered and tranquil lifestyle by setting aside adequate time to connect with our deep essence.

Wealth-Creation Secret #46
Many people misconceive that only the amassing of external
wealth can bring about an abundance mindset.
The higher truth is that if we are disconnected
with our divine essence, the more fervently we hoard external
wealth, the greater is our sense of insecurity, of being vulnerable
to the vagaries of life. A healthy abundance mindset arises not
from external possessions and status, but from the simple ability
to enjoy the natural abundance surrounding us and
from recognizing the range of inner assets at our disposal
to become constructive partners of Divinity.

---

(3)   Practicing Relaxation And Letting Go

A third effective antidote to emotional negativities is learning how to relax. Deep breathing is the building block of healthy relaxation and healthy living. It oxygenates the cells of our body and keeps our brain fresh. As emphasized by Anthony Robbins, fully oxygenating our body should be a number-one priority. Deep breathing for 10 minutes a day is invaluable.

Let me share with you the most effective way to breathe in order to cleanse your system. You should breathe in this ratio: inhale one count, hold four counts, exhale two counts. If you inhaled for four seconds, you would hold for sixteen and exhale for eight. Why exhale for twice as along as you inhale? That's when you eliminate toxins via your lymphatic system. Why hold four times as long? That's how you can fully oxygenate the blood and activate your lymphatic system.

Anthony Robbins
Unlimited Power

Besides deep breathing, there are many other healthy ways to relax, like listening to soothing music, undertaking silent meditation and simple yogic exercise, reading inspirational literature, strolling along a tranquil beach, allocating time to pursue our hobby, watching our favorite movie show, cycling, leisure swimming, jogging, brisk walking, hiking, and so forth. The important point is to let go of our sense of urgency, emergency and haste. It means that we learn to gently surrender and dissipate erroneous notions that we need to be at the center of the world in order to be joyful and contented. It means that we learn to cease clinging to narrow-minded egocentric thoughts, desires and viewpoints, to release ourselves from inner strife and resistance against what we habitually perceived as "unacceptable" life circumstances. It means that we learn to creatively re-interpret such "unacceptable" life circumstances as valuable learning opportunities, as trajectories to catapult ourselves to new heights of wisdom, as stimulants which induce us to tap upon our immense inner resources and find creative ways to solve practical daily problems and transform them into nuggets of golden experiences. We have the choice to relish the infinite richness and vitality of each kaleidoscopic moment, to nurture a vision and broadmindedness as wide as the blue ocean.

Letting go means just what it says. It's an invitation to cease clinging to anything – – – whether it be an idea, a thing, an event, a particular time, or view, or desire..............It's akin to letting your palm open to unhand something you have been holding on to.

Dr Jon Kabat-Zinn
Wherever You Go, There You Are

Wealth-Creation Secret #47
Practicing insightful "letting go" and insightful acceptance of events and circumstances that are beyond our control are the fundamentals of positive growth.

---

(4)   Adopting The Wiser Perspective

Avoid   weatherproofing..............Weatherproofing   means that you are on the careful lookout for what needs to be fixed or repaired. It's finding the cracks and flaws of life, and either trying to fix them, or at least, point them out to others. Not only does this tendency alienate you from other people, it makes you feel bad, too.

Dr Richard Carlson

An effective way to dispel inner negativities is to adopt the wiser perspective. The proverbial advice is: we should not take ourselves too seriously. We should not put the whole world on our shoulders. We should not be hunting for the imperfections in our life situations, for the foibles and inadequacies of other people. We should not spend our lives deploring that we are unable to fix and rectify the blemishes of the world. Rather, we should sustain a healthy long-term perspective, gaining insight into our deep potential as well as our natural limitations, particularly mindful that we can be assaulted or hijacked by egocentric thoughts.

It is my belief, you cannot deal with the most serious things in the world unless you understand the most amusing.

Winston Churchill

Reflecting on our finitude and mortality can be liberating. Some Tibetan monks are initiated to the higher wisdom by undergoing a phase of spiritual training where they devote many hours to contemplate the "emptiness" of life, its lack of intrinsic permanent selfhood. Reflecting on our finitude unveils the futility of putting on a long sullen face all day long whenever we encounter an unpleasant incident. In accordance with a Chinese saying, disagreeable events occur nine times out of ten. By sustaining a healthy optimistic mindset and attitude, we can creatively re-interpret disagreeable events as learning opportunities. In this way, we reinvent our inner reality whereby nine incidents out of ten are perceived as beneficial learning opportunities. We learn to nurture a healthy sense of humor, to occasionally laugh at ourselves when we lapse into egocentric puffed-up thinking and to laugh at the world when it becomes arrogant and conceited, preoccupied with outward honors and trophies. We learn to survey, like an eighteenth-century explorer telescope, the ironies and paradoxes, the flux, impermanence and multi-faceted dimensions and possibilities of life, whose secret appears to crystallize in four words: *This too shall pass.*

Four words I will train myself to say until they become a habit so strong that immediately they will appear in my mind whenever good humor threatens to depart from me. These words, passed down from the ancients, will carry me through every adversity and maintain life in balance...............This too shall pass.

I will laugh at the world.

And with my laughter all things will be reduced to their proper size. I will laugh at my failures and they will vanish in clouds of new dreams; I will laugh at my successes and they will shrink to their true value...............

Og Mandino
The Greatest Salesman In The World

More importantly, as we contemplate on our physical finitude, the time will come when our consciousness rises to the higher plane. We arrive at the sacred deathless dimension of our being. We arrive at the higher understanding that we are embraced by Divinity before we became an embryo in our mother's womb, that Divinity continues to envelop us after we were born into this world, after we slept in the cradle, after we became an adolescent, matured into a full-grown adult, got married, became a parent, a grandparent and finally returned to the sanctified source of our being. In addition, none of the "unacceptable" life circumstances and events could impair our inner sanctity. To arrive at this higher understanding is to reenter the arena of authentic living.

Wealth-Creation Secret #48
To be able to smile compassionately at our imperfections and at the foibles and imperfections of others is an important step to allow our natural affectionate heart to ripen further.

---

(5) Redefining Our Inner Criteria For Contentment

Many of our feelings of satisfaction or dissatisfaction have their roots in how we compare ourselves to others. When we compare ourselves to those who have more, we feel bad. When we compare ourselves to those who have less, we feel grateful. Even though the truth is we have exactly the same life either way, our feelings about our life can vary tremendously based on who we compare ourselves with.

Dr David Niven

To diminish and heal emotional negativities, we need to redefine and lower our inner criteria and self-imposed rules for contentment. In many instances, our inner criteria and rules for happiness are excessive, crippling and sky-high. They forbid us to congratulate ourselves and celebrate the many little successes in our life journey.

Ponder deeply on what are the inner criteria that we impose on ourselves before we allow ourselves to feel contented. Can we really feel at ease and peaceful when we have achieved our worldly prizes, when we have several million dollars in our bank account, when we have two bungalows, two BMWs, a yacht and a private helicopter? Are we confident that when we possessed all these items, our galloping mind will automatically cease its endless comparison with the rich and famous? Are we confident that we can thereby dissociate ourselves from further self-centered pursuits and yearning? Are we confident that we will automatically emerge from the abyss of self-fixation, that we can resolve the gamut of negative emotions induced by our egocentric competition-driven mindset, that we can automatically heal our gnawing sense of fear and apprehension of our physical vulnerability?

The foremost secret of contented living which is free from the festering grip of inner negativities is to have a low threshold for happiness. We allow ourselves to feel contented and happy by strolling along the beach, by having a simple picnic near a mountain lake, by hiking in a tranquil forest, by watching the fascinating activities of dragonflies and butterflies near a lotus pond. We allow ourselves to feel contented and happy by simplifying our personal needs, by dislodging from self-centered pursuits, by attuning our daily activities to the guidance of heart wisdom. We allow ourselves to feel contented and happy by not cluttering, clogging and burdening our daily living with excessive material requirements and attachment to material comfort.

By redefining and lowering our inner criteria for contentment, we will awaken to our immense inner assets. We will feel contented and peaceful by awakening to the higher truth that we are always enveloped by the affection of Divinity, that our inner wholesomeness cannot be undermined by external events and life circumstances. We will feel contented and peaceful by enjoying a cup of tea, by breathing the clean fresh air, by relishing our ability to connect with our deep essence, to practice mindfulness, to attune our words and deeds to the generous spirit and broadmindedness of our heart wisdom. We will feel contented and peaceful by resting in the inner sanctuary designed by the grit and grace of honesty and built from the enduring bricks and mortar of ethical commitment.

Wealth-Creation Secret #49
How do we practice contentment?
To nurture an affectionate heart that does not differentiate between "yours" and "mine" achievements, that appreciates the unity of humankind, that shares the joys of others and sympathizes with the misery of the needy and lends a helping hand.

---

(6)   Practicing "Slowing Down"

An effective method to de-stress is to slow down our pace in life, to heal the gnawing sense of desperation, emergency, urgency and frenzy. Slowing down is liberating and refreshing. We relearn to be receptive to the beauty and radiance of the dancing daffodils along the pedestrian walks. We relearn to enjoy watching the placidity of the white clouds with countless permutation of shapes and sizes floating leisurely across the blue heaven. We relearn to enjoy watching the playful movements of goldfish in a clear garden pond. We relearn to imitate the leisurely yawning of little kittens ensconced in a simple wooden shelter in our backyard. We relearn to intelligently melt into the sparkling eyes and innocent laughter of our children and grandchildren. We relearn to embrace the supreme joy of resting our heart in the inherent simplicity of life that avails itself to the graceful fashioning hands of cosmic affection.

The human tendency is always want more. A better approach is to remember where you started and appreciate how much you have accomplished.

Dr David Niven

(7)   Practicing Inner Silence, Inner Peace, Non-Judgment, Acceptance And Forgiveness

"Be still and know that I am God." I am desperately concerned that we slow down and quiet down and gear down our lives so that intermittently each week we carve out time for quietness, solitude, thought, prayer, meditation, and soul searching. Oh, how much agitation will begin to fade away............how insignificant petty differences will seem............how big God will become and how small our troubles will appear............"

Charles Swindoll
Growing Strong In The Seasons Of Life

A time-honored way to ameliorate stress and sustain our physical, emotional and spiritual health is to practice the five basic tenets of the perennial wisdoms: inner silence, inner peace, non-judgment, acceptance and forgiveness.

Firstly, inner silence is the nutrition and sustenance for our emotional, mental and spiritual vitality. We access inner silence when we practice meditation, when we rein in and tame our galloping mind, when we avail ourselves to the countless gaps of silence that punctuate our streams of thoughts. By resting our body and soul in these sacred gaps, we merge with the sanctified source of our being. A deep sense of serenity will gently course through the cells of our body, defusing stress and emotional negativities. We become attuned to the eternal throb and vitalism of Life.

Secondly, inner peace is the wellspring of fulfillment. If we ponder deeply, we will realize that most of our frenzied pursuits of worldly prizes ultimately aim to attain peace of mind. However, owing to years of negative environmental conditioning and losing touch with our divine essence, our yearnings for peace of mind have mutated into egocentric cravings, into contorted desires for material comfort, for worldly status, power and fame. To return to the sanctuary of inner peace, to restore a healthy perspective of life priorities, we should muster the courage to lift the veil of self-delusion and re-embrace the higher wisdom of cultivating present-moment awareness and watering the seeds of inner freedom.

Thirdly, practicing and cultivating a non-judgmental attitude is an effective way to defuse stress and dissipate the underlying sense of dread and desperation that arise from hectic fast-paced living. We need to tame and discipline the galloping mind which is always judging, evaluating, speculating, planning, forecasting, comparing, measuring, fretting and worrying. To enter the higher arena of peaceful living, we need to see through the tricks, gimmicks and stratagem of the galloping egoistic mind. By seeing though its ruses, we liberate ourselves from its egoistic energies. We become wary of the danger in pre-judging others. We awaken to the value and virtue of nurturing a non-judgmental attitude. We learn to let go of our hypercritical, hyper-defensive and faultfinding habit where we spend many hours of our lives in contending, protecting, defending and fortifying our viewpoints. We dissipate the compulsive need to belittle, attack and denigrate the views and opinions of others, to flaunt our learning and intellectual superiority. We shed the pernicious belief that we must always project mental acumen and that we must always be seen to be correct in our views. We learn to let go of the crippling misconception that mental cleverness and intelligence determines our worth and acceptance by others. We learn to let go of the devastating habit of defending, parading and propping up our mental cleverness and intelligence at all costs. Dissociating from the neurotic belief that our endlessly judging, evaluating and thinking mind is our most prized possession, we learn to practice open-mindedness and extend inner spaciousness to the views and opinions of others.

Fourthly, as discussed in chapter 1, accessing inner peace and embracing broadminded acceptance and non-resistance can heal inner strife and negativities. Once again, it should be emphasized that we are not lapsing into negative surrender. Insightful acceptance and non-resistance are not similar to passivity, insouciance, pessimism or a fatalistic-defeatist attitude. Such insightful acceptance and non-resistance evolve from gaining insight into our inner sanctity, from the higher conviction that we are always guided by divine cosmic intelligence. Thus, we are nurturing a healthy proactive type of higher acceptance and non-resistance which align our words and deeds with the natural laws of abundance. Inner strife, struggles and resistance are not conducive to fulfilling our deep potential. In contrast, by nurturing a relaxed abundance consciousness based on inner peace, acceptance and non-resistance, we are planting and watering the seeds of broadmindedness, fortitude and perseverance.

Fifthly, practicing forgiveness is crucial to healing emotional negativities. By extending forgiveness to ourselves and others, we pierce through the baneful effects and consequences of harboring an unforgiving attitude. We learn to rise above the mediocre crowd which wallows in recriminations, counter-accusations, discord and retaliation. This important subject is discussed in the next chapter.

> *Wealth-Creation Secret #50*
> *The route to inner affluence is inner peace.*

(8)   Practicing Positive Affirmations

An effective method for dissipating pessimism and fostering healthy self-esteem is to undertake positive affirmation by repeating the following sentence for at least three times a day, ie. during the early morning when we wake up, during noontime, and during the evening after work. We can also repeat it five times when we catch ourselves slipping into disempowering mental-emotional states and negative internal dialogue. When repeating the affirmation, we can do so silently in our heart or repeat it aloud in a private place. It is important that we repeat it with enthusiasm by adopting an assertive hand-motion.

With the help of divine consciousness and intelligence, I can do all positive things and overcome adversities.

Or

With the help of God (or Divine Power, the Buddha, Jesus Christ, Holy Spirit, Allah, etc), I can do all positive things and overcome adversities.

When we become aware that egocentric thoughts are attacking us, we should immediately take a few deep breaths and repeat the following affirmations ten times:

These negative and egocentric thoughts are not my divine essence. There is no need to react mindlessly. Calm down. My divine essence is inviolate and wholesome.

> *Wealth-Creation Secret #51*
> *Undertaking positive affirmations on a daily basis will*
> *sustain our inner vivacity and optimism to work*
> *toward worthwhile goals.*

(9) Reinterpreting Our Sensory And Perceptual Experiences And Managing Our Mental-Emotional States

Our thoughts are causes.
You sow a thought, you reap an action.
You sow an action, you reap a habit.
You sow a habit, you reap a character.
You sow a character, you reap a destiny.
It all starts with a thought.

Ralph waldo Emerson

Another fruitful approach in healing negative emotions is to develop a skilful mindset whereby we regain our autonomy to proactively "participate" in creating our thoughts and mental-emotional state. This approach is life-rejuvenating. It underpins the positive reinvention of our phenomenal self. Guided by heart wisdom, we learn to proactively transform negative emotions into positive energies which attune our thoughts, words and deeds to worthwhile goals.

There was once a scientist who planned to demonstrate before a group of alcoholics the pernicious effects of alcohol. He placed before them two glass containers, one filled with water and the other with undiluted alcohol.

The scientist placed a worm into the container filled with water. The worm swam around and headed for the side of the glass. It slowly crawled to the top of the glass. Thereupon, the scientist took the same worm and placed it into the container filled with alcohol. The worm disintegrated rapidly.

"What can you gather from this demonstration?" the scientist asked the class.

A voice from the rear said, "If we drink alcohol, we will never have worms in our stomach."

Let us share another story concerning the Sufis' well-known trickster Nasrudin.

One evening, Nasrudin encountered a woman who was weeping under a tree. He decided to enquire what was the matter.

The woman lamented, "I am so poor. All my possessions are contained in this small bag. When will I ever become wealthy."

Nasrudin pondered for a few moments. Thereafter, he seized the woman's bag and fled out of sight. The woman was shocked. She tried to catch up with Nasrudin, but in vain.

"Now I have nothing," wept the woman as she trudged along the dusty road in the direction where Nasrudin had fled. After walking for half a mile, the woman caught sight of her small bag lying in the middle of the road. She rushed toward it and found that its contents were intact, with no item missing. Filled with huge relief and happiness, she knelt down and said, "Thank you, God. Thank you for your kindness."

The mischievous Nasrudin was watching the woman from behind a tree and whispered to himself, "How miraculous. The same small bag can make this woman weep as well as rejoice in gratitude........."

There is a factual story of two brothers who grew up in a broken family terrorized by an alcoholic father. The father was unemployed and always came home beating his wife and two sons.

Years passed and the two brothers grew up. One became a drug addict while another became a highly successful businessman.

When asked, the drug addict said, "How can I possibly be different from my father? He was an alcoholic and a drug addict. I'm merely following his footsteps............"

The other successful businessman said, "Since young, I grew up in a broken family tyrannized by an alcoholic father. I resolved to myself everyday that when I grew up, I shall never become an alcoholic. Instead, I should continuously strive to improve myself and become a useful member of society......"

What makes the young woman weep over her lack of possessions and later rejoice in happiness when she recovered her small bag? What induces a young man to become a drug addict and his brother to become a successful businessman? What makes David, the young man in the story told at the beginning of this chapter, not to react angrily at the disheveled beggar who unreasonably insulted him?

What makes the following famous people to triumph over adversities and succeed in realizing worthwhile goals?

- Being a cripple did not prevent William Shakespeare from writing the world's finest plays.

- Blindness did not prevent John Milton from writing England's greatest poem, Paradise Lost.

- Deafness did not prevent Beethoven from composing some of the world's most beautiful and inspiring music

- Numerous setbacks did not prevent Abraham Lincoln from becoming one of the greatest American Presidents: failed in business in 1831, defeated in legislature in 1832, again failed in business in 1833, suffered a nervous breakdown in 1836, defeated while running for speaker in 1838, defeated while running for post of elector in 1840, defeated while running for congress in 1843, elected to congress in 1846, defeated while running for congress in 1848, defeated while running for senate in 1855, defeated while running for vice-president in 1856, finally elected as the 16th president of the United States of America in 1860.

- Muteness, deafness and blindness did not prevent Helen Keller from becoming a renowned author and speaker.

- One day, a young child came home with a note from his teacher and showed it to his mother, "Your Tommy is too stupid to learn, get him out of school." Tommy did not give up, persevere in his self-education and transformed himself into the renowned inventor Thomas Edison. Before Edison invented the light bulb and brought light to the world, he failed more than 10,000 times. Deafness also did not prevent him from inventing the phonograph.

- Walt Disney visited more than three hundred banks before he found one which would invest in his theme park idea.

- Noah Webster, the famous lexicographer, spent thirty-six years to compile his great dictionary.

- Leonardo da Vinci spent a decade to complete The Last Supper, which was considered as one of the finest works of art in the world.

- John Wesley preached an average of 3 sermons per day for 54 years, traveling by horseback and carriage for more than 200,000 miles. At the age 86, he was embarrassed to admit that he could not preach more than twice per day and that he would sleep until five in the morning.

- Dr Sun Yat Sen, the father of Modern China, failed ten times before he succeeded in overthrowing the decadent Manchu Dynasty.

- Mahatma Gandhi, revered as the father of modern India, advocated non-violence for more than 40 years when he was leading his countrymen in their struggle for independence.

- Stricken by polio and paralyzed from the waist down at the age of 39 did not prevent Mr Franklin Delano Roosevelt from becoming one of the greatest American presidents.

- As First Lord of the Admiralty during World War I, Winston Churchill's first major offensive, the Dardanelles Campaign was a great failure in which thousands of British troops died and he resigned. However, he did not give up. Learning from his mistakes, Winston Churchill successfully led his country as Prime Minister during the Second World War and prevented the Nazis from defeating Britain.

- Stricken by polio and barely able to walk at a young age did not prevent Wilma Rudolph from winning three Olympic gold medals as the "fastest woman on Earth" in the 1960 Rome Olympics.

- Being imprisoned for 27 years did not prevent Mr Nelson Mandela from succeeding in his fight against racial discrimination in South Africa where he finally became the President at the age of 76.

We are born to make manifest the glory of God that is within us. It is not just in some of us; it is in everyone. And as we let our light shine, we unconsciously give other people permission to do the same. As we are liberated from our own fear, our presence automatically liberates others.

Nelson Mandela

Satisfaction lies in the effort, not in the attainment. Full effort is full victory.

Mahatma Gandhi

The answer lies in their *mental interpretations or reinterpretations of their sensory and perceptual experiences.* The secret of inner and outer success is to realize that it is our innate capacity to proactively interpret and re-interpret our sensory and perceptual experiences which enables us to recreate ourselves and remake our destiny. It is our mental interpretations of our sensory and perceptual experiences that influence our mental-emotional state and our behavioral response to external events. To attain self-mastery, we need to proactively manage our mental interpretations of sensory and perceptual experiences. We need to awaken to our sacred ability to choose and decide on our mindset, attitude and behavioral response to external events.

I am liken to a grain of wheat which faces one of three futures. The wheat can be placed in a sack and dumped in a stall until it is fed to swine. Or it can ground to flour and made into bread. Or it can be placed in the earth and allowed to grow until its golden head divides and produces a thousand grains from the one.

Og Mandino
The Greatest Salesman In The World

They took away what should have been my eyes, but I remember Milton's Paradise. They took away what should have been my ears, Beethoven came and wiped away my tears. They took away what should have been my tongue, but I had talked to God when I was young. He would not let them take away my soul — — — possessing that, I still possess the whole.

Helen Keller

302

- ### Three Models Of Mental Interpretations/Reinterpretations Of Sensory And Perceptual Experiences

The basic principle of spiritual life is that our problems become the very place to discover wisdom and love.

Dr Jack Kornfield
A Path With Heart

Because they have done me such generous favors.
Every time I turn back toward the things they want
I run into them. They beat me and leave me
In the road, and I understand again, that what they want
Is not what I want.
Those that make you return, for whatever reason,
To the spirit, be grateful to them.
Worry about others who give you
Delicious comfort that keeps you from prayer.

Rumi writing about a priest
who prays for thieves and robbers

Once upon a time, there was an elderly man standing on a high hill. Three travelers passed by in the distance and noticed him. They began to discuss what the elderly man was doing.

"He's probably looking for a friend," the first traveler said.

"No, he is up on the hill to watch the sunset," the second traveler said.

"No, I disagree. I believe he is looking for his pet," the third traveler said.

In view of their disagreement, the three travelers decided to ask the elderly man himself. They walked up the hill and spoke to him.

"Are you looking for a friend?" the first traveler enquired

"No, I am not looking for a friend," the elderly man smiled.

"Then you must be waiting to watch the sunset," said the second traveler.

"No, I am not here to watch the sunset," the elderly man said.

"Are you looking for your pet?" asked the third traveler.

"No, I am not looking for a pet."

"What are you doing here then?" the three travelers asked in unison.

"I am merely standing," the elderly man replied.

I want you to know that there are no colors in the real world, that there are no fragrances in the real world, that there's no beauty and there's no ugliness. Out there beyond the limits of our perceptual apparatus is the erratically ambiguous and ceaselessly flowing quantum soup. And we're almost like magicians in that in the very act of perception, we take that quantum soup and we convert it into the experience of material reality in our ordinary everyday waking state of consciousness.

Sir John Eccles

We can identify three useful models relating to mental interpretations/reinterpretations of sensory and perceptual experiences.

Model (A): Passive Mode Of Mental Interpretation

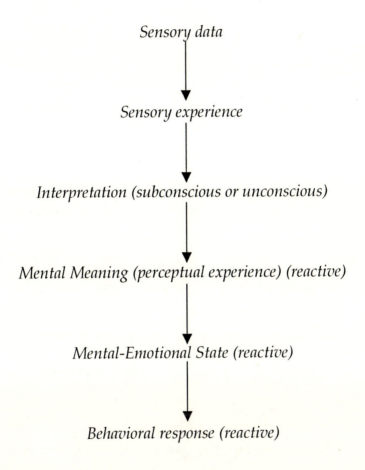

Sensory data

Sensory experience

Interpretation (subconscious or unconscious)

Mental Meaning (perceptual experience) (reactive)

Mental-Emotional State (reactive)

Behavioral response (reactive)

Model (B): Creative Mode Of Mental Interpretation (Type I)

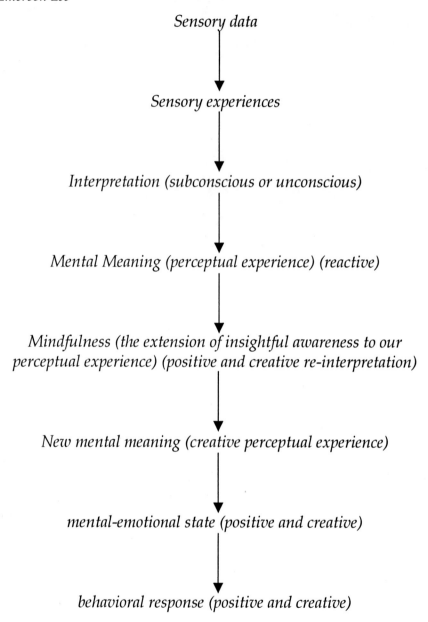

Sensory data

↓

Sensory experiences

↓

Interpretation (subconscious or unconscious)

↓

Mental Meaning (perceptual experience) (reactive)

↓

Mindfulness (the extension of insightful awareness to our perceptual experience) (positive and creative re-interpretation)

↓

New mental meaning (creative perceptual experience)

↓

mental-emotional state (positive and creative)

↓

behavioral response (positive and creative)

Model (C) Creative Mode Of Mental Interpretation (Type II)

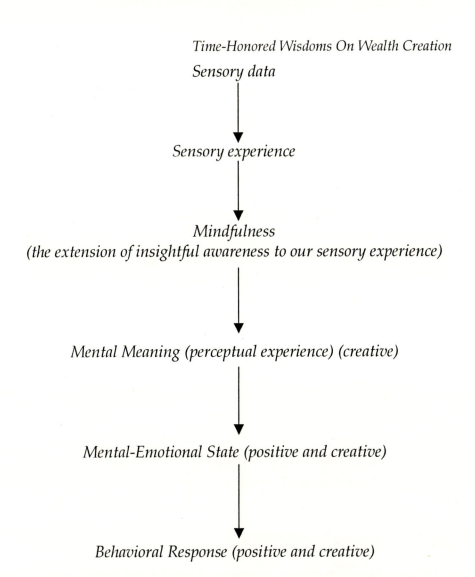

The above three models reflect that when external stimuli (eg. rays of light, sounds, food, objects, etc) come into contact with our sense organs, they are stimulated and transmit signals to our brain. Sensory data are produced in the brain. These sensory data give rise to vision, hearing, smell, taste and tactile sensations which can be identified as basic sensory experiences.

Thereafter, the cognitive-organizing-interpretative functions of the brain confer meaning onto our sensory experiences, transforming them into "mental meaning" or perceptual experiences. In turn, our perceptual experiences influence our mental-emotional state and behavioral response.

Meditation and mindfulness practice sharpen our awareness of the sacred gap between sensory experiences and perceptual experiences. This inner gap underpins our freewill and autonomy to effectively manage and recreate our responses to external stimuli and events. We need not react mindlessly and negatively to adverse events. By nurturing a skilful mindset, we have the innate capacity to effectively manage our behavioral response.

Model A: This model depicts the passive mode of perceptual experiences. Essentially, we adhere to the auto-pilot mode of existence. Our perceptual experiences are mainly determined by environmental conditioning as well as habitual thinking and emotional patterns. We did not proactively manage our perceptual experiences, our mental-emotional states and behavioral responses. This is a unconstructive reactive mode of existence that impedes the realization of our deep potential.

We should awaken to and become wary of the pitfalls, dangers and snares of leading a reactive, impulsive and spiritually apathetic existence. If not, our authentic life purpose would elude us. The realization of our talents and deep potential would elude us. Thus, we should nurture a skilful mindset and reconnect with our inner autonomy to effectively manage our mental-emotional states and behavioral responses. We should nurture a skilful mindset and slough off our mental and spiritual torpor, guarding against succumbing to a fatalistic or defeatist attitude in the face of adverse circumstances. Committed to nurturing resilience and broadmindedness, we gradually awaken to the deep significance of Dr Victor Frankl famous words in *Man's Search For Meaning*: "We who lived in concentration camps can remember the men who walked through the huts comforting others, giving away their last piece of bread. They may have been few in number, but they offer sufficient proof that everything can be taken from a man but one thing: the last of the human freedoms— —to choose one's attitude in any given set of circumstances................ Every day, every hour, offered the opportunity to make a decision, a decision which determined whether you would or would not submit to those powers which threatened to rob you of your very self, your inner freedom; which determined whether or not you would become the plaything of circumstance........."

Model (B): Under this model, we learn to catch ourselves slipping into negative perceptual experiences and negative mental state that corrode inner peace and reinforce negative emotions. By extending our insightful awareness to our perceptual experiences, we can recreate positive perceptual experiences and positive mental states that align with the deep harmony of our divine essence. This leads to more positive and empowering behavioral responses to external events.

Model (C): Under this model, we seek to nurture mindfulness over our sensory experiences, to the extent that we proactively attune the cognitive-interpretative functions of our brain to our healthy awareness that afflictive emotions (like resentment, hostility, vindictiveness and aggressiveness) should be dissipated and nipped in the bud before they generate destructive mental-emotional states. We also learn to proactively create positive empowering mental-emotional states which in turn imbue us with enthusiasm to work toward worthwhile goals.

Furthermore, by expanding insightful awareness, we awaken to the quality and type of our inner dialogue, to the type of inner reality that we continuously represent to ourselves, to the kind of subtle motivations that drive our behavior. If not, our thinking, emotional and behavioral patterns would be driven by environmental conditioning and self-seeking urges. We become quasi-automatons whereby our words and deeds would become largely "unfree" in a higher sense.

Conversely, by committing ourselves to re-interpreting our sensory and perceptual experiences in a positive light, we seek to cultivate healthy internal dialogue and thinking patterns. By minimizing negative disempowering thoughts and emotions, when we encounter obstacles and adversities, we reinterpret them as catalysts for positive growth, as valuable opportunities for cultivating spiritual qualities like patience, endurance, broadmindedness, acceptance, fortitude and empathy.

Major premise: I can control my thoughts.
Minor premise: My feelings come from my thoughts.
Conclusion: I can control my feelings.

Dr Wayne Dyer
Your Erroneous Zones

Let us share a traditional Indian story on a poison tree which is retold by Dr Jack Kornfield in his classic A Path With Heart.

When we encounter a difficult person or an unpleasant event, many of us regard it as a poison tree. When we first encounter this poison tree, many of us would focus on its danger and harm. Our immediate reaction is to chop it down and destroy it.

As we progress in our inner cultivation, we learn that we need to be more receptive to the positive and negative aspects of life. We become aware that the poison tree can be treated sympathetically. We say to ourselves, "Let us not chop it down. Let us regard it with kind understanding and compassion, and learn from it."

As we progress further along the spiritual journey, we would regard the poison tree as a rare and precious opportunity to learn about life. We would pick up the poisoned fruit, investigate its property, treat it with kindness and understanding, and consider whether we can turn it into a beneficial medicine to cure the ills of the world.

Thus, by changing our perspective and mental interpretations of external events and circumstances, we become more broadminded and receptive to the changing vicissitudes of life. We realize that obstacles and setbacks can emerge as catalysts for positive growth, as valuable lessons to ripen our heart.

The Earth school is a 3-D, full-color, big-screen, multi-media, interactive movie. Getting carried way is easy because it is intimate, exciting, and always changing. If you study this movie —

— — the Earth school — — — like a student of cinema studies movies, you see that nothing in it is accidental. Everything happens for a reason...............This movie is your life. The more you use your intuition, the more you see how it is constructed and what it is telling you.

Gary Zukav
Soul Stories

In his classic *Man's Search For Meaning*, Viktor Frankl quoted the memorable example of Jerry Long, who is described as the living testimony to the "defiant power of the human spirit". Jerry Long was paralyzed from his neck down due to a diving accident which rendered him a quadriplegic when he was 17 years old. Nevertheless, he did not give up hope. He learned to use a mouth-stick to type. He continued to enrich himself by reading, watching television and writing. In 1983, he wrote to Professor Viktor Frankl, "I view my life as being abundant with meaning and purpose. The attitude I adopted on that fateful day has become my personal credo for life: I broke my neck, it didn't break me. I am currently enrolled in my first psychology course in college. I believe that my handicap will only enhance my ability to help others. I know that without suffering, the growth that I have achieved would have been impossible."

............man is ultimately self-determining. Man does not simply exist but always decides what his existence will be, what he will become in the next moment.

Viktor Frankl

Problems, depending on their nature, evoke is us frustration or grief or sadness or loneliness or guilt or regret or fear or anxiety or anguish or despair. These are uncomfortable feelings...............

Yet it is this whole process of meeting and solving problems that life has its meaning. Problems are the cutting edge that distinguishes between success and failure. Problems call forth our courage and our wisdom; indeed, they create our courage and our wisdom..

M. Scott Peck The Road Less Traveled

Let us share an oft-quoted story about W. Mitchell who encountered several crippling accidents. In June 1971, Mitchell was riding his brand-new motorcycle in downtown San Francisco. However, he met with an accident and smashed into a truck. Two and a half gallons of gasoline spread on his body and both Mitchell and his bike went up in flames. With burns over 65% of his body, he underwent many surgeries and survived. In 1975, he was again struck with a plane accident which left him permanently paralyzed. Now, more than two decades later, he is still in a wheelchair, unable to walk, confined to a body that lacks fingers and toes. Nevertheless, he has become a successful businessman, earning millions and seeking to help the less fortunate. He said, "............before I was paralyzed, there were ten thousand things that I could do. Now there were nine thousand. I could dwell on those one thousand things and spend the rest of my life doing that or I could focus on the nine thousand that I have left. If, in my lifetime, I am able to do a few hundred of those things, I'll be one of the most remarkable people on this planet."

> *Wealth-Creation Secret #52*
> *To exercise our immense inner freedom to change and modify*
> *our perceptual experiences and to align them with*
> *our higher perspective of life is to empower ourselves*
> *with the broadmindedness and wisdom to bravely*
> *face the challenges in life.*

Become an alchemist. Transmute base metal into gold, suffering into consciousness, disaster into enlightenment.

Eckhart Tolle

(10) Practicing Creative Visualizations

In the inner world, anything that you can imagine is actually a part of you right now. Your proclamation of being wealthy and happy, if taken to that inner nonjudgmental world, will lead you to feel wealthy and happy. This, in turn, will lead you to begin acting in new ways. You will begin to create a new concrete reality of wealth and happiness within yourself as you generate a positive attitude toward all that you encounter.

Dr Wayne D Dyer

In his influential book *Unlimited Power*, Anthony Robbins discussed about the neuro-linguistic programming (NLP) techniques which were originated by prominent linguist Richard Bandler and mathematician cum computer expert John Grinder. By applying NLP techniques, we can "run our brain" more effectively.

NLP postulates that our beliefs are sending consistent messages to our neuro-physiological system which affects our thinking and emotional patterns; that the way we organize our thoughts influence our inner reality; and that the mind and body are linked. NLP suggests that the way we use our physiology, the way we breathe and speak, the way we hold our body, posture, facial expressions, the type and quality of our body movements determine our mental and emotional states. By effectively managing our physiology and internal dialogue, we can more effectively manage our mental-emotional states.

NLP also introduces us to the important concepts of the primary modalities through which we experience the world and the submodalities of our mental pictures or internal representations. Internal representations refer to what and how we represent images in our mind, and the content and quality of our internal dialogue. The five modalities through which we experience the world are in the form of visual, auditory, kinesthetic, gustatory, or olfactory sensations. Primarily, our sensations arise from the visual, auditory and kinesthetic modalities. The submodalities refer to the exact quality of our sensations.

For example, regarding the visual submodality of our mental pictures, we are referring to their degree of clarity and steadiness, their colors, the intensity and range of colors, the number of mental pictures and their relative sizes, their focus, the type and color of their background, their degree of movement, their quality of brightness and dimness, etc.

Regarding the auditory submodality of our mental pictures, we are referring to their volume (ie. loudness or softness), the degree of clarity and steadiness of the volume, their cadence, rhythm, tempo, the uniqueness of these sounds, etc.

Regarding the kinesthetic submodality of our mental pictures, we are referring to their texture, their movement and vibration, their focus and steadiness, their temperature, pressure, weight and density, etc.

By creatively changing, varying and transforming the submodalities of our mental pictures, we can more effectively manage our interpretations of our sensory and perceptual experiences. We can thereby more effectively manage our mental-emotional states, feelings and emotions, and behavioral responses.

By training our mind and nurturing a healthy insightful awareness, we become more conscious of the quality of our mental pictures and their submodalities. From this perspective, meditation and mindfulness training have the benefit of enabling us to utilize NLP techniques to "run our brain" more creatively, so as to realize our deep potential and fulfill our talents. Let us undertake the following visualization exercises which incorporate NLP concepts.

Visualization Exercise: Managing Our Mental Picture Of A Difficult Person

- Let us close our eyes and undertake silent meditation for five minutes.

- Thereafter, let us recall a difficult person who has mistreated or committed a wrong against us. By steadying and focusing our awareness, we can learn to observe the visual, auditory and kinesthetic submodalities of this mental picture, ie. its degree of clarity and steadiness, its size and color, its brightness and dimness, its loudness and softness, its distance from our mental focus, etc.

- If we are uncomfortable or distressed by our mental picture of this person, we can creatively diminish its brightness. Besides dimming it, we can shrink it gradually to a comfortable size, reduce its volume, lessen its weight, pressure and density, etc. We can vary the submodalities of this mental picture until it is comfortable to us and no longer appear threatening.

- Thereafter, visualize that this mental picture is enveloped by a golden bubble. Visualize that this person is diminishing in size and growing younger and younger until he or she becomes a harmless infant. Visualize that the golden bubble has infinite divine quality and kindness to heal all the negative emotions, sorrow and pain inflicted on us by this difficult person.

- Visualize that the golden bubble is slowly and gently floating away, further and further away, until it disappears from the bright horizon in our mind.

- Repeat this visualization on a daily basis until our mental picture of this difficult person no longer triggers negative emotions or hostile energies in us.

Visualization Exercise: Managing Our Mental Picture Of A Distressing Event

- Let us recall a distressing event. Notice the size, movement, color, brightness and dimness, loudness and softness of this mental picture. Imaginatively shrink its size, dim its brightness, lower its volume and lessen its weight, pressure and density, until it becomes a comfortable mental picture.

- Visualize that this mental picture is enveloped by a golden bubble. Visualize that the negative emotions, pain and sorrow stemming from this event are softening and diminishing, becoming dimmer and dimmer. Visualize that the golden bubble has the divine quality of healing this event and enabling us to reconnect with our innate wholesomeness.

- Visualize that this golden bubble which engulfs our mental picture of this event is slowly and gently floating away, further and further away, until it disappears from the bright horizon of our mind.

- Repeat this visualization on a daily basis until our mental image of this distressing event no longer triggers negative emotions and hostile energies in us.

Visualization Exercise: Seeking The Daily Guidance Of A Hallowed Figure

- Begin we commence the day, it is rejuvenating to seek the companionship, guidance and sacred presence of a hallowed figure. Close our eyes and meditate for 5 minutes. Thereafter, identify a hallowed figure with whom you have a special preference or affection (eg. the Buddha, Jesus Christ, prophet Mohamed, God Vishnu, Confucius, Kwan-Yin, etc). Picture Him or Her clearly in our mind.

- Gently remind ourselves that His or Her Holy Presence is permeating the phenomenal realm and that we can always invite Him or Her to sit in our heart and guide, support and encourage us in our daily activities.

- Visualize that this hallowed figure is the embodiment of compassion and wisdom, and as long as we are willing to open our heart, He or She will sit in our heart, offer intimate guidance and encouragement to us, and lead us to the inner wellspring of peace and joy.

- Visualize that this hallowed figure is sitting comfortably and peacefully in our heart for the rest of the day. Visualize that the serenity, lovingkindness and compassion emanating from this hallowed figure has diffused to all parts of our body.

- Slowly repeat the following phrases three times:

"Thank you for your Holy Presence in my heart. I am grateful for your continuous guidance, affection, support and encouragement. With your holy guidance, I can do all positive things."

Visualization Exercise: Focusing On A Worthwhile Life Goal

- Let us close our eyes and recall a moment in our lives where we experience great enthusiasm, positive energy, fulfillment and contentment in having attained a worthwhile objective. Observe the degree of brightness and clarity, color, size and sound of this mental picture. We can further increase the brightness, size and color of this positive mental picture, until we feel comfortable surges of positive energies within us. Maintain this positive and colorful mental picture.

- Visualize that we are now working toward a worthwhile life goal. Visualize that in 3 years' time, we will attain this worthwhile life goal.

- Visualize that we have taken a quantum leap in time and arrived at the moment in the future whereby we have attained this worthwhile life goal. Picture clearly the sense of inner fulfillment, joy and contentment at the moment when we have attained our life goal.

- Picture clearly the huge amount of joy and happiness that we can bring to the people around us. Picture clearly that our worthwhile life goal has significantly enhanced the well-being of the people around us, ie. when we are working toward it as well as at the point of time when we attain it.

- Visualize that streams of golden light are emanating from the depths of our heart, filling us with positive energies and enthusiasm in working toward worthwhile activities. Visualize that our body is merging with the streams of golden light and that we are bathed in inner peace and fulfillment.

- Sustain this mental picture and experience of inner peace and fulfillment for the rest of the day. Undertake this positive visualization exercise at least once a week.

- Whenever we catch ourselves slipping into negative mental states, learn to use our insightful awareness to immediately recall this enthusiastic mental state to dissipate depressive thoughts and feelings. We should also remind ourselves of the Holy Presence of Divinity in our heart, and that regardless of external events and circumstances, we are receiving unending love, support and encouragement from Divinity.

Wealth-Creation Secret #53
Creative visualizations enable us to explore, survey, probe and discover the vast creativity and ingenuity of the human mind.

It helps me if I remember that God is in charge of my day............While He is pleased with the wise management of time and intelligent planning from day to day, He is mainly concerned with the development of inner character. He charts growth toward maturity, concerning Himself with the cultivation of priceless, attractive qualities that make us Christlike down deep within.

Charles Swindoll
Growing Strong In The Seasons Of Life

* * * * * *

Wealth-Creation Wisdom 7
Nurturing Our Divine Capacity To Forgive

Then Peter came and said to him, "Lord, if another member of the church sins against me, how often should I forgive? As many as seven times?" Jesus said to him, "Not seven times, but I tell you, seventy-seven times."

The Bible

Do you want happiness, a quiet mind, a certainty of purpose, and a sense of worth and beauty that transcends the world?.........All this forgiveness offers you, and more.

A Course In Miracles

Forgiveness is the shortest route to God.

Dr Gerald Jampolsky

The gateway to inner peace is labeled "Forgiveness". Inner cultivation is an ongoing process of forgiving and accepting the limitations and imperfections of our phenomenal self as well as those of others. Extending forgiveness to ourselves and others is pivotal to healing inner negativities, dislocation and self-rejection. It reveals our potential for broadening and deepening our constricted five-sensory worldview. It reveals the futility, morbidity and self-imposed punishment of clinging to our "skin-encapsulated ego", to a vindictive eye-for-eye tooth-for-tooth mindset. It reveals our capacity for nurturing healthy self-esteem, positive growth and a constructive relationship with ourselves and others. Our inherent capacity to forgive is divine, the wellspring of inner healing and spiritual rejuvenation.

It was recorded that when Guatama Buddha was in his sixties, he and his sangha did not support the coronation of King Ajatasattu who had earlier plotted to kill his father, the old king. The Buddha's decision not to attend the coronation ceremony offended the new king.

Late one night, while sitting in meditation, the Buddha became aware of a man hiding behind a nearby tree. The Buddha motioned to him to step forward. Filled with fear, the man laid a long sword at the Buddha's feet and prostrated before him.

"Who are you and why are you concealing yourself behind the tree?" enquired the Buddha.

The man replied in a remorseful tone, "Allow me to bow before you, Great Teacher. I was ordered by my Master to murder you. I raised my sword several times while you were sitting in deep meditation. However, I could not summon enough courage to kill you. Now, I am afraid that my Master would kill me."

"Who is your Master?" asked the Buddha.

"I do not dare to reveal his name," replied the man tearfully.

"Very well. You need not tell me his name. Do you have a wife and children?" asked the Buddha.

"No, I am not married. But I have an elderly mother."

"Dear friend, listen to me and follow my advice closely. Return home at once and escape tonight with your mother across the border into neighboring Kosala. Start a new peaceful life there. Do not return by the road that your master had led you. I believe his men would ambush and kill you. Go now quietly and be careful," said the Buddha with compassion and forgiveness.

When someone whom I have helped,
Or in whom I have placed great hopes,
Mistreats me in extremely hurtful ways,
May I regard him still as my precious teacher.

The Dalai Lama

Wealth-Creation Secret #54
The practice of compassion and broadmindedness begins with self-forgiveness. Genuine self-forgiveness is not easy. In fact, many of our emotional negativities arise from subtle self-hatred and non-forgiveness of our imperfections.
In fact, many of us spend our entire lives amassing external possessions and scoring external victories to mask our non-forgiveness of our inadequacies and finitude.

What Is Forgiveness?

To forgive is to touch the sacred region of our heart and be attuned to its tenderness, purity, inner wisdom and pristine vivacity. To forgive is to extend our compassion and kind understanding to ourselves and others with regard to those thoughts, words and deeds which are not aligned with our heart wisdom. To forgive is to touch our intuitive sense of deep kinship with humanity, to feel and share its aspirations and striving, its affection and fear, its joy and suffering, its endurance, grit and vulnerability. To forgive is to rise to the higher plane where we embrace the interwoven fabric of life, its triumphs and debacles, its exultation and disillusionment, its faith and hope.

To forgive is to feel the compassion, gentleness, tenderness, and caring that is always within our hearts, no matter how the world may seem at the moment. Forgiveness is the way to a place of inner peace and happiness, the way to our soul.

Dr Gerald Jampolsky

Hating yourself and hating the Universe are the same thing. Loving yourself and loving the Universe are the same thing. Not forgiving the Universe is a heavy burden to carry. Why not lighten your load?............If forgiving the Universe seems more than you can do, start by forgiving another person. Put down one suitcase at a time.

Gary Zukav

Let us share a memorable story from Paul Rep's classic *Zen Flesh, Zen Bones*:

One evening, a Zen master named Shichiri was reciting sutras when he was interrupted by a thief carrying a sharp sword.

"Do not disturb me," said Shichiri. "The money is kept in that old drawer. But do not take all. I need some to pay taxes tomorrow."

The thief took most of the money and as he was leaving, Shichiri said, "Thank a person when you have received a gift." The surprised thief thanked him and departed.

A few weeks later, the thief was caught while trying to steal from a rich merchant. The thief was put on trial who confessed, among others, his offence against Shichiri. When called upon as a witness, Shichiri told the magistrate, "This man was not a thief as far as I know. I gave the money to him and he had thanked me."

The Zen master's forgiveness deeply touched the thief. After his release from prison, he returned to Shichiri and became his disciple.

Why Is It Difficult For Us To Forgive?

Genuine forgiveness is difficult and rare, to the extent that it has become proverbial to identify forgiveness as a divine quality. The common reasons are:-

- We are confused about the nature of forgiveness

- We are unaware of the harmful effects of harboring an unforgiving mindset and attitude.

- Our phenomenal self lost connection with its deep essence and innate capacity to forgive

- We lack understanding of how to practice forgiveness.

Confusion About The Nature Of Forgiveness And Non-awareness Of The Harmful Effects of Non-forgiveness

Malice drinks one-half of its own poison.
                                    Marcus Annaeus Seneca

Many of us subtly cling to past grievances. We harbor anger, resentment and hatred against someone who mistreated, disappointed, humiliated or committed some wrongdoing against us. We may erroneously believe that this is the correct way to protect ourselves and to punish the wrongdoer. We may erroneously think that if we were to extend forgiveness to the wrongdoer, it would imply that we agree with his wrongdoing. We may think that to forgive is to admit that we were wrong and that the wrongdoer was correct. We may think that to forgive is to reveal that we are weak or cowardly.

It is important to clarify to ourselves that these beliefs are not accurate. To harbor an unforgiving mindset is to cripple the wings of our broadmindedness, surround our heart with barbed wires and imprison ourselves in a dark dudgeon. To harbor an unforgiving mindset is to subtly recycle and reinforce inner negativities, anger, resentment and hostility. We exude "attack thoughts" against others. Harboring negative and hostile energies corrode our inner peace and physical health, preventing us to realize our deep potential. As explained by the Buddha, "Holding on to anger is like grasping a hot coal with the intent of throwing it at someone else; you are the one who gets burned."

............*when we perceive another person as attacking us, we usually feel defensive, and find a way, directly or indirectly, to attack back. Attack always stems from fear and guilt. No one attacks unless he first feels threatened and believes that through attack he can demonstrate his own strength,, at the expense of another's vulnerability.*

Dr Gerald Jampolsky
Forgiveness

The idea of getting rid of our anger by giving vent to it has some dramatic appeal....... but the problem is that this method simply does not work. Many studies over the past four decades have consistently shown that the verbal and physical expression of our anger does nothing to dispel it and just makes things worse.

Dr Howard Cutler

In Life Strategies, Dr Philip McGraw wrote, "Hatred, anger and resentment eat away at the heart and soul of the person who carries them......When you harbor hatred, anger, resentment and bitterness, our body's chemical balance is dramatically disrupted. Your fight or flight responses stay aroused continuously and they are incompatible with a relaxed state of mind." Dr Jampolsky also stressed that, "Our lack of forgiveness can eat us alive, creating tension that limits our relationships and attacks our bodies."

Common symptoms associated with an unforgiving mindset may include headaches, backaches, stomach ulcers, fatigue, lack of energy, anxiety, irritability, depression, tenseness, sleeplessness, etc. Thus, to harbor an unforgiving mindset is self-punishing. We are choosing to harm our physical health and to sink deeper into the abyss of self-imposed misery and inner negativities.

Psychologists also explained that to a certain extent, our unforgiving mindset, our frequent criticisms and harsh judgments of others, may reflect hidden guilt. They may also reflect some darker aspects of our personality that we could not openly acknowledge. We may thereby unconsciously project our anger, fear, sense of insecurity, hidden guilt or subtle non-acceptance of the darker aspects of our personality onto others' behavior and launch criticisms against them. As observed by Herman Hesse, "If you hate a person, you hate something in him that is part of yourself."

How do we gain deeper insight into the truths that forgiveness does not mean that we agree with wrongdoing and unethical acts; that forgiveness manifests broadmindedness and moral vision, rather than a sign of weakness or cowardice; that forgiveness is a stepping-stone to inner peace and happiness? The following pages will explore these questions.

Connecting With Our Innate Capacity To Forgive

Many of us could not forgive ourselves. We could not forgive ourselves for not meeting our high expectations and not achieving our goals. We could not forgive ourselves for not meeting the expectations and standards of our parents, spouses, children, siblings, bosses and colleagues. Subtle self-dislike and self-rejection begin to germinate, corroding our healthy self-esteem.

To heal and resolve inner strife, discontent, frustrations and emotional negativities, we need to nurture a forgiving mindset. We need to extend insightful compassion, kind understanding and affection to ourselves and others.

By undertaking inner cultivation, we realize that on many occasions, we have been too harsh and demanding on ourselves. Our galloping mind is prone to endless comparisons with the rich and successful. We tend to disallow ourselves to celebrate and enjoy little successes on our journey toward positive growth and maturation.

To experience self-forgiveness, we need to touch our higher dimension. By nurturing a healthy insightful awareness and gently reminding ourselves that external events and failures cannot impair our innate wholesomeness, we gradually dislodge unhealthy preoccupation with external success and self-aggrandizement. Our sense of inadequacy relating to jealousy over the achievements of others will also soften.

When low self-esteem and self-dislike assault us, we gently remind ourselves that our commitment to worthwhile goals is commendable and intrinsically fulfilling. We gently remind ourselves that external success depends on many conditions that are not entirely within our control. Guided by heart wisdom, we channel positive energies in working toward constructive goals that create value for others. Regardless of whether the outcomes finally materialize, we learn to derive intrinsic fulfillment from engaging in worthwhile activities.

With ripening wisdom, our capacity to forgive the imperfections of our phenomenal self as well as those of others will mature. From the higher perspective, improvement does not apply to our divine essence which is intrinsically wholesome. Nonetheless, the physical, mental and emotional aspects of our phenomenal self need to be nurtured for they have been subject to years of negative environmental conditioning. If we are not mindful, we can slip into spiritual unconsciousness and become non-receptive to our heart wisdom.

During these moments of spiritual unconsciousness, our thoughts, words and deeds are not attuned to our heart wisdom. They lack kind understanding and kind intentions. When we slip into spiritual unconsciousness, we need to quickly catch ourselves and realign our intentions, words or deeds with the deep harmony of our soul. Such mindfulness practice serves to fulfill our deep potential and minimize the emergence of unkind behavior.

By extending kind understanding to the imperfections of our phenomenal self, we learn to forgive ourselves. We learn to forgive our past spiritually unconscious thoughts, words and deeds. Self-forgiveness serves to heal feelings of guilt and confusion over past mistakes. It serves to restore healthy self-esteem. We can thereby commit ourselves to learn from our past mistakes, identify worthwhile life goals that create value for others, and re-commit ourselves to become constructive members of our family and society.

There are no chains like hatred............
Dwelling on your brother's faults multiplies your own.
You are far from the end of your journey.

The Buddha

We also extend kind understanding to occasional feelings of self-dislike and self-rejection for not achieving external goals, for not living up to our expectations, for not living up to the expectations of our parents, spouses, teachers, relatives, colleagues and friends. We gently remind ourselves of our inherent wholesomeness and goodness. We commit ourselves to improve our shortcomings. Gradually, we dissipate the compulsive need to score external victories, to obtain the approval and recognition of others. We learn to be guided by our heart wisdom and pure-hearted commitment to worthwhile goals.

We also learn to soften, dissolve and let go of our guilt, self-dislike and unhappiness through compassionate self-understanding, through compassionate exploration of our weaknesses, egoistic urges and the darker aspects of our

331

personality. We understand that our negative urges originate from having lost touch with our innate wholesomeness; from years of negative environmental conditioning; from an erroneous belief that we are a conglomerate of animal instincts without a spiritual dimension; and from skepticism and cynicism of human kindness. Through self-forgiveness, by committing ourselves to mindful ethical living, we retouch our innate wholesomeness. We redefine our values and life goals, and gradually rebuild a healthy self-esteem.

In addition, through undertaking meditations on a daily basis, we learn that anger, resentment and hostile energies are non-substantial and evanescent in nature. By nurturing a healthy insightful awareness during meditative moments and during normal waking hours, we cultivate the skilful mindset to watch them arise and pass away. We learn to liberate ourselves from the pernicious habit of venting anger and hostile energies on others.

............*I believe that generally speaking, anger and hatred are the type of emotions which, if you leave them unchecked or unattended, tend to aggravate and keep on increasing. If you simply get more and more used to letting them happen and just keep expressing them, this usually results in their growth, not their reduction. So, I feel that the more you adopt a cautious attitude and actively try to reduce the level of their force, the better it is.*

The Dalai Lama

The power of self-forgiveness is divine. It is miraculous and liberating. We experience a profound sense of inner freedom and vibrancy. It is as if we are given a new lease of life. Upon extending kind understanding and forgiveness to the imperfections of our phenomenal self, our compassionate heart can breathe again. A healthy sense of self-esteem, self-acceptance and self-appreciation can blossom again. The cultivation of spiritual qualities and forgiveness of others can truly commence. Without experiencing self-forgiveness, our efforts to nurture a constructive relationship with ourselves and others are tenuous.

Upon experiencing self-forgiveness, we learn to extend insightful compassion and kind understanding to others. We learn to empathize with their spiritually unconscious thoughts, words and deeds, their inner negativities for harboring an unforgiving eye-for-eye tooth-for-tooth mindset. We gently remind ourselves that we are all human beings implanted with the sacred seeds of innate wholesomeness. By forgiving the spiritually unconscious words and deeds of others, by forgiving their slippage into spiritual unconsciousness, we allow our compassionate heart to mature and ripen.

Wealth-Creation Secret #55
As we progress along the spiritual path, we will occasionally stumble. Self-forgiveness based on insightful understanding of our natural limitations offers the inner nutrition to sustain our commitment to positive growth.

How Do We Practice Forgiveness?

(1)   We Learn To Effectively Manage Our Expectations

To practice forgiveness, we need to be realistic. As a starting point, we learn to effectively manage our expectations, guarding against idealism. In being realistic about the shortcomings and imperfections of other people around us, we can more effectively manage our disappointment and disillusionment when we encounter the darker aspects of human personality. In *Life Strategies*, Dr Philip McGraw highlighted "ten common characteristics of human functioning":-

- *The number one fear among all people is rejection.*
- *The number one need among all people is acceptance.*
- *To manage people effectively, you must do it in a way that protects or enhances their self-esteem.*
- *Everybody approaches every situation with at least some concern about "what's in it for me".*
- *Everybody prefers to talk about things that are important to them personally.*
- *People hear and incorporate only what they understand.*
- *People like, trust and believe those who like them.*
- *People often do things for other than the apparent reasons.*
- *Even people of quality can be, and often, are petty and small.*
- *Everybody wears a social mask.*

To effectively practice forgiveness, we need to bear in mind the above common characteristics of human behavior. We can thereby more effectively manage our expectations when interacting with others. Specifically, we remind ourselves to focus more on giving, contributing and creating value for others, surrendering unhealthy notions of gain and reward. We also learn not to expect others to be grateful to us when we perform kind deeds.

Recall the incident when Jesus was traveling along the border between Samaria and Galilee. As he was going into a village, ten men who had leprosy met him. They stood at a distance and called out to him, "Jesus, Master, have pity on us!"

Thereupon, Jesus healed them and they were cleansed. However, only one of them turned back and thanked him.

"Were not all ten cleansed? Where are the other nine?" Jesus asked.

This story serves to remind us that gratitude is rare. We need not expect people to express gratefulness to us when we performed kind deeds. Rather, we learn to derive intrinsic fulfillment by performing kind deeds, and not to seek the commendation and recognition of others.

Wealth-Creation Secret #56
We need to nurture realistic expectations of the many people around us, be it in our families, neighborhood or workplaces, and be cognizant of their spiritual unconsciousness and inadequacies. We need to learn to forgive their spiritually unconscious words and deeds, their foibles and idiosyncrasies. Such forgiveness will connect us with the unity of humanity and enable us to touch the higher dimension of our being.

---

(2)   We Learn To Cease Clinging To The Past

Can sand flow upward in the hour glass? Will the sun rise where it sets and set where it rises? Can I relive the errors of yesterday and right them? Can I call back yesterday's wounds and make them whole? Can I become younger than yesterday? Can I take back the evil that was spoken, the blows that were struck, the pain that was caused? No. Yesterday is buried forever and I will think of it no more.

Og Mandino
The Greatest Salesman In The World

To be born again is to let the past go, and look without condemnation upon the present............You are but asked to let the future go, and place it in God's Hands. And you will see by your experience that you have laid the past and present in His Hands as well............

A Course In Miracles

In his book How To Get What You Want And Want What You Get, Dr John Gray wrote, *"Some people carry guilty feelings an entire lifetime for stealing bubble gum at the drugstore, or for saying something mean and hurting in grade school. Little mistakes can haunt us for a lifetime when we don't know how to get unstuck from guilt."*

To nurture a broadminded forgiving mindset that nourishes inner peace and harmony, we should let go of unhealthy clinging to the past. We should commit ourselves to learn from our past mistakes and recommit ourselves to worthy life goals. We gently remind ourselves that the past resembles an evening mist. Its haziness cloaks the impermanence and transitory nature of phenomenal events. We need not grasp at it. Our future need not be fettered and constricted by past traumas or distressing events. Rather, we can allow our inner Light to shine on them and let it reveals that by forgoing unhealthy clinging to the past, we can awaken to the rejuvenating bountiful present, its rich tapestries and nuances of possibilities. Each moment is a fresh new moment. Each kaleidoscopic moment blossoms and comes to fruition in a unique way. By becoming attentive to each burgeoning moment, we participate viscerally and vibrantly in creating a new inner reality. Our inviolate wholesomeness shines forth. We relearn to commit ourselves to focus positive attention on the present moments, to engage in worthwhile activities that create value for ourselves and others. This is the stepping stone to fulfilling our talent and deep potential.

Finish every day and be done with it. You have done what you could. Some blunders and absurdities no doubt crept in; forget them as fast as you can. Tomorrow is a new day; begin it well and serenely...............

Ralph Waldo Emerson

Wealth-Creation Secret #57
We gain access to inner affluence by discarding attachment to the past, by stopping the habit of mentally recycling unpleasant events in the past. Gently affirm to ourselves that past events cannot undermine our inner sanctity.

---

(3) We Learn To Be Non-Judgmental And To Dig For Hidden Gold

When multi-millionaire Andrew Carnegie was interviewed on how he managed his employees, his reply was, "Dealing with people is like digging gold. When you go digging for gold, you have to remove tons of dirt to get an ounce of gold. But when you go digging for gold, you don't go looking for the dirt. You go for the gold."

In fostering constructive relationships with others, we identify the strengths and good points of others, and ponder on how we can learn from them. We hunt for the nuggets of wisdom hidden in others. We gently remind ourselves that all human beings are innately wholesome, that they can awaken to their divine spark.

By nurturing a broadminded attitude, we learn to respect others and their different viewpoints. As advised by Dr Denis Waitley, we practice empathy by becoming *"more open and sensitive to the needs and differences of others. Successful individuals look toward relative viewpoints rather than absolutes. We empathise and understand that each human being has the right to fulfill his own positive potential."*

By dislodging our judgmental faultfinding mindset, we learn not to focus on the failings and shortcomings of others. Instead, we seek to deeply understand their frame of mind, their past experiences, family and educational backgrounds, and perceive things from their perspective. In this way, we can better understand their concern and feelings and can more effectively search for win-win solutions.

Years ago, I had several colleagues who were prone to emotional outbursts. As my relationship with them deepened, I realized that they were harboring subtle discontent and insecurity. Hence, they were highly self-protective and frequently exuded negative energies. By extending kind understanding to their inner turmoil, I could better sympathize with their work-related stress. Gradually, I learn to extend forgiveness to their occasional emotional outbursts. In hindsight, I could now extend thankfulness to these difficult people for offering the opportunity to cultivate patience and compassion.

As I continue to nurture a forgiving mindset, whenever I encounter difficult persons, I seek to adopt their perspective. Usually, I discover that they are driven by the fear of being taken advantage of, by the fear of having an unfair bargain, by skepticism about human kindness or an inflated sense of self-importance. With this understanding, we can step into the shoes of these difficult persons, comprehend their main concerns and sincerely discuss with them on how to arrive at win-win solutions.

...........it is in fact the presence of this hateful state of mind in the enemy, the intention to hurt us, that makes the enemy's action unique. Otherwise, if it is just the actual act of hurting us, then we would hate doctors and consider them as enemies because they adopt methods which can be painful, such as surgery. But still, we do not consider these acts as harmful......because the intention of the doctor was to help us. So, therefore, it is exactly this willful intention to harm us that makes the enemy unique, and gives us this precious opportunity to practice patience.

The Dalai Lama
The Art of Happiness

Wealth-Creation Secret #58
By viewing difficult people, our competitors and rivals
as God-given opportunities to practice forbearance, patience
and empathy, we can more easily forgive
their spiritually unconscious words and deeds.

---

(4)   We Learn To Look Beyond The Masks Worn By People

In nurturing broadmindedness and a forgiving mindset, we learn to look beyond the social masks worn by people around us. We should not be deceived by their smug appearance, pretense and pseudo-confidence.

Many of the people around us are suffering from inner dislocation, existential confusion, loneliness, self-dislike and self-alienation. By learning to extend kind understanding and empathy to the people around us, we become little flames of warmth and kindness that brighten their lives. By shining our inner Light into the baffled and perturbed souls of others, we can cast positive rays of hope and joy into their inner reality. We learn to be receptive to the cracks in their social masks, the chinks in their social armor, the pores in their steel-like egos. By extending compassionate understanding to their compulsiveness to maintain a variety of social masks and pretences, we lend a willing ear, a sincere hand and a forgiving heart to their suppressed fear. Our compassionate hearts become mutually strengthened in precious moments of awakening to the sacred regions of our being. As revealed by the following anonymous confession, we all need sincere acceptance and love:-

"Don't be fooled by me. Don't be fooled by the face I wear. I wear a mask. I wear a thousand masks — — masks that I am afraid to take off; and one of them are me.

Pretending is an art that is second nature to me, but don't be fooled. For my sake, don't be fooled, I give the impression that I am secure, that all is sunny and unruffled within me as well as without; that confidence is my name and coolness my game, that the water is calm and I am in command; and that I need no one. But don't believe me, please. My surface may seem smooth, but my surface is my mask...............

Beneath lies no smugness, no complacence. Beneath dwells the real me in confusion, in fear, in aloneness. But I hide that. I don't want anybody to know it. I panic at the thought of my weakness and fear being exposed. That's why I frantically create a mask to hide behind — a nonchalant, sophisticated façade — — to help me pretend, to shield me from the glance that knows. But such a glance is precisely my salvation, my only salvation, and I know it. That is, if it's followed by acceptance; if it's followed by love……"

Anonymous letter,
extracted from Denis Waitley's Seeds of Greatness

Wealth-Creation Secret #59
By nurturing the ability to see through the pretence and social masks of the people around us,
we learn to touch their inner confusion, frustration and turmoil.
Our capacity to sympathize and to forgive would be enhanced.

---

(5)   We Learn That Forgiveness Does Not Involve Forgoing Moral Reasoning And Ethical Principles

As mindful living is embedded in everyday living, forgiveness does not involve forgoing moral reasoning, ethical principles and values which are valuable for sustaining our ethical vision. We therefore continue to engage in moral reasoning, to distinguish between ethically correct and incorrect thoughts, words and deeds. We continue to uphold ethical norms and rules. We also inculcate in our children correct ethical principles and values, teaching and enjoining them not to commit wrongdoing.

Thus, forgiveness does not mean that we agree with the wrongdoing of other people. We continue to cognitively and rationally identify them as morally wrong. We continue to advocate that we should not commit wrongdoing, that we should not transgress basic ethical principles like the Golden

Rule and the Silver Rule. We continue to denounce immoral and law-violating deeds that are detrimental to human well-being.

For example, if we became aware that one of our neighbors is a terrorist who is planning to plant a bomb in a shopping mall, although we forgive his spiritual unconsciousness, we should proactively take actions to stop him from harming innocent people (eg. notifying the local authorities). Forgiveness does not mean that we agree with or support actions that undermine the well-being of other people.

Furthermore, forgiveness does not mean that we passively accept or endure unjust or harmful actions against us. We should honor our own well-being as well as that of others. Forgiveness is an inner process of releasing ourselves from the festering grip of resentment, enmity, vindictiveness and aggressive energies. It is an inner healing and life-rejuvenating process. Inner negativities are transmuted into positive energies, into broadminded acceptance of the ugly aspects of human personalities. It also awakens us more deeply to the preciousness of our body as a sacred vessel to manifest the higher dimension of our being. We therefore treasure our soul and body in a healthy balanced way. In forgiving difficult people who have mistreated or harmed us, we do not mindlessly expose ourselves to their mistreatment or spiritually unconscious deeds. If these difficult people did not awaken to their reprehensible deeds and improve their character, we can extend kind understanding to them and choose to leave the situation. Sharon Salzberg highlighted this issue in *Lovingkindness*:-

Forgiveness does not mean condoning a harmful action, or denying injustice or suffering. It should never be confused with being passive toward violation or abuse. Forgiveness is an inner relinquishment of guilt or resentment, both of which are devastating to us in the end. As forgiveness grows within us, it may take any outward form: we may seek to make amends, demand justice, resolve to be treated better, or simply leave a situation behind us.

Wealth-Creation Secret #60
We should adopt the Middle Way approach to practicing forgiveness and broadmindedness, ie. although we forgive the spiritually unconscious words and deeds of others, we continue to uphold moral principles and values.
Only by denouncing, opposing and using all appropriate means to prevent immoral behavior can we contribute to the education, reformation and positive growth of spiritually unconscious people.

---

(6)   We Learn To Positively Re-Interpret Distressing Experiences

Forgiveness is letting go of our tendency to hold others responsible for our plight in this world. We do not hold grudges or resentment against them.

John Gray

Forgiveness involves nurturing and exercising our healthy insightful awareness to re-interpret our perception of distressing events. Specifically, when we encounter difficult persons who mistreat or commit some wrongdoing against us, we gently remind ourselves that our inner wholesomeness remains intact. The spiritually unconscious words and deeds of others cannot impair our inner wholesomeness. This serves to sustain healthy self-esteem and a broadminded forgiving mindset, to heal our misperception that others can genuinely destroy us. Their spiritually unconscious words or deeds may hurt our physical body. However, they cannot harm or impair our divine essence and inner sanctity. This is the higher truth, the wellspring of genuine peace.

By attuning our internal dialogue to this higher truth, we can positively transform our interpretations of the unkind, spiritually unconscious, defensive, judgmental and faultfinding behavior of others. We learn to regard them as catalysts and opportunities for ripening our heart wisdom. We gently remind ourselves that these difficult people are already acting to the best level of their emotional and spiritual consciousness. For them to reach higher planes of fruitful existence, they need to awaken to their deep essence. We gradually learn to sympathize with their fearful, protective, defensive and faultfinding behavior as surreptitious calls for our affection.

A group of students were studying how a caterpillar turned into a butterfly. The biology teacher instructed them to watch carefully how the butterfly would struggle to emerge from the cocoon. However, the students should not assist the butterfly to free itself from the cocoon. The teacher went out of the classroom for a while.

The students waited impatiently and it happened. The butterfly struggled to free itself from the cocoon. However, one of the students did not heed the teacher's instruction. He broke the cocoon so that the butterfly need not struggle to disentangle itself. To their dismay, the butterfly began to shrivel and die.

When the teacher returned, he explained that the butterfly died as it was deprived of the opportunity to struggle out of the cocoon and to strengthen its wings.

In encountering adversities, we should gently remind ourselves that we need to undergo trials in order to strengthen our character. This is tersely captured by the English proverb: A smooth sea never made a skilful mariner. By nurturing our capacity to positively reinterpret adversities and our perceptions of the behavior of difficult people, we learn to be responsible for our own thoughts and feelings toward others. We let go of an unhealthy mindset which constantly pictures ourselves as helpless victims and we learn to cease blaming others for our inner negativities.

Wealth-Creation Secret #61
When we encounter adversities and unfortunate events,
we are prone to lament, to hate the configurations of the universe
and wonder why God did not create a less blemished world.
Let us compose ourselves. Let our afflictive emotions arise and
pass away naturally. Gently remind ourselves that it is the
impermanence and flaws of this phenomenal world that can
accelerate our deep awakening.

---

(7)   Forgiveness Is An Ongoing Process

As authentic living involves nurturing constructive relationships with ourselves and others, forgiveness is an ongoing process. It is a moment-to-moment connection with our heart wisdom. As explained by Dr Gerald Jampolsky, *"Forgiveness is not one of those things which we never complete in our lives. It is ongoing, always a work in progress."*

Being an ongoing process, we seek to nurture a broadminded forgiving mindset and kind intentions by connecting with our inner sanctity on a daily basis. Gradually, we understand that forgiveness does not prescribe other people to change. It does not require other person to conform to our expectations and ethical standards. Rather, genuine forgiveness is pure kind understanding. It is whole-hearted acceptance of the inadequacies, failings, weaknesses and faults of others, trusting that in due course, they will awaken to their deep essence and tread the spiritual path.

Genuine forgiveness also does not anticipate return or commendation. Rather, we forgive silently in the bottom of our heart. In many instances, it is appropriate that we do not inform others that we have forgiven them. We silently extend our kind understanding toward them and wish them well. Inner peace and tranquility are the natural fruits of our commitment to cultivate a forgiving mindset.

Forgiveness releases us from inner strife and warfare, from a sense of being victimized, exploited and controlled by others, from the compulsive recycling of hostile emotions. Forgiveness releases us from being imprisoned in the past, from morbid fixation on the past. By healing and letting go of past grievances, we stop strangling our compassionate heart and let it breathe again. By letting go of the past, we discover our inner freedom to reinvent ourselves and realize our deep potential.

When someone has hurt us deeply, to extend forgiveness is not easy. However, in due course, we will realize that forgiveness is the miraculous antidote that can heal our deep wounds. We discover that our inner capacity to forgive is truly divine, the doorway to positive self-transformation, inner healing and rejuvenation. By extending forgiveness and kind understanding to persons who committed wrongs against us, we retouch our inner wholesomeness. By tapping upon our heart wisdom to positively re-interpret and lessen recurring mental images and episodes of the harm done against us, we gradually heal our deep wounds. Once again, we gently remind ourselves that external events and the wrongs done against us cannot impair our innate wholesomeness and sanctity. Our divine essence remains intact. Letting go of our grief, sorrow and attachment to dualistic notions of right and wrong, we discover our inviolate access to the higher arena of fruitful living.

For most people forgiveness is a process. When you have been deeply wounded, the work of forgiveness can take years. It will go through many stages — — grief, rage, sorrow, fear, and confusion — — and in the end, if you let yourself feel the pain you carry, it will come as a relief, as a release for your heart. You will see that forgiveness is fundamentally for your own sake, a way to carry the pain of the past no longer.

Dr Jack Kornfield
A Path With Heart

Wealth-Creation Secret #62
The precious seed of forgiveness will take shoot if we water it everyday. Its roots will deepen and it will grow and strengthen to become the redwood of compassion, patience, empathy and inner affluence.

---

(8)   We Learn That The Time Is Always Ripe To Forgive

The time is always ripe to forgive, to nurture a broadminded forgiving mindset. The time is always ripe to forgive ourselves and others, to surrender our perfectionist idealistic standards that arise from years of negative environmental conditioning.

Guided by heart wisdom, we learn to renounce unrealistic expectations and standards that we imposed on ourselves and others. We learn to appreciate and treasure our strengths and unique talents, our divine capacity to forgive, our innate capacity to sprinkle kind intentions into our thoughts, words and deeds. The following is an inspiring example of forgiveness on the national level which is eloquently expressed by Dr Roger von Oech in *Expect The Unexpected:-*

After World War I the victorious countries.............. demanded reparations from Germany. This imposition turned out to be the most costly political decision of the entire World War I era. Not only did it undermine Germany's economic recovery and weaken its already enfeebled political system, it also fostered the conditions that led to the rise of Hitler and the Nazis.

A generation later, after World War II, Europe again faced economic and political chaos. But instead of demanding reparations from the vanquished Axis powers, the Allies took the opposite approach in dealing with the situation. Through its massive Marshall Plan aid, the United States helped to rebuild much of the continent's economic infrastructure, including Germany's. In doing so, it created conditions that encouraged both economic health and political stability.

To tread the royal road to inner and outer success, we need to cultivate constructive relationship with ourselves and others. We need to extend kind understanding, patience, compassion, empathy, broadmindedness and generosity to others. We need to continuously probe and hunt for the nuggets of wisdom hidden in each person. Forgiveness is the glittering golden thread that sews all these elements together into a beautiful garment for our soul. Forgiveness is also the sacred flaming torch that lights up the higher dimension of our being, revitalizing and remolding us into a constructive force in the world.

Whenever I meet people I always approach them from the standpoint of the most basic things we have in common. We each have a physical structure, a mind, emotions. We are all born in the same way, and we all die...............Looking at others from this standpoint rather than emphasizing secondary differences such as the fact that I am Tibetan, or a different color, religion, or cultural background, allows me to have a feeling that I'm meeting someone just the same as me, I find that relating to others on that level makes it much easier to exchange and communicate with one another............

The Dalai Lama
The Art of Happiness

We learn to look at life from the perspective that we are spiritual beings who are just temporarily in these bodies of ours.......... And what forgiveness teaches us is that it is possible to choose love over fear and peace over conflict, regardless of the circumstances affecting our lives.

Dr Gerald Jampolsky

Spiritual Exercise: Meditation On Forgiveness

Get rid of all bitterness, rage and anger, brawling and slander, along with every form of malice. Be kind and compassionate to one another, forgiving each other, just as in Christ God forgave you.

Ephesians: 4: 31 - 32

Undertake breath-counting meditation for ten minutes and creative visualization to touch our inner wholesomeness. Thereafter, repeat the following phrases slowly ten times. We do not need to recall or conjure up any images. Repeating the following phrases has significant effect on healing patent or hidden guilt, grudges, enmity and aggressiveness. We can do this simple exercise on a daily basis to cleanse and purify emotional negativities. Alternatively, if there are specific difficult people whom we wish to extend our forgiveness, we can visualize them as newborn babies and repeat the pertinent phrases.

If I have consciously or unconsciously hurt anyone, I sincerely seek their forgiveness.

I am touching my divine capacity to forgive. If I have intentionally or unintentionally hurt or harm anyone, I seek God's forgiveness (or the forgiveness of the Higher Power). Please forgive me. I am grateful for divine forgiveness.

I am touching my divine capacity to forgive. If I have intentionally or unintentionally hurt or harm anyone, I extend kind understanding to myself. I forgive myself.

I am touching my divine capacity to forgive. If I did not meet the expectations and standards of my parents, spouse, friends or colleagues, I extend kind understanding to myself. I have tried my best and will commit myself to improve. I forgive myself.

I am touching my divine capacity to forgive. I forgive all the people who have intentionally or unintentionally hurt or harm me. I extend kind understanding and compassion to their spiritual unconsciousness.

* * * * * *

Wealth-Creation Wisdom 8
Practicing And Embodying
The Eight Pillars Of Genuine Wealth

Keep on sowing your seed, for you never know which will grow — — perhaps it all will.

Ecclesiastes 11:6

If in your heart you make a manger for His birth, then God will once again become a child on this earth.

Angelus Silesius

There are two ways to live your life, one is as though nothing is a miracle, the other as if everything is.

Albert Einstein

First Pillar Of Genuine Wealth: Practicing The Eightfold Path of Higher Wisdom

Let us share Loren Eiseley's memorable story of The Star Thrower, which was retold in Denis Waitley's Seeds of Greatness.

Once there was a young man who noticed that the shell collectors at a beach resort during the busy tourist season sought to outdo each other in collecting, hoarding and amassing different types of glimmering sea shells of various colors, shapes and sizes. They were attempting to collect life and its prized possessions and amass outward happiness.

However, the young man also noticed a solitary figure engaged in certain activity near the edge of the coming waves at a quiet corner of the beach resort. The figure would persistently stooped over, picked up something and vibrantly threw it away.

The young man decided to walk over and enquire what was the older man doing. When the older man saw him approaching, he smiled and waved at him.

"May I ask what are you doing?" the young man shouted across the beach.

"I am a star thrower," the older man replied with a sincere broad grin. He stooped over again, briskly scooped up another starfish and gracefully threw it far out into the sea. "It may live if the offshore pull is strong enough," he explained.

Are we acting like the tourists who are preoccupied with collecting, hoarding and amassing outward prizes? Do we lull ourselves into believing that happiness and joy depend on amassing material wealth, gaining social status, chasing after romantic relationships and other chimerical trophies? Are we mesmerized by these outward prizes? Are we oblivious of the deep significance of authentic living, of the need to dissipate self-fixation, so as to creatively participate in life and contribute to the well-being of others, be it starfishes, a "fainting robin", a needy person, our neigbors and friends, our aged parents or lovable children?

If I can stop one heart from breaking,
I shall not live in vain;
If I can ease one life the aching,
Or cool one pain,
Or help one fainting robin
Unto his nest again,

I shall not live in vain.

Emily Dickinson

Life cannot be collected. Happiness cannot be traveled to, owned, earned, worn, or consumed. Happiness is the spiritual experience of living every minute with love, grace and gratitude. The gift of life is not a treasure hunt...............the treasure is within you. It only needs to be uncovered and discovered. The secret is to turn a life of collection into a life of celebration.

Denis Waitley
Seeds of Greatness

To taste the deep significance of fruitful living, to turn a life of frenzied, hectic and aimless collection into a life of epiphanic celebration, to cultivate genuine wisdom and spiritual qualities, it is useful to avail ourselves to the insights of treading the eightfold path as taught by the Buddha. This Noble Eightfold Path which is also known as the Fourth Noble Truth comprises the foundational steps in building and positively transforming our phenomenal self. By patiently and constantly practicing them, we will align the physical, cognitive and emotive aspects of our phenomenal self to the deep harmony and potential of our deep essence. This Noble Eightfold Path consists of the following:-

- Wise Speech
- Wise Action
- Wise Livelihood
- Wise Effort
- Wise Mindfulness
- Wise Concentration
- Wise Intention
- Wise Understanding

Wise Speech means to abstain from saying untruths; from spreading falsehoods or slander that foster misunderstanding, disharmony, enmity and discord; from using harsh and abusive language with unkind intentions; and from idle babble and harmful gossip. We should extend our insightful awareness, to pierce through the unkind intentions of using abusive or harmful words. We should apply mindfulness and catch ourselves slipping into unkind intentions. It will dawn on us that part and parcel of our inner cultivation consists of ensuring that our words and language are conducive to positive communication, to promoting harmony, accord and understanding, to enhancing the maturation of others as well as our own. It will dawn on us that ensuring that our words arise from kind intentions and are guided by inner wisdom is to quantum leap to the higher plane of mindful living. With ripening wisdom, we realize that much of the discord, enmity, contentions and disputes in this world arose from abusive or harmful words that were motivated by spiritual unconsciousness and torpor. Using compassionate and sympathetic words is a valuable conduit to planting, gardening, fertilizing and cultivating the seeds of fruitful living in our hearts.

Wise Action means engaging in deeds that are sincere, honest, peace-loving, honorable and accord with our authentic life purpose. It means that our behavior and daily activities should be guided by heart wisdom and compassionate intentions, rather than by self-centeredness and selfish motives. Our deeds should be conducive to the cultivation of positive spiritual qualities, to personal maturation and to the well-being of others. We should therefore abstain from behavior and deeds that would physically or emotionally harm others. Our deeds should reflect our insight into the innate sanctity of all sentient beings. Thus, we should refrain from harming and destroying life, from indulging in sense pleasure and amassing material wealth at the expense of others, from engaging in sexual misconduct, from engaging in dishonest, immoral or illegal acts that would undermine the well-being of others.

I awoke and saw that life was service.
I acted and behold, service was joy.

Rabindranath Tagore

Christ has no body now on earth but yours,
no hands but yours, no feet but yours;
Yours are the eyes through which is to look out
Christ's compassion to the world;
Yours are the feet with which he is to go about doing good;
Yours are the hands with which he is to bless men now.

St. Teresa of Avila

Wise Livelihood means that we should abstain from earning our living through dishonest, immoral, fraudulent or illegal means, like cheating, lying, stealing, embezzling others' money, deceiving the young and guileless, etc. We should choose an occupation that accords with our integrity and authentic life purpose, that is conducive to our positive growth and would create value for others.

Always do right. This will gratify some and astonish the rest.

Mark Twain

Wise Effort, in the context of Buddhist wisdom, means using our positive willpower (a) to prevent unwholesome states of mind from arising; (b) to dissipate unwholesome states of mind that have already arisen; (c) to produce and to cause to arise wholesome states of mind that are not yet arisen; and (d) to nurture and cultivate wholesome states of mind that already arose. In the contemporary context, by undertaking daily meditation and mind concentration exercises, we nurture a healthy insightful awareness and mindfulness that enable us to catch ourselves slipping into negative or unwholesome mental-emotional states. As discussed in chapter 6, by re-interpreting our perceptual experiences and mental-emotional states, we can thereby positively transform them into healthy, wholesome and positive mental states. We are thereby induced to engage in constructive activities that create value for ourselves and others.

Wise Mindfulness means that we can focus our attention on the activity at hand in a healthy way. We should not let our roaming mind from being negatively distracted and preoccupied about the past or future. We should cultivate a healthy awareness of our bodily activities, our physical sensations and feelings, our mental energies and dynamics, our thoughts, ideas, conceptions, rationalizations and thinking patterns. By undertaking daily meditation, we nurture an in-depth awareness of how our sensations, perceptual experiences, thoughts, mental states, feelings and emotions arise and pass away, and that there is no permanent independent "self" orchestrating and chereographing the complex dance of our thoughts.

Wise Concentration, in the Buddhist context, refers to four main stages of Dhyana (ie. meditation). In the first stage of Dhyana, unwholesome thoughts, passions, energies and desires are calmed down and gradually dissipated. Nevertheless, feelings of joy, composure and happiness are maintained. In the second stage, intellectual activities are dispelled, and one-pointedness of the mind is developed.

Feelings of joy, tranquility and happiness are being maintained. In the third stage, the active sensation and feeling of joy is gradually dissipated, although a general sensation of equanimity, tranquility and inner peace remains. In the fourth stage of Dhyana, all sensations and feelings are surrendered, where our individuated subjective consciousness merges with the cosmic consciousness. Only a pure vibrant awareness remains.

Wise Intention refers to nurturing intentions and thoughts that are not controlled by egocentric urges. It refers to nurturing intentions and thoughts of affection, kind understanding and insight into the innate sanctity of all sentient beings. By expanding an insightful awareness, we learn to catch ourselves slipping into negative intentions or thoughts that reflect envy, jealousy, hatred, self-rejection, frustrations or enmity. As discussed in chapter 6, by undertaking creative visualization exercises and learning to reinterpret our perceptual experiences, we can generate healthy and wholesome intentions and mental-emotional states.

Wise Understanding means to gain insight into the higher truths and avail ourselves to the inner Light. We attain and sustain "wise understanding" by undertaking meditation and creative visualizations on a daily basis, whereby we learn to dissipate self-fixation, to tap upon our heart wisdom, to forgive our imperfections and those of others, to understand the interwoven nature of life. Human beings are imbued with divine luminosity and intelligence. We have the potential to awaken to the sanctified source of our being and quantum-leap to the higher plane of fruitful living congruent with the natural laws of inner and outer abundance. In his delightful book *Winning In The Game of*

Life, Tom Gegax wrote that the signs of spiritual maturity are as follows:-

- *Smiles appear. Those that were there before become wider.*
- *Dangerous curves no longer seem so dangerous. You have a sense that you can handle whatever lies ahead.*
- *You feel a sense of adventure about where you're going.*
- *You start to notice the scenery in way you didn't before.*
- *You don't feel guilty about stopping to rest.*
- *You enjoy being on the road with other people......*
- *You stop worrying about why other people are the way they are. Instead you start exploring and wondering why you are the way you are.*
- *You feel less need to judge other people and instead approach them with openness.*
- *You appreciate other people for their uniqueness, ready to learn from them.*
- *You notice that you feel grateful and happy more often.*

When you see life from within, you see wisdom, purpose, and faith as cornerstones of your family's foundation. You see through the eyes of love and reach our and touch all those with whom you come in contact. Seeing from within is having the courage to adapt to change and to persevere when the odds seem overwhelming. Seeing from within is believing that beauty and goodness are worth planting every day.

Denis Waitley
Seeds of Greatness

Wealth-Creation Secret #63
The path of higher wisdom and inner affluence is multi-dimensional,covering all aspects of everyday living.

Second Pillar of Genuine Wealth: Nurturing Inner Leadership And A Noble Character

If you want to be a leader, the good news is that you can do it. Everyone has the potential, but it isn't accomplished overnight. It requires perseverance...........Leadership doesn't develop in a day. It takes a lifetime.

John Maxwell

...........maturity will be the prime quality of the CEO of the future, permitting him or her the self-awareness to avoid unconscious programming, self-deception, the urge for power, and other temptations that ensnare less developed personalities. The achievement of this kind of maturity is at the very heart of spirituality.

Michael Thompson
The Congruent Life

One evening, a boy was learning from his grandfather the basic techniques of keeping a kite high in the sky. He enquired whether it was the strong wind which kept the kite flying. The grandfather patted the boy and explained that it was the string which made the kite to fly high. Puzzled, the boy said, "But I always thought that it was the string which prevents the kite from flying high." Thereupon, the grandfather decided to plant a seed of wisdom into the boy's supple mind. He walked away, returned with a pair of scissors and cut the string of the kite. Within a minute, the kite which was flying high in the sky came flickering down.

In a world that bombards us with messages on the overriding importance of quick gains, do we occasionally lapse into thinking that our uprightness, ethical values and beliefs are keeping us down? Do we occasionally lapse into thinking that we should hunt for shortcuts, that we could arrive at genuine success without nurturing honesty, integrity, temperance, discipline, ethical commitment and a noble character? Do we lapse into thinking that we could arrive at genuine success without developing inner leadership ability?

If you would lift me, you must be on higher ground.
Warren R. Austin

The first duty of a university is to teach wisdom, not trade; character, not technicalities.
Winston Churchill

Leaders are widely recognized to be crucial to organizational effectiveness and success. Although organizational procedures, policies and authority structures can facilitate control, it is the leader who offers the vision, identifies organizational goals and provides the direction to achieving them. Effective team-building from leaders is needed to provide the enthusiasm and inspiration to enhance group performance. Thus, modern corporations spend huge sums annually to recruit, evaluate and train individuals for leadership positions. In modern workplaces, many of us have encountered different types of leadership behaviors. Many of us have assumed or are assuming leadership roles. Hence, how do we interpret leadership?

In an organizational context, leadership can be interpreted, studied and analyzed in various ways. Conventional management literature identified leadership as a "follower-leader" process which is embedded within the dynamic processes of group activities, team-building, communication, delegation, employee motivation and interpersonal relationships. It involves effectively influencing employees and securing their support, commitment and effective performance to pursue organizational goals.

For the past few decades, most management theorists do not hold that leadership abilities are inborn and cannot be learned. Nevertheless, they recognize that some individuals have more leadership potential than others.

Conventional management literature also differentiated between managers and leaders. Broadly speaking, managers are concerned with the more routine well-defined management duties in the areas of planning, organizing, directing and controlling. They adopt a relatively impersonal attitude toward organizational goals and display a lower level of emotional involvement when interacting with their subordinates.

On the other hand, leaders or leader-managers seek to secure a high degree of work commitment, loyalty and enthusiasm from the employees. Thus, Robert Blake and Jane Mouton defined leadership as "the managerial activity that maximizes productivity, stimulates creative problem solving, and promotes morale and satisfaction".

Studies also indicated that leaders are intrinsically motivated. They adopt a more personal, proactive and passionate attitude toward the achievement of organizational goals. They display higher levels of emotional involvement and interest in the well-being and developmental needs of their followers. They continuously seek ways to motivate and inspire their followers to achieve idealized goals.

............*the Seeds of Greatness are not dependent upon the gifted birth, the inherited bank account, the intellect, the skin-deep beauty, the race, the color or the status. The Seeds of Greatness are attitudes and beliefs that begin in children as baby talk, as do's and don'ts, as casual family chatter, bedtime stories............*

Denis Waitley
Seeds of Greatness

John Maxwell, an authority on leadership, postulated the Law of the Lid. It states that "a person's leadership ability determines a person's level of effectiveness. The lower an individual's ability to lead, the lower the lid on his potential." This Law highlighted that it is our leadership ability that determines our effectiveness and the potential impact of our organization. This is particularly true for knowledge-based organizations with increasingly complex, non-routine and less procedurized task activities. To optimize individual and group performance in knowledge-based organizations, we need to fully tap our creativity and innovativeness. We need to motivate and inspire our subordinates and colleagues to contribute their best toward achieving challenging goals.

Since the 1950s, conventional management literature and leadership training emphasized the development of interpersonal and human relations skills, communication and influence techniques. Nonetheless, the conventional personal development framework was not adequately inner-oriented. It did not given sufficient emphasis on genuine character development. It is mainly concerned with questions like: How do I acquire superior interpersonal, communication and persuasion skills and techniques which will enable me to effectively influence other people? How do

I gain the trust of other people through self-image management and leveraging on a "winning attitude"?

Years of managerial experiences convince me that the focus of these questions is unclear. Leadership development is, first and foremost, not about influencing, motivating, guiding, coaching, mentoring and directing other people. Leadership development is, first and foremost, about leading, motivating, guiding, coaching, directing, inspiring and uplifting ourselves. It is an inner-oriented process. As emphasized by Dr Stephen Covey in *Principle-Centred Leadership*, "private victories precede public victories". John Maxwell's *The 21 Irrefutable Laws of Leadership* also stressed that "The first ability that every leader must have is the ability to lead and motivate himself". Paul Wharton's *Stories and Parables for Preachers and Teachers* contained the following confession of a Middle-Eastern mystic, "I was a revolutionary when I was young and all my prayer to God was: "Lord, give me the power to change the world." As I approached middle age, with my life half gone and without changing a single soul, I changed my prayer to: "Lord, give me the grace to change all those who come into contact with me, just my family and friends." Now that I am old and my days are numbered, I have realized my impudence. My one prayer now is: "Lord, give me the grace to change myself." If this had been my prayer from the beginning, most of my life would not be frittered away."

In reconceptualizing leadership, we need to awaken to the higher truth that before we can effectively influence, motivate, inspire and lead other people, we need to effectively motivate, inspire and lead ourselves. We need to develop constructive relationships with ourselves. If we cannot effectively motivate, inspire and lead ourselves, our intentions and efforts to positively motivate, inspire and lead others will be undermined. When the "rains came and the winds blew", when the trials and temptations arrive, when we encounter adverse events within and beyond the workplaces, our spiritual and emotional immaturity will be unveiled. The shallow "foundationless" nature of our leadership skills will be unveiled, exposing cosmetic self-assurance and confidence. John Maxwell cogently pointed out, "Leaders can never take others farther than they have gone themselves, for no one can travel without until he or she has first traveled within." Without a noble character, we are unable to chart a worthwhile course for ourselves, let alone charting a worthwhile course for others and for our organization.

Thus, the critical questions are, "How do we effectively motivate, inspire and lead ourselves? How do we effectively tap our inner resourcefulness and realize our leadership potential?"

This brings us back to the Wisdom Paradigm on personal development as discussed in Chapter Two. We plant and water the seeds of inner leadership by cultivating wisdom, by touching our deep essence, by nurturing positive spiritual qualities, like patience, empathy, compassion, forgiveness and broadmindedness. We plant and water the seeds of inner leadership by upholding the Golden Rule and the Silver Rule in our daily activities, by practicing the eightfold path of higher wisdom, by gradually healing inner negativities and egoistic urges, by attuning our words and deeds to our authentic life purpose. When the fruits of inner leadership ripen, our ability to effectively motivate and inspire others will also mature. If our outer leadership abilities are not built upon these inner fruits, they will be inadequate and shallow. When the trials and tribulations arrive, their "foundationless" nature is exposed. In the famous words of former US President Harry S. Truman, "In reading the lives of great man, I found that the first victory they won was over themselves.............."

Wealth-Creation Secret #64
The fruits of genuine leadership, maturity and inner wealth are borne by the tree of inner cultivation.

Third Pillar of Inner Wealth: Practicing Resolve, Commitment And Perseverance

I long to accomplish a great and noble task, but it is my chief duty to accomplish small tasks as if they were great and noble.
Helen Keller

Since younger days, I have inscribed the following words on the tablet of my heart:

Calvin Coolidge's Law Of Persistence

Nothing in the world can take the place of persistence.
Talent will not; nothing is more common that unsuccessful men with talent.
Genius will not; unrewarded genius is almost a proverb.
Education will not; the world is full of educated derelicts.
Persistence and determination alone are omnipotent.

To arrive at genuine success, persistence, perseverance and fortitude are pivotal. They are the golden rays that nourish the shoots of our latent gifts and talents. They give rise to imposing temples, cathedrals, monuments and pyramids; to uplifting poems, novels and speeches; to great discoveries, inventions and innovations; to constructive epoch-making social reforms. They give birth to bards, sages, statesmen, scientists, explorers, inventors, to Shakespeare, John Milton, Beethoven, George Washington, Thomas Jefferson, Benjamin Franklin, Ralph Waldo Emerson, Abraham Lincoln, Booker T. Washington, John Wesley, Dr Sun Yat-Sen, Helen Keller, Thomas Edison, Franklin Roosevelt, Winston Churchill, Mahatma Gandhi, Albert Schweitzer, Mother Teresa, Alva Myrdal, Margaret Thatcher and Nelson Mandela.

Keep on going, and the chances are that you will stumble on something perhaps when you are least expecting it. I never heard of anyone ever stumbling on something while sitting down.
Charles Kettering

Let us share two inspiring stories which exemplify the indefatigable human spirit when galvanized by worthwhile objectives.

The first is the memorable barefooted odyssey of Legson Kayira, an African lad, who aspired to obtain a college education in America. He literally walked thousands of miles across the rugged African terrain to achieve his dream. This touching story was retold in Dr Vincent Peale's *Enthusiasm Makes The Difference* as well as in Cynthia Kersey's *Unstoppable*. It is condensed below.

Legson Kayira grew up in the poor village of Mpale, in northern Nyasaland, East Africa. His father had died since he was young. His mother was illiterate. In 1952, his mother was touched by the words of the missionaries of the Church of Scotland and their family converted to Christianity. From the missionaries, young Legson learned not only to love God and his neighbors, but also of the importance of having an education. His teachers also gave him a Bible and a copy of Pilgrim's Progress.

As time elapsed, Legson became deeply moved by stories of Abraham Lincoln who rose from poverty to become an American president and Booker T. Washington who sloughed off the fetters of slavery to become a renowned reformer and educator. In October 1958, at about sixteen years old, Legson decided to go to America to obtain a college education. With a five-day supply of maize wrapped in banana leaves, an axe, his two treasured books and meager belongings, he left his home. He planned to walk to Cairo to board a ship to America. However, he was uncertain of the distance that he need to cover. He was unaware that Cairo was 3,000 miles away from his village and in between there were dozens of tribes as well as wild animals. However, Legson was determined to undertake this journey.

After walking for five days across the rugged African terrain, he had covered only 25 miles and already out of food. But he was not discouraged. He told himself that he would continue walking and would not stop until he reached America. He learned to develop a pattern of travel whereby he would cautiously enter each village and enquire whether he could work and earn some food and temporary shelter. If that were possible, he would spend the night there and move on to the next village the next morning. This pattern of travel lasted more than a year. He also bartered away his axe for a easily concealed knife, as the axe might give the impression that he was hostile. Based on this pattern, Legson sometimes found work and shelter as he traveled. However, he was alone most of the time and slept under the stars. When his food was finished, he would survive on wild fruits and edible plants. He was also struck by a fever and fell ill. Kind strangers treated him with herbal medicines and offered a place for him to recover. When he became better, despite being thin and weak, he continued his long journey and kept walking............

On 19 January 1960, fifteen months after he left his village, he had walked nearly a thousand miles to Kampala, the capital of Uganda. He found a job making bricks for government buildings and remained there for six months. During his spare time, he visited the USIS library at Kampala. In that library, he came across an illustrated directory of American colleges. One particular picture caught his eye: the Skagit Valley College in Mount Vernon, Washington. Legson was captivated by the clear blue sky, the fountains, lawns and majestic mountains as shown in the picture. He decided to write to Skagit Valley College to apply for admission. However, he was uncertain whether Skagit Valley College would accept him. Hence, he also wrote to other colleges.

Dean Hodson at Skagit was impressed with Legson's determination and granted him admission. The Dean also offered to help him find a job, so that he could pay for his room and board. Legson was overjoyed. Nevertheless, he needed a passport and a visa. He quickly wrote to the missionaries who had taught him since childhood. They helped him to obtain a passport through government channels. However, Legson still lacked the airfare required for a visa. Undeterred, he continued his journey to Cairo, spending his last savings on a pair of shoes, so that he would not need to walk through the door of Skagit Valley College barefooted. In the meantime, the students of Skagit Valley College raised sufficient money to cover Legson's airfare to America. When he learned of their generosity, Legson fell to his knees in gratefulness and joy.

In December 1960, more than two years after his journey began, Legson Kayira arrived at Skagit Valley College, carrying his two treasures, the Bible and the Pilgrim's Progress. A few years later, after graduating from Skagit Valley College, he continued his academic journey and finally became a professor of political science at Cambridge University, England.

I learned I was not, as most Africans believed, the victim of my circumstances but the master of them.

Legson Kayira

We cannot lose once we realize that everything that happens to us has been designed to teach us holiness.

Donald Nichol

Our second story is that of Wilma Rudolph whose exemplary perseverance is retold in many books, including Denis Waitley's *Seeds of Greatness*. It is condensed below.

Wilma was born prematurely, with complications that led her to contract pneumonia twice and scarlet fever. She was also a victim of polio, which crippled her left leg whose foot was turned inward. Around the age of six, Wilma need to wear leg braces. She also need to undertake bus journeys to Nashville hospital for routine treatment. This continued for 6 years. During each visit to the hospital, she would ask the doctor whether her braces could be removed. The doctor did not give her a firm reply and said, "We'll see............" During the homeward bus trips, Wilma would visualize herself being a parent, surrounded by happy children. She would tell her mother of her dreams. Her mother was very supportive and would encourage her, "If you keep on believing and trying, you can definitely succeed."

At the age of 11, Wilma began to tell herself constantly that she could learn to walk without braces. Against the doctor's advice to exercise a little, Wilma secretly began to learn to walk without her braces. She patiently and courageously strengthened her legs. She would painfully walk around the house everyday for hours, without informing anyone. A year later, when Wilma visited the Nashville Hospital for regular treatment, she decided to demonstrate the strength of her legs in front of her doctor and mother. She walked across the office to her doctor's desk without the help of braces. Both her mother and the doctor were astonished.

When Wilma turned 12, she discovered that girls can engage in a range of athletic activities. Now that she could walk without her braces, she decided that she would learn to run. She was determined not to be homebound anymore. Wilma began to train and strengthen her legs. Soon she ran in a competition. The first time she ran, she could beat her best friend. Subsequently, she beat all the other girls in her high school — —then, every high school in the state of Tennessee. When she turned 14, as a high school student, she joined the Tigerbelles' track team and went into serious training at Tennessee State University, aspiring to win a gold medal at the 1956 Olympic Games in Melbourne. Wilma trained hard and came in second at the 200-meter dash qualifying heats at the American University in Washington. However, Wilma was eliminated in the semifinals of the 200-meter dash at the 1956 Olympic Games in Melbourne, although she won a bronze as a member of the team finishing third in the women's 400-meter relay.

Upon returning home, she intensified her training. She would run at six o'clock in the morning, at ten o'clock and then in the afternoon at three o'clock. Day after day, she would practice, adhering to this rigorous schedule for twelve hundred days.

When Wilma stepped into the stadium field in the summer of 1960 in Rome for the Olympic Games, she was well prepared. Her performances in the 100-meter and 200-meter dashes and 400-meter relay became history. She won three gold Olympic medals, the first woman ever to win three gold medals in track and field. Above all, she completed each race in world record time. Wilma was once a homebound crippled girl who, for more than 6 years, need to travel to Nashville hospital for routine treatment. Manifesting the indomitable human spirit, she refused to be shackled by her illness and became a legend.

There may be world class athletes, and superstars, but that doesn't set them apart as world class people. I've had many of the same problems growing up as you have, and I hope my story in some small way can help one person believe that he or she can change, improve, and grow.

Wilma Rudolph

When nothing seems to help, I go and look at a stonecutter hammering away at his rock perhaps a hundred time without as much as a crack showing in it. Yet at the hundred and first blow it will split in two, and I know it was not that blow that did it, but all that had gone before.

Jacob Riis

Be of good cheer. Do not think of today's failures, but of the success that may come tomorrow. You have set yourselves a difficult task, but you will succeed if you persevere; and you will find a joy in overcoming obstacles. Remember, no effort that we make to attain something beautiful is lost forever.

Helen Keller

God permits evil only in so far as he is capable of transforming it into a good.

Saint Augustine

Wealth-Creation Secret #65
Tap our inner autonomy to reinterpret external obstacles and hurdles as valuable opportunities to enhance our maturation, ripen our heart, strengthen our resolve to do good and deepen our commitment to embrace the higher dimension of life.

Fourth Pillar of Genuine Wealth: Practicing Humility And A Spirit of Continuous Learning, Acceptance And Surrender

Let us recall the famous Greek story about Icarus.

Icarus' father, Daedalus, was an ingenious craftsman. Originally from Athens, Daedalus traveled to Crete where he assisted King Minos to design an amazing labyrinth that held captive the deadly Minotaur. However, when Daedalus fell out of favor with King Minos, he and Icarus were imprisoned in a stone tower overlooking the ocean.

For many days and nights, Daedelus and his son sought to conceive of an effective plan to escape. They saved the crumbs from their food and enticed the seagulls into their prison cell at the tower and patiently collected their feathers. They also began to hoard the wax drippings from their candles. Finally, they could produce two sets of wings from the feathers that are held together by thread and wax.

When they were ready, Daedulus advised Icarus not to fly too high, lest the sun will melt the wax. Late one night, they dismantled the prison window and soared upwards. After flying for several hours, they saw the sun appearing. Icarus rejoiced in his new freedom and began to soar higher and higher, feeling as if he could touch the heavens.

Alarmed, Daedalus shouted to his son and told him not to soar so high. But Icarus did not listen. Soon the morning rays melted the wax on his wings, and more and more feathers began to drop off. Icarus suddenly realized that he had flown too high and was rapidly losing his balance. He cried out to his father, as he began to plunge toward the sea. Daedalus tried his best to fly toward his son to reach out for him, but to no avail. Icarus plunged into the deep seas and were drowned by the waves. Daedalus flew to a quiet place in Athens and retired, depressed over the death of his son.

Look for inspiration in many different areas, but above all look within yourself. Indeed, a sense of yourself is vital to your success as a creative human being. If, however, this sense of self-worth is carried to extremes, your judgment may become clouded and you risk cutting yourself off from the deep ocean of Being that sustains you.

Roger Von Oech
Expect The Unexpected

If I were asked, how do we effectively sustain the cultivation of higher wisdom and the maturation of spiritual qualities, my answer would be: practice humility. It is a higher form of wise humility that pierces through our inner sanctity as well as the divine spark immanent in others. It is a higher form of wise humility that galvanizes us to awaken to our inner assets. It is a higher form of wise humility that recognizes our deep potential as intimate partners of Divinity. It is a higher form of wise humility that accepts and extends compassionate understanding to our imperfections, limitations and finitude.

If I were asked what is the primary and most dangerous pitfall of our spiritual path, my answer would be: non-humility. If we do not learn to nurture a humble spirit, mindset and attitude, we would gradually succumb to the arch-rival of wisdom: pride. In Christian literature, pride is frequently depicted as the ultimate cause of the downfall of men as well as angels. Pride is the main source of energy of our Ego, of self-centered thinking and emotional patterns. As we progress in our inner cultivation, we will realize that our egoistic thinking can mutate and transmute itself into many different forms and guises. Spiritual pride or hubris is one of them.

Such transmutation is subtle, surreptitious and insidious. During the initial stages of our awakening when we catch glimpses of our divine spark, our egoistic thinking patterns may stealthily mutate itself into spiritual pride and an inflated sense of self-importance. We rationalize that in view of our divine potential, we are above all others. We should be accorded respect above all others. We are spiritually superior to all others.

According to Christian teachers, the essential vice, the utmost evil, is Pride. Unchastity, anger, greed, drunkenness, and all that, are mere fleabites in comparison: it was through Pride that the devil became the devil: Pride leads to every other vice: it is the complete anti-God state of mind.

C. S. Lewis

The symptoms of spiritual pride and spiritual materialism are many. They may include the followings:-

- Subtle conceptualization in our thinking and emotional patterns of a new spiritual identity. We erect new barricades in our mind to prop, protect and fortify it. We experience irritation, anger and hostility if someone attacks our new spiritual identity or transgresses upon the spiritual territory that we build in our mind.

- We trap ourselves into thinking that since our divine essence is inviolate and inalienable, we are self-sufficient and do not need to participate in the marketplace. We begin to lose touch with our inner wisdom and its holistic vision of the interwoven fabric of life, of the importance of cultivating compassion. We become subtly attached to and fixated on our new inflated spiritual identity where we view others who are spiritually untrained as unworthy of our care and attention. Subtly or subconsciously, we view ourselves as quasi-Godly beings who are above the marketplace.

- We misconceive that attaining higher spiritual states are the sole purpose of inner cultivation. We begin to cloister ourselves and deem others as threats to our inner peace and quietness. We become subtly attached to the false sense of solace and security that we derive from erroneous concepts of a new spiritual identity.

- We display subtle resistance to accept that inner peace and tranquility are also transient mental-emotional states which we should not cling to. We display subtle resistance to accept hardship and adverse circumstances as learning opportunities for deeper awakening. We refuse to recognize the innate sanctity and wholesomeness of others, to extend respect and compassionate understanding to others. We refuse to accept our finitude and mortality, to accept the imperfections and rowdiness of the marketplace as valuable avenues for nurturing inner qualities.

By availing ourselves to the twelve gateways of higher wisdom as discussed in chapter 3, by listening to our heart wisdom, we can shine our inner luminosity onto the various guises and transmutations of an inflated spiritual identity. We can thereby learn to see through the fortifications that we erect to prop up our sense of inward security and learn to sustain a healthy vigilance against erecting a specious spiritual identity. We also learn to nurture a healthy spirit of continuous learning, committed to ongoing positive growth.

In his book *The Unknown Craftsmen*, the world-famous potter Shoji Hamada wrote, "If a kiln is small, I might be able to control it completely, that is to say, my own self can become a controller, a master of the kiln. But man's own self is but a small thing after all. When I work at the large kiln, the power of my own self becomes so feeble that it cannot control it adequately. It means that for the large kiln, the power that is beyond me is necessary. Without the mercy of such invisible power, I cannot get good pieces." By practicing humility, by recognizing and submitting ourselves to the immensity and higher intelligence of the transcendental realm, our potential to do good will flower manifold.

Wealth-Creation Secret #66
Nurture the insightful awareness to detect pride, over-confidence, arrogance and hubris. Guard against subtle conceits when we pursue worthwhile ends.
Foster a resilient spirit of humility, continuous learning and service to humanity in daily living.

Fifth Pillar of Genuine Wealth: Practicing Forgiveness And Broadmindedness

Dream of your brother's kindnesses instead of dwelling in your dreams on his mistakes. Select his thoughtfulness to dream about instead of counting up the hurts he gave.

A Course In Miracles

To forgive is more than divine. To forgive is to manifest the broadmindedness of our humanity and the luminosity of our divine essence.

As discussed in the previous chapter, not to forgive is to imprison ourselves in a dark dudgeon, to seek to snuff out

378

the glimmering of our divine broadmindedness. In his touching book, *The Bait of Satan*, John Bevere discussed the subject of how do we respond when we have been "offended", when someone has hurt or harmed us. If we do not awaken to our heart wisdom and extend kind understanding to the transgressors and perpetrators, if we succumbed to an unforgiving mindset, we would have yielded to the inner "demon", which is a transformation of our egoistic thinking and emotional patterns. By adhering to an unforgiving mindset, we have been hooked by this demon's bait. Without liberating ourselves from this bait and lethal trap, we would be barred from touching our higher dimension. By holding onto our hurt feelings, we would imprison ourselves in a vicious cycle of inner strife.

It was recorded that when the Buddha and his disciples passed by some rice fields, he was accosted by a wealthy farm owner. It was a season of plowing and the wealthy farm owner was supervising dozens of laborers plowing and sowing seeds. The wealthy farm owner deliberately stood in the Buddha's way and said with disdain, "You and your disciples do nothing. You produce nothing, yet you still eat. You don't plow, sow, fertilize, tend or harvest."

Instead of being offended and angered by these words, the Buddha explained in a tone filled with kind understanding, "But we do plow, sow, fertilize, tend and harvest."

"If so, where are your plows, buffaloes and seeds? What crops do you tend and harvest?" the wealthy farmer retorted.

The Buddha replied serenely, "We sow the seeds of compassion and kind understanding in the soil of a true heart. Our plow is mindfulness and moment-to-moment awareness. Our buffalo is commitment, diligence, constant effort and persistence. Our harvest is broadmindedness, forgiveness, compassion and love."

Thich Nhat Hanh's *Old Paths, White Clouds* recorded that on another occasion, the Buddha taught his son, Rahula, on the lessons of how we should practice compassion, broadmindedness, acceptance and forgiveness like the basic elements. The Buddha said, "Learn from the earth. Regardless of whether people spread pure and fragrant flowers, perfume or fresh milk on it, or discard filthy foul-smelling feces, urine or mucus on it, the earth receives them without aversion, but with patience and forgiveness. Learn also from the water. When people wash dirty things in it, the water is not resentful or disdainful. Learn from the fire, which burns pure and impure things without discrimination. Learn from the air, which carries all types of fragrances, whether sweet or foul."

Anyone who proposes to do good must not expect people to roll stones out of his way, but must accept his lot calmly, even if they roll a few more upon it.

Albert Schweitzer

Wealth-Creation Secret #67
On a daily basis, contemplate and dwell on
the natural abundance surrounding us and
how the radiant sunlight does not discriminate against anyone.
This can sustain a spirit of forgiveness and lovingkindness.

Sixth Pillar of Genuine Wealth: Practicing Simplicity, Uncluttered Living And Inner Peace

God made us plain and simple, but we have made ourselves very complicated.

Ecclesiastes 7: 29

Happiness and suffering are states of mind, and so their main causes cannot be found outside the mind. The real source of happiness is inner peace. If our mind is peaceful, we shall be happy all the time, regardless of external conditions, but if it is disturbed or troubled in any way, we shall never be happy.........External conditions can only make us happy if our mind is peaceful.

Geshe Kelsang Gyatso
Transform Your Life

By nurturing an insightful awareness of the sanctified source of our being, we reconnect with the purity and simplicity of our divine essence. It will dawn on us that our frenetic and cluttered lives arise from warped beliefs that external possessions are the bedrock of inner peace. By listening to our heart wisdom, we learn to pare down and divest the non-essentials and showy embellishments of our life. We learn to re-focus and re-prioritize our life goals and daily activities.

We do not chase after the chimerical approval, applause and admiration of others. We do not orient our lives to hunting, collecting and hoarding outward prizes to prop up a false sense of security, invulnerability, bravado and self-sufficiency. We do not orient our lives to avoid adversities that can forge a resilient character. We do not orient our lives to indulge in luxurious living, oblivious to the pleas for assistance by the needy, the handicapped, the less fortunate members of our society. Rather, by embracing a pure-hearted simple lifestyle that touches the purity and simplicity of our deep essence, we avail ourselves to the wholesome joys of authentic living. We retouch the profundity, wonders and grace of the present moment. We relish the miracle of our sentient aliveness. We learn to treasure the simple joys in life, the glimmering insatiable curiosity in the eyes of our children, the humid freshness of the late autumn breeze, the sprightly chirping of birds, the gentle fragrance of chrysanthemum, the pristine radiance of blooming daffodils, the vitality of forest deers and squirrels, the tranquility of white swans gliding gracefully across a forest pond whose surface reflects the placidity of floating white clouds, the vastness and profound beauty of Mother Nature, her infinitely colorful garment of tranquil lakes, flowing rivers, trickling streams, lush green hills, white-peaked mountains, majestic canyons and magnanimous blue oceans.

To reorder one's own private world, the need to simplify is imperative. Otherwise, we find ourselves unable to be at rest within, unable to enter the deep, silent resources of our hearts, where God's best messages are communicated.

Charles Swindoll

*There is a word in Buddhism that means "wishlessness".......
The idea is that you do not put something in front of you and run after it, because everything is already here, in yourself. While we practice walking meditation, we do not try to arrive anywhere. We only make peaceful, happy steps. If we keep thinking of the future, of what we want to realize, we will lose our steps.*

Thich Nhat Hanh

By practicing simplicity, contentment, inner peace and tranquility, another miraculous fruit would blossom: gratefulness. We awaken to the affection showered on us by many people around us since when we were born. Let me retell a touching story about an apple tree who loved a boy. It is based on *The Giving Tree* by Shel Silverstein and retold in Charles Swindoll's classic *Growing Strong In The Seasons Of Life*.

There was once an apple tree which often played "hide and seek" with a boy. The boy would swing from her branches, climb over her, eat her apples and sleep in her shade.

As the boy grew into a young man, he spent lesser time with the tree. On one occasion, when the young man returned home, the apple tree invited him, "Come, let us relax and play........." However, the young man was worried about money-making and was not in the mood to play. The tree said, "Take all my apples and sell them. I am confident that you can garner a handsome little profit." The young man brightened up and followed the tree's advice, plucked all the apples and sold them.

The young man did not return home for a long time. Years later, when he was already middle-aged, he passed by the apple tree. "How are you, my dear son?" the tree asked affectionately.

The middle-aged man replied in a sad voice, "Not so good. I do not have money to purchase a house." The tree thought for a while and said, "Why don't you chop down all my firm branches. They should enable you to build a comfortable tiny cabin." The middle-aged man brightened up and followed the tree's advice.

Nevertheless, the man soon grew tired of living in his tiny cabin. One day, he passed by the apple tree with only a trunk and several frail branches left. "How are you today? Are you feeling better with your cabin?" the tree enquired. Thereupon, the middle-aged man explained that he would like to travel around the world to gain exposure and widen his prospects.

The apple tree thought for a while. "Chop down my trunk. You can thereby build a boat and sail away to your dream destination. But do remember to come back and visit me," said the tree. The middle-aged man brightened up, chopped down the trunk, made himself a boat and traveled to a faraway place to seek his fortune.

Many seasons passed and the man, now old and alone, returned home. As he walked past the tree stump, she welcomed him home, "My dear friend, I have a good stump left. Please sit down and rest a while. We can reminisce on our carefree days…………"

How many people have contributed to our lives like the broadminded and altruistic apple tree? Did we learn to be contented and touch the depths of our soul? Did we connect with our innate sense of gratitude, silently expressing thankfulness to all the people who have in one way or another, during the changing seasons of our life, assisted us in our positive growth? Did we in turn manifest this generous and altruistic spirit in our daily words and deeds?

Constant comparison with those who are smarter, more beautiful, or more successful than ourselves……tends to breed envy, frustration, and unhappiness. But we can use this same principle in a positive way; we can increase our feeling of life satisfaction by comparing ourselves to those who are less fortunate than us and by reflecting on all the things we have.

Dr Howard Cutler

The cessation of suffering — — well-being — — — is available if you know how to enjoy the precious jewels you already have. You have eyes that can see, lungs that can breathe, legs that can walk, and lips that can smile.

Thich Nhat Hanh

Wealth-Creation Secret #68
Nurture the positive habit of constantly appreciating the range of inner assets within us.
We can thereby counter negative habits to ignore our inner worth and to become preoccupied with egoistic achievements.

Seventh Pillar of Genuine Wealth: Practicing Compassion, Kind Intentions, Patience and Empathy

Compassion is the wish that others be free of suffering.

The Dalai Lama

Compassion is the quivering of our heart. It is an insightful compassion that we are planting, watering and nurturing. It is compassion permeated by insights into the common aspirations, strivings, disillusionment, frustrations, anguish as well as the evolving maturation, fortitude, faith and hope of humankind. It is compassion permeated by insights into how spiritual torpor and inertia have trapped many of us in a vicious cycle of pursuing chimerical prizes and bounties. It is compassion permeated by insights into our innate ability to blend the voices of our individual soul with the euphonic chorus of Divinity.

385

Lord, make me a channel of Thy peace that, where there is hatred, I may bring love; that where there is wrong, I may bring the spirit of forgiveness; that where there is discord, I may bring harmony; that where there is error, I may bring truth; that where there is doubt, I may bring faith; that where there is despair, I may bring hope; that where there are shadows, I may bring light; that where there is sadness, I may bring joy.

St Francis of Assissi

Mother Teresa is an embodiment of divine compassion, lovingkindness and patience. For five decades, she worked among slum-dwellers, children's homes, homes for the dying and a leper colony. In the words of Professor John Sanness who gave the presentation speech during the ceremony in awarding the 1979 Nobel prize to Mother Teresa: "She sees Christ in every human being, and this in her eyes makes man sacred...............The hallmark of her work has been respect for the individual's worth and dignity."

There is a well-known story of a hard-hearted baker who was touched by Mother Teresa's non-selfishness and broadminded spirit. One day, Mother Teresa approached a bakery to request for some bread for the poor children in her orphanage. The baker not only refused, but became infuriated and spat on her. However, Mother Teresa did not react angrily at his unreasonable and uncouth behavior. Instead, she said, "Now that you have vented your unhappiness and frustrations, please spare some bread for my children?" The baker was astounded and became remorseful. He gave her loaves of bread and became a convert to her philanthropic cause.

I am neither spurred on by excessive optimism nor in love with high ideals, but am merely concerned with the fate of the individual human being — — that infinitesmal unit on whom a world depends, and in whom, if we read the meaning of the Christian message aright, even God seeks his goal.

Carl Jung

Another embodiment of compassion, patience and lovingkindness is Mahatma Gandhi who advocated non-violence for decades. When leading his countrymen to seek for independence. He was acknowledged, even by his critics, as one of the greatest Hindu of modern times. On 30 January 1948, Gandhi was shot by a fanatic Hindu for his acquiescence in the partition of their country into India and Pakistan. Gandhi, instead of cursing the fanatic who shot at him, reverentially closed his palms together as a gesture of forgiveness, uttered his mantra and passed away. Years of meditation and practicing the higher truths contained in his beloved Bhagavad Gita enabled Gandhi to gracefully accept all external events with equanimity, compassion and broadmindedness.

Ahimsa (non-violence) is for Gandhi the basic law of our being. That is why it can be used as the most effective principle for social action, since it is in deep accord with the truth of man's nature, and corresponds to his innate desire for peace, justice, order, freedom, and personal dignity.

Thomas Merton

I have known from early youth that non-violence is not a cloistered virtue to be practiced by the individual for his peace and final salvation, but it is a rule of conduct for the whole of society.

Mahatma Gandhi

In Tibet, there was a famous Dharma practitioner called Geshe Ben Gungyal who focused on watching the thoughts in his mind. Whenever he noticed negative thoughts surfacing, he would refuse to follow the train of his negative thoughts. To gauge his progress, he would put a black pebble in his room whenever a negative thought arose, and a white pebble when a wholesome thought arose. At the end of each day, he would count the number of black and white pebbles. Initially, the black pebbles significantly outnumbered the white ones. Nevertheless, by patiently undertaking meditation and nurturing broadmindedness and kind intentions, as time passes, his room was full of white pebbles at the end of each day.

In the end, that is what the love and worship of God is all about: to turn our minds, and if possible, our bodies too, away from earthliness to perfection, from doubt to certitude, from the self to goodness, and from the flesh to the spirit. This act of turning is something we should do every day of our lives, and as often as we can in each day, so that in the end it becomes second nature and we cease to need to turn, but become one with the great spirit in whom alone we find peace and our destiny.

Paul Johnson
The Quest For God

Let us share the story of the spiritual quest of Asanga, a famous Buddhist saint who lived in the fourth century. Before he became enlightened, he went to a mountain to meditate, hoping that he would be blessed to meet Buddha Maitreya.

After six years of meditation and contemplation, he did not experience any epiphanic vision. Deeply disappointed, he began to walk down the mountain. Halfway, he saw an elderly woman rubbing an iron bar against a rock. Asanga asked what she was doing. "I am seeking to make a fine needle out of this iron bar", she replied.

Amazed by her determination and perseverance, Asanga decided to return to his mountain to meditate.

Another three years elapsed and Asanga still did not attain enlightenment. Once again, he was very depressed and walked down the mountain. He came to a bend and saw a middle-aged man scraping a silver spoon against a boulder. Asanga enquired what he was doing. "This rock is so huge that it is blocking the sunlight from reaching my cottage at the foot of this mountain. Hence, I am scraping it with a silver spoon to get rid of it."

Asanga was inspired by the man's patience and determination and once again, he went up the mountain to practice.

Another three years passed and he still did not have any vision of Buddha Maitreya. Totally dejected, he decided to return home. When he reached the foot of the mountain, he saw an old diseased dog. The lower part of its body was rotting and covered with maggots. This old dog had been begging for many weeks for passers-by to help it to get rid of the maggots, but none of them rendered any assistance. Out of compassion for the pitiful condition of the dog, Asanga obtained a pail of water and began to wash the festering wounds and gingerly remove the maggots one by one. Initially, he used his fingers to remove the maggots. However, the old dog felt immense pain. Asanga decided to use his mouth to suck and spit the maggots. He closed his eyes and leaned closer to the festering wounds...........The next thing he knew, he was touching the ground. His eyes met an immense radiance. Standing before him was Buddha Maitreya. He realized that the old dog was Buddha Maitreya in transformation to test him. At that moment, Asanga attained enlightenment, touching the higher dimension in his being............

............compassion............is glimpsed in those moments when the barrier of self is lifted and individual existence is surrendered to the well-being of existence as a whole. It becomes abundantly clear that we cannot attain awakening for ourselves: we can only participate in the awakening of life.

Stephen Bachelor
Buddhism Without Beliefs

To be alive is to be in a state of progress, a singular experience unique to each of us. Every one of us is a unique gem of incomparable worth to ourselves, not by what we accomplish or what we obtain but rather by the way in which we learn to live and by the discovery of who we essentially are.

Dr Carlos Warter
Who Do You Think You Are

It was recorded that after his Great Awakening, the Buddha contemplated on whether he should remain silent on the great truths that he had penetrated or should he commit himself to disseminate them. He wondered whether the people would be receptive to the higher teaching and wisdom which defy conventional logic and thinking. Guided by the seeds of altruism in his heart, the Buddha decided that he should reveal the Way to the higher truths.

The Buddha's first sermon on the Four Noble Truths was to his former spiritual friends, the five ascetics at the Deer Park. In *Old Path, White Clouds*, Thich Nhat Hanh recounted, "........ please listen, my friends. You will be the first to hear my Teaching. I have found the Great Way, and I will show it to you. You will be the first to hear my teaching. This Dharma is not the result of thinking. It is the fruit of direct experience. Listen serenely with all your awareness." The Buddha thereby spoke on the existence of suffering, the origin of suffering, the cessation of suffering and the eightfold path leading to the cessation of suffering. The Buddha was sincerely concerned that his friends should experience the depth of awakening and inner liberation that he had undergone. Thus, for the next forty-five years, the Buddha embodied compassion, kind intentions, patience and empathy in reaching out to the people to show the Way to the higher truths.

It was recorded that during the Buddha's final hours of his earthly life, an ascetic named Subhadda attempted to seek audience with him. The Buddha's attendant initially refused, explaining that the Buddha was not feeling well and too tired to receive anyone. However, the Buddha overheard their conversation and told the attendant to allow Subhadda to see him. Subhadda had heard about the Buddha's teaching but had not met him in person. He knelt before the Buddha and enquired, "Venerable Teacher, I have heard that many spiritual leaders have attained enlightenment. I would like to enquire whether, in your view, did they genuinely attain enlightenment?"

The Buddha opened his eyes and gazed at Subhadda with compassion and kind understanding. He replied slowly, "Subhadda, whether or not these spiritual teachers and leaders attain enlightenment is not really important. What is of ultimate importance is that you should awaken and attain enlightenment yourself." Using the final strength remained in his physical body, the Buddha spoke to

Subhadda about the Four Noble Truths and concluded by saying that, "Subhadda, if we practice this path, we all could attain enlightenment." Before the Buddha passed away, his final words were, "...........If there is birth, there is death. Be diligent in your efforts to attain liberation............"

Uncreated is the truth that is not made, that has always been, and will always be. It is the safe refuge, the true home, the long-sought goal, the supreme bliss.... This truth transforms death into bliss, and life into fearless freedom. It is what lies behind the Buddha's smile.

Robert Thurman
Inner Revolution

Wealth-Creation Secret #69
What can be more enriching and enlightening than to awaken to the deathless dimension within us?

Eighth Pillar of Genuine Wealth: Practicing Insightful Awareness And Reverence For Life

If an Arab in the desert were suddenly to discover a spring in his tent, and so would always be able to have water in abundance, how fortunate he would consider himself; so too when a man who......is always turned toward the outside, thinking that his happiness lies outside him, finally turns inward and discovers that the source is within him.

Soren Kierkegaard

............if we just act in each moment with composure and mindfulness, each minute of our life is a work of art.

Thich Nhat Hanh

By rekindling our vibrant insightful awareness, we have taken a quantum leap toward the miracles and mysteries of fruitful living. We learn to connect deeply and spontaneously with the present moment, immersing into its infinite richness. The intricate nuances of our sensations, thoughts, feelings, emotions, inner communication as well as the subtle intentions and complex motives of our spoken words and behavioral patterns unveil before our insightful attentiveness.

During our meditative moments, we learn to listen to the gentle rhythm of our pulse and we thereby pulse along with it. We learn to relish the tingling of the breath flowing gently into and out of our nostrils and lungs, and we become the sacred breath itself. We become alive to the vibrant cosmic intelligence coursing through the cells of our body.

Man has not invented God;
He has developed faith,
To meet a God already there.

Edna St. Vincent Millay

During our waking moments, we learn to watch the arising and passing away of our thoughts, feelings, emotions, conceptualizations and rationalizations against the vast spacious background of insightful awareness. We penetrate through the transitory nature of pleasant and unpleasant sensations and mental states. We pierce through the fleeting nature of our thoughts and emotional patterns. We thereby learn to de-condition and de-fixate ourselves from unhealthy concepts, notions and beliefs in a substantial separate self. We have plunged into the depths of our being, rediscovering that our phenomenal bodies emanate from the sacred realm, that we are offspring of God, children of Divinity. We have plunged into the depths of our being, rediscovering that our phenomenal bodies are permeated by cosmic consciousness and intelligence, as well as divine love and affection. We have plunged into the depths of our being, rediscovering that Divinity cares for us in inexplicable ways that contribute to our ultimate well-being, that the magnitude of God's love for us reflects the depth and profundity of the cosmos. We have plunged into the depths of our being, rediscovering the ultimate secret of positive inner transformation and genuine success.

To laugh often and love much;
To win the respect of intelligent persons
and the affection of children;
To earn the approval of honest critics
and endure the betrayal of false friends;
To appreciate beauty;
To find the best in others;
To give of one's self without the
slightest thought of return;
To have accomplished a task, whether
by a healthy child, a rescued soul,
a garden patch, or a redeemed social condition;
To have played and laughed
with enthusiasm and exaltation;
to know that even one life has breathed easier
because you have lived; this is to have succeeded.

Ralph Waldo Emerson

During our waking moments, we learn to replicate healthy meditative attentiveness. We feel more vibrantly the rays of sunlight warming our retina during our evening strolls. We feel more intensely the refreshing coolness of the breezes. We become more receptive to the beauty of the sunset, the pinkish skyline and the fading vestiges of golden sunlight. Suddenly, the greenery before us becomes transformed and transfigured, unveiling its bountiful secret in an epiphanic moment. The holistic unity and interconnectedness of all beings and all things, their spiritual foundation and sacred source, become clear. Non-harming, non-violence and reverence for life become the guideposts in our daily living. We have taken the quantum leap toward authentic living. We have embarked on a fruitful path to relearn the infinite possibilities of rejoicing in the present moment.

We shall not cease from exploration
And the end of all our exploring
Will be to arrive where we started
And to know the place for the first time.

T. S. Eliot

With a sudden shock of the utterly obvious, you recognize your own Original Face, the face you had prior to the Big Bang, the face of utter Emptiness that smiles as all creation and sings as the entire Kosmos — — and it is all undone in that primal glance, and all that is left is that smile, and the reflection of the moon on a quiet pond, late on a crystal clear night.

Ken Wilber

Wealth-Creation Secret #70
To awaken to the kaleidoscopic richness and possibilities of
each present moment is to participate in divine co-creation.
As observed by William James,
"For the moment, what we attend to is reality..............."

Our journey has arrived at a full circle. We have returned home. I am grateful that we are able to share some precious moments together. I am confident that Divinity and our inner luminosity will affectionately guide us along this fruitful path where our final reunion will be filled with joy and abundance.

Blessed is the man who finds wisdom,
the man who gains understanding,
for she is more profitable than silver
and yields better returns than gold.

Proverbs 3:13-14

With spiritual maturity the basis for these practices shifts away from ambition, idealism, and desire for self-transformation. It is as if the wind has changed, and a weather vane — — still centered in the same spot — — now points in a different direction: back to this moment. We are no longer striving after a spiritual destination, grasping for another world different from the one we have. We are home. And being home, we sweep the floor, make nourishing meals, and care for our guests.

Dr Jack Kornfield
After The Ecstasy, The Laundry

May all beings everywhere
be awakened, healed, peaceful, and free;
May there be peace in this world,
and an end to war, poverty,
violence, and oppression;
and may we all together
complete the spiritual journey,

Lama Surya Das

Being mindful and spiritually conscious, divine qualities manifest through us. Our innate worth exceeds the treasures of the world. Being mindful and present-moment-oriented, we are all miracles, emerging as intimate partners of Divinity in co-designing, co-molding and co-creating the present and the future. Being mindful and insightfully aware, undiminishing inner Light radiates forth, illuminating the truth that there is no basic difference between our inner wholesomeness and the eternal verities.

In fulfilling our sacred life mission as partners of Divinity, may we be guided by the perennial wisdoms: Nothing is more valuable than the continuous awakening of the human mind. Nothing is more miraculous than the blossoming of altruistic intentions. Nothing is more nourishing than the insight that sincerity in providing services to the needy unveils our divine qualities. Nothing is more inspiring than the fortitude ignited by an unflinching dedication to worthwhile causes. Nothing is more uplifting than in devoting ourselves to implanting the seeds of the perennial wisdoms in the fertile minds of our children and grandchildren. Nothing is more precious than the patient, incessant and resolute practice of compassion. Nothing is more golden than our pure altruistic heart.

* * * * * *

397

Bibliography

When Things Fall Apart by Pema Chodron, published by Shambhala Publications, 1997.

Manifest Your Destiny by Dr Wayne D. Dyer, published by HarperCollins Publishers, 1999.

Awaken The Giant Within by Anthony Robbins, published by Fireside Publisher, 1992.

The Seven Spiritual Laws of Success by Dr Deepak Chopra, published by Amber-Allen Publishing, 1994.

Awakening To The Sacred by Lama Surya Das, published by Bantam Books, 2000.

Living Buddha, Living Christ by Thich Nhat Hanh, published by Riverhead Books, The Berkeley Publishing Group, 1997.

After The Ecstasy, The Laundry by Dr Jack Kornfield, published by Bantam Books, 2000.

The Heart of The Buddha's Teaching by Thich Nhat Hanh, published by Broadway Books, 1999.

Essential Spirituality by Dr Roger Walsh, published by John Wiley & Sons, 1999.

The Road Less Traveled by Dr M. Scott Peck, published by Arrow Books, 1990.

The Road Less Traveled And Beyond by Dr M. Scott Peck, published by Simon & Schuster, 1997.

A History of God by Karen Armstrong, published by Ballantine Books, 1993.

How To Know God by Dr Deepak Chopra, published by Rider, an imprint of Ebury Press, Randon House, 2000.

The Art Of Happiness by The Dalai Lama and Dr Howard Cutter, published by Coronet Books, Hodder & Stoughton, 1998.

The Tao of Physics by Dr Fritjof Capra, published by Shambhala Publications, 1999.

Ageless Body, Timeless Mind by Dr Deepak Chopra, published by Rider, an imprint of Ebury Press, Random House, 1998.

The Cosmic Game by Dr Stanislav Grof, published by State University of New York Press, 1998.

The Seat Of The Soul by Gary Zukav, published by Fireside Publisher, 1990.

Communion With God by Neale Donald Walsch, published by Hodder And Stoughton, 2000.

Lovingkindness by Sharon Salzberg, published by Shambhala Publications, 1995.

The Holotrophic Mind by Dr Stanislav Grof, published by HarperCollins Publishers, 1993.

Awakening The Buddha Within by Lama Surya Das, published by Broadway Books, 1998.

Everyday Enlightenment by Dan Millman, published by Hodder and Stoughton, 1998.

Old Paths, White Clouds by Thich Nhat Hanh, published by Parallax Press, 1991.

Transform Your Life by Geshe Kelsang Gyatso, published by Tharpa Publications, 2001.

Man's Search For Meaning by Dr Victor Frankl, published by Beacon Press, 1992.

The Congruent Life by Michael Thompson, published by Jossey-Bass Publishers, 2000.

The Gospel Of Good Success by Kirbyjon H. Caldwell, published by Fireside publisher, 1999.

Soul Stories by Gary Zukav, published by Simon & Schuster, 2000.

Journey of Awakening by Ram Dass, published by Bantam Books, 1990.

Ancient Wisdom, Modern World by The Dalai Lama, published by Abacus, a division of Little, Brown and Company, 1999.

A Path With Heart by Dr Jack Kornfield, published by Rider, an imprint of Ebury Press, Random House, 1994.

The Tibetan Book Of Living And Dying by Sogyal Rinpoche, published by HarperCollins Publishers, 1994.

The Power Of Now by Eckhart Tolle, published by New World Library, 1999.

Wherever You Go, There You Are by Dr Jon Kabat-Zinn, published by Hyperion, 1994.

A Brief History Of Everything by Ken Wilber, published by Shambhala Publications, 1996.

The Marriage Of Sense And Soul by Ken Wilber, published by Newleaf, 1998.

The Spectrum of Consciousness by Ken Wilber, published by Quest Books, 1977.

Unlimited Power by Anthony Robbins, published by Simon & Schuster, 1988.

The Greatest Salesman In The World by Og Mandino, published by Frederick Fell Publishers, reprint 1997.

Life Strategies by Dr Philip McGraw, published by Hyperion, 1999.

Expect The Unexpected by Dr Roger von Oech, published by The Free Press, a division of Simon & Schuster, 2001.

Seeds of Greatness by Dr Denis Waitley, published by Pocket Books, a division of Simon & Schuster, 1984.

Winning In The Game Of Life by Tom Gegax, published by Harmony Books, 1999.

The Seven Habits Of Highly Effective People by Dr Stephen Covey, published by Simon & Schuster, 1989.

Who Do You Think You Are? by Dr Carlos Warter, published by Bantam Books, 1998.

The Quest For God by Paul Johnson, published by The Orion Publishing Group, 1996.

The River Of Fire, The River Of Water by Taitetsu Unno, published by Doubleday, a division of Bantam Doubleday Dell, 1998.

Buddha's Nature by Wes Nisker, published by Rider, an imprint of Ebury Press, Random House, 1998.

Zen Mind, Beginner's Mind by Shunryu Suzuki, published by Weatherhill Inc, revised edition, 1999.

Peace Is Every Step by Thich Nhat Hanh, published by Bantam Books, 1992.

Buddhism Without Beliefs by Stephen Batchelor, published by Riverhead Books, The Berkeley Publishing Group, 1997.

The Myth Of Freedom by Chogyam Trungpa, published by Shambhala Publications, 1976.

The Way of Zen by Alan Watts, published by Vintage Books, 1985.

Inner Revolution by Robert Thurman, published by Riverhead Books, the Berkeley Publishing Group, 1998.

About the Author

With post-graduate degrees in Accountancy and Business Administration, Emerson Lee has worked as a senior finance manager for many years. In addition, he is an earnest student of the perennial wisdoms for more than fifteen years, attaining an in-depth knowledge of their essential teachings. He discovers that the liberating "secrets" of the perennial wisdoms can be fruitfully applied to enhance personal motivation and work performance in modern stress-laden workplaces, as well as to lay a firm foundation for constructive wealth creation. Presently, he is devoting more time to disseminate these insights, focusing on the importance of undertaking inner cultivation to nurture emotional-spiritual intelligence and leadership qualities, of tapping our inner assets to fulfill our deep potential and rise to higher levels of fruitful living.

Printed in the United States
1011200003B